D0551820

First edition published 2009
by Pencil-Sharp Publishing Ltd

ISBN 978-0-9562573-0-7

The publisher would like to thank the author, Geoffrey Hill, and Penguin Books for their kind permissions to use an extract from the poem A Triumph of Love as the epigraph for this book. Extracts from University of London and Edexcel past examinations papers are reproduced by kind permission of Edexcel Limited. Extracts from University of Cambridge and OCR past examinations papers are reproduced by kind permission of OCR (Oxford Cambridge and RSA Examinations). Extracts from AQA past examinations papers are reproduced by kind permission of AQA. Extracts from DCSF, QCA and HMSO published documents are reproduced under the terms of the PSI Click-Use License.

The publisher would also like to thank Harrow School for permission to reproduce extracts from the Harrow School Literacy Test 2008; the Independent Schools Examinations Board, for permission to quote a question from the 1957 Common Entrance examination; University of Cambridge International Examinations, for permission to quote from the Pre-U publicity brochure for schools; Professor Colin MacCabe, for permissions to quote from his open letter to Charles Clarke, published in the Observer; and to Civitas, for permission to quote extensively from Nick Cowen's book Swedish Lessons.

Every effort has been made to obtain permissions. Any omissions will be rectified in the next edition.

A CIP catalogue record for this book is available from the British Library.

Typeset by Bookcraft Ltd, Stroud, Gloucestershire
Printed and bound in Great Britain by CPI Antony Rowe, Chippenham

For Christine

Contents

List of Illustrations

And yes – bugger you, MacSikker et al., – I do
mourn and resent your desolation of learning:
Scientia that enabled, if it did not secure,
forms of understanding, far from despicable,
and furthest now, as they are most despised.
By understanding I understand diligence
and attention, appropriately understood
as actuated self-knowledge, a daily acknowledgement
of what is owed the dead.

The Triumph of Love, Geoffrey Hill

Acknowledgements

All sorts of people have influenced the writing of this book. Few, if any, will agree with every aspect of its argument. Special thanks are due to my friends John Clare and Anthony O'Hear, whose inspired comment on the absurdity of Government education policy used to lighten many a weary hour as we plodded through the Cuillin Hills. John kindly tracked down many of the references I had, stupidly, mislaid. Peter Newsam offered trenchant insight into the propaganda surrounding City Academies. Edmund Lazarus helped sharpen my thinking about the economics of private schooling. Matt Allcock filed courageous dispatches from the front line of state primary education. Nick Seaton has been, as always, a mine of useful information on just about everything. Peter Ireland, who wrote me the rudest letter I received when I was Chief Inspector and who is now a friend and colleague at the University of Buckingham, has shown me what real educational leadership can achieve. Neither he nor Philip Fawkes, whose maverick brilliance cheers me up every time I visit Bruern Abbey, would ever have achieved the National Professional Qualification for Headship.

Sunday Times readers and others have sent me a fascinating array of examination papers, dating, in one case, back to 1929. Thank you.

My editor, James Croft, could not have been more supportive and thorough in his scrutiny of my drafts. Geoffrey Hill, whose poetry I have read with deepening admiration for forty years, kindly gave me permission to use an extract from his poem, *The Triumph of Love*, as my epigraph and title.

Christine, my wife, has propped me up throughout.

Hendre Gwenllian
March 2009

Introduction

I WROTE *Class War*, an analysis of what was wrong with state education and New Labour education policies, in the months following my resignation as Chief Inspector of Schools in November 2000. I thought then that that was that. There was not anything else I could say or wanted to say on the subject. I would write newspaper articles and comment on radio and television, but the last thing I envisaged was another book. I wanted to do more walking and climbing. With my friend, Anthony O'Hear, I had set up an anti-department of education at the University of Buckingham and I was planning to launch a company which would run private schools. Cognita, the education company, now owns fifty schools. Buckingham is training ninety or so PGCE students, and this year started to run a masters degree in education leadership. And, I find, rather to my surprise, that I have written another book.

I changed my mind for three reasons. The first is that problems in state schools are, again to my surprise (because I did not think it was possible), worse than they were in 2001. Locked into its compulsion to run things from the centre and desperate to find the initiative which might save ministers' skins, the Government has continued its strategy of hyperactive intervention. The story of how the Government has failed since 1997 and what this failure has meant for millions of children needs, I think, to be told. In particular, and this is my second reason, it needs to be told because it is possible that in the next two years we will have a change of government and an opportunity, therefore, to effect change. Mr Cameron has, no doubt, drawn his own conclusions from the failures of the last twelve years. Those conclusions need, however, to be translated into a genuinely Conservative education policy, which, as yet, we do not have. I have sought, therefore, to outline such a policy.

The third reason is personal. I have two granddaughters: a five-year-old who has just started school and another, aged two, who will soon follow in her footsteps. I want them to benefit from the educational opportunities I was lucky enough to experience. If things continue as they are, this is not going to happen.

Switching on the radio last summer I heard Secretary of State for Education, Ed Balls, talking about the new Diploma qualification which was about to be introduced into schools and colleges. He was, as you might expect, extolling the virtues of the Diploma. Everyone in education, he said, was really enthusiastic. The interviewer commented that Chris Woodhead wasn't. 'Chris', Mr Balls replied, 'is out of step.'

With whom, I wondered? With Mr Balls, yes, indeed. I am not so much out of step with the policies he and his predecessors have pursued as disappearing fast over the opposite horizon. With headteachers in state secondary schools? I am not sure. In private a good number are very willing to admit that they share my concerns about the Diploma and many other aspects of Government policy. In public, they find it harder to be honest. Mavericks are not welcome in what has become a heavily policed thought world, and most tend to choose their words carefully. The majority of independent headteachers certainly agree with me about the Diploma. A mere three per cent of them, according to a recent survey,[1] have even bothered to discuss it as a possible qualification for their pupils. Many worry, as I worry, about the dumbing down of the curriculum, the fads that are pursued in the never-ending drive to 'modernise' every aspect of our children's lives at school, the substitution of social engineering for education. Parents worry, too, if my *Sunday Times* postbag is anything to go by. I may be out of step with politicians and their apparatchiks, but I might, I feel, be speaking for a good number of ordinary teachers and anxious parents.

The Diploma is but one disagreement in what has proved to be a long and fundamental quarrel – a quarrel this book seeks to explain. Chapter 1 discusses the state of public examinations. I compare the demands of O Level and A Level papers from thirty years ago with the demands (I use the word loosely) of examinations set in 2008. Ministers might fulminate against commentators like myself who dare question 'the achievements of hardworking students and their deeply committed teachers', but the evidence speaks for itself. More students have been awarded top grades in recent years because the examinations they sit have become progressively easier.

Chapters 2 and 3 analyse what I take to be the two core beliefs that have driven Labour's education reforms. The first is that if opportunity could be equalised, whatever this might mean, everyone would succeed, and, in particular, working class children would claim their fair share of places at successful schools and top universities. As Chief Inspector of Schools, I did everything in my power to expose the inadequacy of schools that blamed family breakdown and endemic unemployment for what in fact were failures of leadership and teaching. My attacks on what I saw as a culture of low expectation did not endear me to the teacher unions and, as some readers will remember, upset a good number of left-leaning pundits. So be it: there were (and still, I am afraid, are) fundamental problems in too many schools. I continue to believe that every child has a right to realise whatever talent he or she might have, but this is not to endorse some spurious ideal of equality of opportunity. Experience tells me that individuals have very different abilities and aspirations and that social engineering will never deliver the utopia ministers, from Tony Blair onwards, have dangled before us. Indeed, the pursuit of utopias can have unintended and negative consequences. If all are expected to win prizes, then the prizes become meaningless. Those left-leaning pundits need to ask themselves why England has become a less socially mobile country than it was in the 1950s, and, more fundamentally, whether equality of opportunity is a goal that is either realisable or even desirable.

Belief two is that we live in 'a knowledge economy', and that students must stay at school for longer and longer in order to develop the ever more sophisticated skills the economy is supposed to need. I do not think that the 'knowledge economy' exists, and, following Professor Alison Wolf, I query the now universal assumption that our economic competitiveness depends upon the never-ending expansion of post-16 education and training. This expansion has wasted millions of pounds of public money. Worse, the Government's utilitarian obsessions have, in my view, undermined belief in the intrinsic value of academic study, and will, if this philistinism continues, threaten the character of universities, like Oxford and Cambridge, that still have a global reputation for academic excellence.

Since what matters most is what we think our children should be taught, Chapter 4 analyses the assumptions underpinning the new National Curriculum introduced into secondary schools in September 2008. This is a curriculum with little time for the teaching of traditional subject knowledge. It aims rather to 'enable young people to become successful learners, confident individuals and responsible citizens', and, in pursuit of these elusive goals, has become a vehicle for political ideas about the 'benefits of diversity', 'global citizenship' and 'sustainability'. Education has become indoctrination.

The primary curriculum appears to be travelling in the same direction. Sir Jim Rose has, at the time of writing, yet to publish his final report on his review of the primary curriculum, but the recommendations of his interim report are unlikely to change. Chapter 5 discusses how his proposals will return primary education to the serendipitous days of the 1960s.

Why, you might be thinking, do teachers put up with it all? The answer is that Labour's greatest achievement has been to create what I can only call an 'educational thought world': a set of ideas about the purpose of education and the nature of teaching that has been imposed upon the profession. New entrants to the profession are trained on courses which have to conform to strict and comprehensive criteria laid down by the Teacher Development Agency. Needless to say, these criteria reflect the Government's agenda. The message is reinforced by Local Authority advisers who run courses designed to ensure that their teachers are fully conversant with and committed to 'good practice'. Pages of Department for Children, Schools and Families (DCSF) 'guidance' descend weekly on schools. Anyone who wants to become a headteacher has to study for the National Professional Qualification in Headship (NPQH), and those who question official orthodoxies are unlikely to qualify. The National Curriculum, with its warped, ideological view of the educational enterprise, exerts its stranglehold daily on classroom activities. Ofsted inspectors lurk in the bushes waiting to report on any failure to conform. Chapter 6 describes the work of these various enforcement agencies.

When Labour came to power the mantra was 'standards not structures'. Mr Blair's Government was going to resist the temptation to fiddle with the structure of, in particular, secondary education and instead dedicate itself to raising standards. Ministerial willpower proved weak, and recent years have seen endless tinkering. For years Lord Adonis laboured heroically in his quest to drum up business support for City Academies. Different labels have been stuck on 'bog standard' comprehensives to demonstrate the vibrant diversity of secondary education under Labour. Chapter 7 asks the obvious question: have these structural changes had the slightest impact on standards? It also examines the controversies surrounding grammar schools and faith schools and discusses the vexed problem of how local authorities should deal with the problem that demand for good schools continues, despite all this ministerial tinkering, to outstrip supply. What constitutes a fair approach to admissions?

The independent sector educates some seven per cent of pupils. Survey after survey reveals that most parents would prefer to send their children to private schools if they could afford the fees. Chapter 8 asks whether this is a sensible aspiration. Does the fact that independent schools dominate the league tables reflect the nature of their intake or tell us something about the characteristics of successful schools? Is it possible to reconcile a commitment to 'social justice' with the continuing existence of the private sector? And what of the future? Can fees continue to rise as they have in the past? How will new demands that charitable trust schools should demonstrate how they benefit the wider community affect provision and, indeed, fees? And what of companies like Cognita, the schools group I chair? What will the independent sector look like in ten years time?

An election is inevitable in the not-too-distant future. Conservative policies need, therefore, to be scrutinised. The trouble, I argue in Chapter 9, is that at the time of writing there are few coherent policies. There are commitments, such as that of allowing no more grammar schools (or maybe one or two in areas where grammar schools already exist) and to a National Curriculum, which run counter to basic Conservative beliefs. An opposition should, in my view, oppose, and I find it very hard to identify real differences between the Conservative and Labour positions. I offer Mr Cameron a way forward that would allow conservative-minded voters interested in education to vote for the Conservative party.

A conclusion ties, as conclusions do, the different strands of the book together.

Finally in this Preface, I would like to ask the question that anyone reading thus far is probably asking: was Mr Balls right? Is this man 'out of step', which is code, of course, for 'isolated, embittered and probably mad'? I know, as I have already suggested, that plenty of people do agree with what I have said about education over the years. But I also know that no other senior public figure has chosen to attack Government policy and the educational beliefs upon which it is based. This might be because everyone else agrees with the beliefs and supports, therefore, the policy. It might be because they have had the wool pulled over their eyes. It might be because they think that they might have more influence if they stay within the machine. It might, less honourably, be because they like the prestige and, indeed, the honours that obedience brings.

This brings me back to why I resigned as Chief Inspector of Schools and, having resigned, made such a fuss. In part, it is because I have spent much of my life thinking about words. I believe that 'we should mean something by our words, and know what we mean'.[2] I have never been able to live with the rhetoric of policy pronouncement: by which I mean the failure ever to argue the case, the unexamined assumptions, the assumption that no examination is necessary. Why, I ask myself, should ministers and the officials who draft the gobbledegook they spout get away with it? Their slipshod prose betrays either a mind that cannot think or a patronising arrogance that does not care.

Neither, to my mind, is acceptable. Of course, it is the substance of the policy that ultimately matters, not the language in which it is clothed, and, as will already be clear, I disagree profoundly with virtually everything that has been done to our schools and universities in recent years. I had little option but to resign.

In that discussions about education are always personal, it is worth, perhaps, saying a little about how these disagreements have been influenced by my own experience as a child in what was a very typical 1950s South London primary school and later at Wallington Grammar School. My teachers at primary school taught me to read and write. I learnt a few facts about history and geography and natural history, enough, certainly, to send me to the library to find out more. I took the 11+ a year early and suffered, as far as I am aware, no long-term trauma.

Wallington was pretty characteristic of the period, too. The uniform included a cap which was meant to be worn to and from school. There were prefects. The cane, as I discovered twice, was the punishment of last resort. We were allocated to different houses and competition between the houses was a major aspect of school life. That competition fed through into classroom life. We were streamed according to academic ability and lists were published each week giving our position in the form. I had done well in primary school, but soon found myself struggling, which might be why I spent a fair amount of time playing the fool and ended up in the headmaster's study with my bottom in the air. The dinners were foul and we had two or three hours of homework a night. I can remember standing in the rain waiting for the bus one November night after a detention thinking that I had one advantage over the teachers who were persecuting me: I was younger than they were, and the odds were they would die first.

So, when I say that the seven years I spent at that school opened my eyes to a world I did not know existed, I am not romanticising a period of my life that was in some ways very difficult. Visiting the school some years ago to give the prizes, I stood in the classroom where on Tuesday mornings we were tested orally on our grasp of the previous night's Latin homework. The old terror flooded back. That said, as I wandered round, poking my nose into the showers to see if there was still mould on the walls (there was, I am glad to say), I knew that this school had given me opportunities I want children today to have if they can benefit from them.

It was, first, a school which functioned as a community. We were expected to contribute to the life of our houses, represent the school in sporting and cultural activities, take responsibility for ourselves and others. Time was not wasted on citizenship and PSHE (personal, social, health education) lessons. The understandings and values these pseudo-subjects now struggle to make explicit were embedded in the everyday fabric of the school, and were transmitted all the more effectively because of that. The focus was unambiguously on the academic. There was no nonsense, to quote from the Government's Children's Plan, about 'successful learners, confident individuals and responsible citizens'. If asked, I am sure the headmaster would have agreed that these were not unreasonable aims, but he would also have pointed out that they were aims that depended as much upon the abilities and personalities of his pupils as the magic wands of his staff, and he would have added, no doubt, that he rather hoped that his pupils might end up knowing a little more science and Latin than they did when they arrived at the school.

At first, of course, the mastery of that knowledge involved a fair bit of grind. The current wisdom is that every lesson must be instantly enjoyable, that children must immediately appreciate the 'relevance' to their everyday lives of everything they are taught. These are misconceptions I touch upon in subsequent chapters. Here I simply want to say that what is worth learning is without exception difficult to learn. We delude ourselves and damage our children if we pretend otherwise. Yes, of course, those Latin lessons were a trial. I cannot even pretend that I ever came to achieve anything other than a very rudimentary competence in the language. My teacher shared my amazement when I passed the O Level examination. But I did learn that if you want to make any progress, you have to struggle, and, in some subjects, like, above all, English, the subject I eventually read at university, the horizons did begin to broaden as I moved through the school. Gradually, very gradually, I began to realise the poverty of ignorance.

Then there were the teachers. Again, I must defend myself against the charge of nostalgia. There were bad teachers at Wallington when I was a pupil. Some simply could not teach, and, looking back, I wonder how they survived our calculated and determined attempts to render their lives miserable. But the good were good: teachers who cared passionately about their subject, who expected their pupils to be interested and to succeed, and who, while more often than not mavericks and eccentrics who would find today's formulaic approach to 'good classroom practice' risible, were masters of their professional craft. Such teachers exist, I know, today. They are, though, a rare breed, and they are getting rarer. This Government, as I show in Chapter 6, has done everything in its power to programme the teaching profession into a robotic conformity. I do not blame our teachers. Their promotion depends upon the enthusiasm with which they espouse the latest modernising fad. Six principals of major city Academies attended a talk I gave recently in which I questioned the 'agenda' they had been appointed to implement. Not one responded. Was my eloquence so compelling that there was nothing anyone could say? I doubt it. The more likely explanation is that these men and women were embarrassed, but whether they were embarrassed by my mentioning the unmentionable (arguing, for example, that it was rather a good idea to teach children new knowledge) or by their agreement and the inauthenticity, therefore, of their position, I shall never know. Whatever: I look back at my own school days and I want my grandchildren to have the chance to attend a similar school.

I knew back in 2000, when I resigned as Chief Inspector, that there was no chance of influencing the direction from within. Everything that has happened has confirmed my judgement. I do not think I am embittered, and I know I am not mad. I know, too, that few issues in social policy are more important than education. I did not plan to write this book, but, in the end, I had no option.

Chapter 1

Dumbing Down: The Proof

What do you think?

HERE IS A QUESTION, more challenging than most you will encounter in today's GCSE examination, but not too difficult really. If you find a paragraph or two of consecutive prose a bit of a struggle, a cartoon will, of course, constitute an equally acceptable answer:

> 'Teenagers at a North Tyneside school have reached nirvana: their headteacher has developed a technique by which they passed an entire GCSE module in the space of 90 minutes – and a third of that time they spent playing basketball. Monkseaton High has introduced a memory technique that saw 80% of a class of 46 13–14-year-olds get at least a D grade in a Science GCSE module. The system involves pupils watching a 20 minute PowerPoint™ presentation of 70 slides covering the entire module, which is narrated by the teacher.'[3]
>
> What does this newspaper report tell you about (a) the latest groundbreaking developments in twenty-first century teaching techniques? (b) the stomach-churning banality of twenty-first century examinations?

The sterile debate: Ofqual to the rescue

Last summer, Secretary of State for Education, Ed Balls, said: 'I sincerely hope that this year with the formation of the new independent standards regulator, Ofqual, we can finally begin to put an end to the annual sterile debate which claims that improved results means "dumbing down".'[4] Warming to his theme, he continued: 'Ofqual will provide a robust, transparent regulatory framework which can continue to give people confidence in the standards of both existing qualifications and tests.'

The Chairman of Ofqual is one Kathleen Tattersall. Ms Tattersall has been involved in examining for 37 years. She ended her examining career as Chief Executive of the Assessment and Qualifications Alliance (AQA), one of the three national examining bodies. Her experience is unrivalled. Her independence, in that she has been a key figure in the world of public examinations through three decades of dumbing down, is a matter of opinion. She may be able to distance herself from her previous work and review what has happened to our public examination system with the fresh and sceptical eye which is so desperately needed. I hope she can. The evidence to date suggests that she will defend the status quo, and that Ofqual, however hard the Secretary of State might try to hype its independence, will be one more toothless quango.

Take the major reforms to the GCSE examination, which were announced in the summer of 2008. The GCSE is to be 'modularised'. This means that each subject syllabus will be divided up into a number of units and that candidates will be tested on each unit as it is completed. If students fail a module they will be allowed to re-take it. Ms Tattersall moved swiftly and predictably to reassure potential sceptics that 'Ofqual will ensure that the GCSE standard will be maintained.'[5] She did not, however, explain how an examination in which candidates are tested on small parts of the syllabus (and can re-take each test if they do not like the mark they achieve) can be compared to a traditional end-of-course examination in which they have just one chance to demonstrate their grip on the totality of the syllabus. You might not like the stress involved in the latter kind of examination, but you cannot pretend that the modular examination is as demanding. Unless, that is, you are the Chairman of the body responsible for defending educational standards.

Perhaps Ms Tattersall failed to explain why she was so confident that nothing untoward was happening because she was so keen to tell us that these 'new GCSEs will ensure that young people are able to demonstrate their skills, knowledge and understanding when studying for a qualification which meets their needs'.[6] The idea that qualifications now have to 'meet young people's needs' is an article of faith for both the new GCSEs and the 14–19 Diplomas which I discuss in the following chapter. Speaking at an event designed to publicise the Diplomas, the Schools Minister, Jim Knight, reported, for example, that 'students tell us that they want flexible qualifications that match their ambitions'.[7] I know I find it hard to keep up with the latest developments in educational policy, but

I had rather thought that the boot was meant to be on the other foot: that the issue was whether examinations identified the candidates who understood the demands of the syllabus, not whether the syllabus had succeeded in 'meeting the candidates' needs' (whatever this last phrase might mean).

In that the Government never takes any notice of the comments made each year by those of us who are not convinced by the ministerial rhetoric, the Secretary of State is right: the annual debate about dumbing down is sterile. Ofqual is unlikely to change anything. The latest GCSE reforms simply show that the Government remains more interested in the 'needs' of students than the maintenance of examination standards. Results get better each year, but the examinations get worse. It is not the students' fault. It is not the teachers'. It is the Government which is to blame. Ministers want to bathe in the warm glow of improving statistics. They have deceived themselves that a system in which everyone wins prizes is one in which the prizes mean something. Sadly, they do not. They do not mean anything.

The ministerial line is that standards improve every year because students work harder and teachers teach better every year. A more sophisticated defence against the accusation that examinations have been dumbed down is that it is impossible to compare today's examinations with those set ten, twenty, thirty years ago. This is what David Hargreaves used to say when he was Chief Executive of the Qualifications and Curriculum Authority, the body which was then responsible for the maintenance of examination standards. The Hargreaves argument is that today's examinations are different from earlier examinations. They test different things in a different way and it is impossible, therefore, to try to establish whether they are more or less demanding than the examinations I, for example, sat in 1962 (O Level) and 1964 (A Level). This argument slides quickly into a value-laden variant. Greg Watson, the Chief Executive of Oxford, Cambridge and RSA Examinations (OCR), one of the three main examining bodies, stated recently that: 'There has been a move away from rote learning and repetition towards using data and processing it.'[8] Today's examinations, in other words, might appear to require candidates to know and remember less than was the case in the past, but this is because, for very good educational reasons, we no longer force-feed pupils with gobbets of useless information. Education has changed, and for the better; examinations reflect this change and should be celebrated for their new, and more effective, focus.

So, the question we need to ask ourselves is whether Watson is right. Has education changed for the better and in the ways he describes? This is the question that lies at the heart of this book. I will not at this stage spell out why I think Watson's assertion is a panglossian caricature of the truth. Instead, let us look at some actual GCSE and A Level papers.

GCSE

Last year, 61 per cent of 16-year-olds achieved a pass (grade C or above) in GCSE English. Most people would expect a GCSE pass to guarantee a basic competence in the language. It does not. Last year the Headmaster of Harrow School, Barnaby Lenon, was quoted as saying that it is perfectly possible to achieve an A* grade in GCSE English and be weak at grammar and spelling.[9] Harrow's solution to this problem is to require its sixth form students to sit a literacy test. Those who make more than twenty mistakes are given extra tuition until they pass. Harrow, of course, is a top public school. If its headmaster has these concerns about the basic literacy of his students, and has gone to the extent of devising such a test, what does this say about standards generally? The test has sections on Spelling, Vocabulary, Apostrophes, Further punctuation and Proofreading. Here are two of them:

1. Spelling

Underline the correct spelling in the following groups of words:

(i) professor/proffessor/proffesor
(ii) committed/comited/commited
(iii) acomodation/accommodation/ accomodation
(iv) unneccessary/unneccesary/unnecessary
(v) embarrass/embarras/embarass
(vi) iridescence/irridescence/iridesence
(vii) similies/similes/simmiles
(viii) pusilanemous/pusillanemous/ pusillanimous
(ix) privilege/priviledge/privelige
(x) viccissitude/vicisitude/vicissitude

Figure 1a Harrow School Literacy Test 2008, Question 1

4. Further punctuation

Write a comma or a full stop beneath the *:

(i) MY MAIN HOBBY IS FISHING * MY SECOND HOBBY IS PLAYING THE TROMBONE.

(ii) WILLIAM * PLEASE COLLECT IN THE WORK.

(iii) SHE SANG WELL * THIS WAS SURPRISING.

(iv) JOHN SWIMS WELL * HOWEVER, MARY HATES THE WATER.

Add full stops and capital letters to:

(v) George was quite clear that he needed to work harder if he was going to achieve the grades he required it was quite possible to get three A grades his sister had got two As and a B and she was far dimmer than he was

Add commas to:

(vi) For lunch the school offered lamb chops pasta baked potatoes yogurt trifle and fresh fruit.

(vii) James the talented but lazy cricketer never seemed to score as highly as the others.

(viii) Henry walked up to his room opened the door ripped off his clothes and dived into bed.

(ix) Sally however always wanted to watch television rather than do her homework.

Add semi-colons to:

(x) I have porridge for breakfast every day it sees me through to lunch.

(xi) The boy's mother wrote to the Head Master to complain about table manners Harrovians ought to know how to hold a knife and fork.

(xii) At Harrow Winston Churchill was dreadful at Latin but he learnt to write English properly we sometimes forget that he won the Nobel Prize for Literature

Figure 1b Harrow School Literacy Test 2008, Question 4

When O Levels were abolished in 1988 we were told that grades A–C in the new GCSE examination would be equivalent to grades A–C in the O Level. A candidate who could answer the following question from a 1963 O Level English paper set by the University of London would not have much trouble with the demands of the Harrow literacy test:

3. (*a*) Analyse the following sentence into clauses, *writing out each clause in full;* give the grammatical description of each clause, and state its grammatical function in the sentence.

When the prisoner was brought to trial, it was believed by the few friends he had that he would be acquitted, since his case had been postponed several times so that evidence might be collected for his defence, which rested on a claim that he had become a naturalized Spanish citizen.

Figure 2 University of London O Level 1963 English Language Paper 2, Summer 1963, Question 3(a)

Nine years later, candidates for the O Level paper set by the same Board were expected to write an essay of 450 or more words, 'planning (their) composition according to the nature of the material and form', writing 'in an appropriate style', and 'taking care with grammar, spelling and punctuation'. I used to teach this paper and I can testify to the fact that the latter instruction mattered. No candidate, however creatively inspired they might be, would pass if they did not know how to spell. This same paper required candidates to summarise a complex passage of 500 words into 150 of their own words and to answer a demanding set of comprehension questions. The comprehension question in January 1972, which totalled more than 1,000 words, was divided into three sections with three accompanying sets of questions. Here is the middle section of the question:

2. Read the following passage (which has been divided into three sections for your convenience) and answer the questions.

[...]

B

Uncle Martha would have behaved quite well, I am convinced, if he had been left alone, and would have acquitted himself with perfect propriety in all the transactions of the day; but it seemed to be Aunt Martha's immovable belief that he was wholly incapable of any action, even the simplest and most obvious, unless impelled by shoves and jerks. Consequently he was shoved into the mourning carriage – we had two – and jerked into the corner opposite to the one he selected; shoved out – almost on all fours – at the cemetery; and, perceiving him entering the little chapel of his own motion, Aunt Martha overtook him and jerked him in there. This example presently impressed the other ladies with the expediency of shoving Uncle Martha at any convenient opportunity; so that he arrived home with us at last in a severely jostled condition.

'Ah well,' said the Fat Aunt, shaking her head, with a deep sigh that suggested repletion, 'ah well; it's what we must all come to!'

There had been a deal of other conversation, but I remember this remark because the Fat Aunt had already made it twice.

'Ah, indeed,' assented another aunt, a thin one, 'so we must, sooner or later.'

'Yes, yes; as I often say, we're all mortal.'

'Yes, indeed!'

'We've all got to be born, and we've all got to die.'

'That's true!'

'Rich and poor – just the same.'

'Ah!'

'In the midst of life we're in the middle of it.'

'Ah yes!'

Grandfather Nat, deeply impressed, made haste to refill the Fat Aunt's glass, and to push the cake-dish nearer. Aunt Martha jerked Uncle Martha's elbow towards his glass, which he was neglecting, with a sudden nod and a frown of pointed significance – even command.

[...]

Figure 3 University of London O Level English Language Paper 2, January 1972, Question 2, Passage Section B (questions on p.16)

Answer the following questions *in your own words as far as possible*. Questions marked with an asterisk (*) should be answered *very briefly*, and in these answers complete sentences are not essential. (For instance, an answer may consist of a clause: 'Because . . . ') Other questions should be answered in complete and correct sentences.

[...]

From Section B:

(*e*) Explain, with particular reference to the words in italics, what is meant by the statement that, left alone, Uncle Martha 'would have *acquitted himself* with perfect *propriety* in all the *transactions* of the day' (ll. 23–25).

*(*f*) (i) Describe in a word or short phrase:

(*a*) Aunt Martha's behaviour towards her husband.

(*b*) Uncle Martha's behaviour towards his wife.

(ii) What does the behaviour of the other women present show about their opinion of Uncle Martha?

*(*g*) Give in a single word or short phrase the meaning of *two* of the following words *as used in the passage*: expediency (l. 34); repletion (l. 38); assented (l. 42); significance (l. 56).

(*h*) In line 41 we are told about a remark that the Fat Aunt had made that she had 'already made it twice'. What *other* evidence is there in this section of this lady's habit of repeating herself?

The O Level was, of course, an examination that was taken against the clock in an examination hall at the end of the course. Not so with today's GCSE, where 40% of the marks are awarded for coursework. Today's examination assesses three criteria: Speaking and Listening; Reading a Text; Writing. Speaking and Listening (to which 10% of the marks are allocated) is assessed entirely on contributions made during the year and is therefore difficult, if not impossible, to authenticate. The Reading and Writing components are assessed through a mixture of examination (60%) and coursework (30%). Questions 1 and 2 from the Higher Tier AQA English Paper 1 for 2008 were as follows:

2

SECTION A: READING

Answer **all** questions in this section.

You are advised to spend about one hour on this section.

1 Read **Item 1**, the article called 'The first greenies' by Michele Hanson.

(a) According to Michele Hanson, what could 'today's green consumers' learn from 'Britain in the 40s and 50s'? *(7 marks)*

(b) What criticisms does Michele Hanson make of other people's behaviour and attitudes? *(6 marks)*

2 Now read **Item 2**, the front page from *The Independent* newspaper.

Now look again at **Item 1** and **Item 2** together.

(a) Write about the ways in which presentational devices are used in each item. *(8 marks)*

(b) Compare the ways in which words are used for effect in each item. *(6 marks)*

M/Jun08/3702/1H R

Figure 4a AQA GCSE English (Specification A) Paper 1 (Higher tier), June 2008, Section A, Questions 1 and 2

Item 1

Ethical living

Today's green consumers could learn a lot from Britain in the 40s and 50s, writes **Michele Hanson** (a woman who would never throw away tinfoil)

The first greenies

The front cover of a government booklet published in the 1940s (printed above)

It is painful for many of my generation, born in the 40s and 50s, to watch the world's resources being needlessly frittered away. We were trained up, after the war, not to waste a scrap of anything. We lived through years of giblets and darning, rationing, gas fires and "make-do and mend", and now, all around us, it's "don't bother and chuck". But perhaps not for much longer. Make-do and mend is starting all over again, but now it's called recycling.

I, and many of my peers, still squeeze all the little bits of nearly finished soap together, re-use tea-bags, share baths, wash and re-use tinfoil, leave the heating off, wear an extra jumper, save elastic bands, old sheets, bits of string and brown paper bags.

Brown paper is perfect for soaking up the excess oil from home-made fish and chips. But who still makes that at home any more? Only me. And how do you make chicken soup if you can't buy giblets and have to beg the organic butcher for a carcass? My mother used every bit of a chicken. Now all those bits of chicken go into pet food or nuggets or bins. Bins! To our parents and still to us, the worst crime is to waste food. Last week, my friend Jennifer – aged 67 – was travelling on a train with a younger person who left the crusts from her sandwiches. Jennifer was appalled. She sees pupils at a local school chuck flour and eggs at each other at the end of term. "It breaks my heart," says she. Good job she isn't outside our local school at lunch times. There pupils hurl their food about, pelting each other with chips, pizzas, kebabs and assorted drecky snacks. And there we were in the war with one egg each fortnight.

Back at home, Jennifer is forever asking her children, now in their 20s and 30s, to turn the lights off, but they only mock and call "Blackout, blackout". Same with me. I come in at night and every room in the house is ablaze with light, and Daughter is in only one of them.

When I was growing up, my mother was at home, doing all the cooking, hand-washing, putting things through the mangle, sewing, knitting, darning, growing vegetables, making stock out of peelings and onion skins, doing all that fiddling about with chickens, steaming puddings wrapped in old cloths and, in 1942, washing my nappies. No disposable ones available. Imagine the workload. No wonder she often had to have a shout. There were very few washing machines, dry cleaning was expensive, we had to spot-clean and brush serge and wool skirts, and hang the washing out to dry.

My friend Andrea collected bottles and returned them to the shop and took papers to a collecting point, both for a few pennies pocket money. It trained her from an early age to recycle. Her mother had a proper string tin – an old cocoa tin with a hole in the top to put your bits of string in.

My friend Andrea's family, like many others, unravelled their old jumpers and re-knitted them. At that time there was no nylon mixed with the wool. It easily became matted, particularly under the arms, so you couldn't use that bit, which meant less useable wool each time. The woollies got smaller and smaller, until you ended up with a tank top, often striped, with different wools from different jumpers. Now woollies cost flumpence. Chuck. Never mind the slave labourers who made them and the world's bursting landfill sites.

Andrea remembers the government booklet 'Make-do and Mend' (above). She still has one. It offered advice: cut old sheets in half down the worn middle, then sew the outside edges together, so that the worn bits are now on the outside edge. Make rag rugs and dolls, polish and repair shoes, re-use wool, steam it straight again, even mend ladders in stockings. And darn socks. My mother had a wooden darning thingy in her sewing bag and darned with it until her arthritis put a stop to it.

She probably remembered when clothing and fabric were rationed. Your coupons added up to one new outfit a year. Imagine that girls. You pampered creatures. Could you bear it? One day, you may have to. Ha ha.

Figure 4b AQA GCSE English (Specification A) Paper 1 (Higher tier), June 2008, Section A, Item 1. The original author of the piece was Michele Hanson. Copyright Guardian News & Media Ltd 2006.

Item 2

THE INDEPENDENT

NEWSPAPER OF THE YEAR

(Ireland, €1) 70p
Monday 22 January 2007
www.independent.co.uk

Today
.media
16-page supplement inside

This is a swede, on sale in a leading supermarket. It is shrink-wrapped in plastic, despite nature providing it with protective wrapping of its own. It is a symbol of the absurd and excessive packaging in our shops – and of the urgent need for...

THE CAMPAIGN AGAINST WASTE

FULL REPORTS PAGES 2 & 3; **LEADING ARTICLE** PAGE 28

Figure 4c AQA GCSE English (Specification A) Paper 1 (Higher tier), June 2008, Section A, Item 2. Reproduced from the original article in *The Independent*, Monday 22nd January 2007. Copyright Independent News and Media Limited Ltd 2007.

Last November, Graham Stuart, the Conservative MP for Beverley and Holderness, read out the following question from a GCSE Science paper to the Children, Schools and Families Select Committee:

> Residents have a variety of thoughts concerning the siting of the new power station. The two views are: 1. The nuclear power station will provide more employment in the area; 2. Any release of radioactive material would be very dangerous.

> Which statements are arguments in favour of siting the nuclear power station here – 1 only, 2 only, both 1 and 2, neither?[10]

He then asked, 'Is the department really sure that we are providing pupils with a rigorous scientific understanding?' 'Yes,' school's minister, Jim Knight, replied, 'I am absolutely happy that we are, and we have set up Ofqual to provide more public reassurance.'

It is good, I suppose, to have one's doubts about the impartiality of Ofqual confirmed, but, if Knight said what he said and kept a straight face, he deserves an Oscar. As with English, so too with Science. Here is a question from the GCSE Physics module (Higher Tier), June 2008:

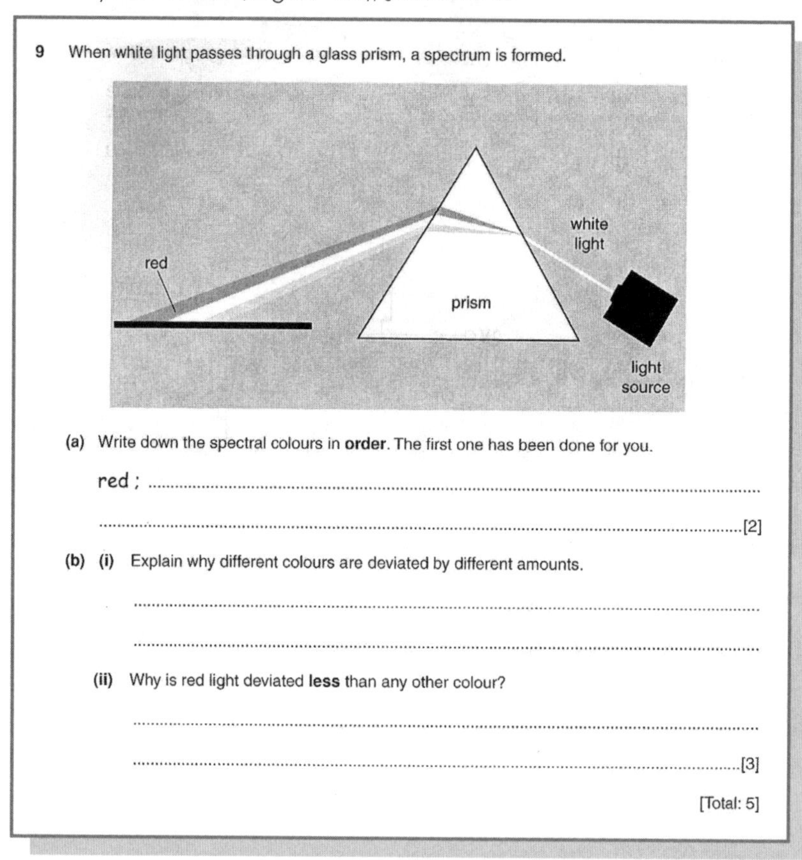

9 When white light passes through a glass prism, a spectrum is formed.

(a) Write down the spectral colours in **order**. The first one has been done for you.

red ; ....

.... [2]

(b) **(i)** Explain why different colours are deviated by different amounts.

....

....

(ii) Why is red light deviated **less** than any other colour?

....

.... [3]

[Total: 5]

Figure 5 OCR GCSE Gateway Science Physics B, Unit 2 Modules P4 P5 P6 (Higher tier), June 2008, Question 9

Compare the above to the following question which was set in the 1972 University of London O Level Physics paper:

B7. Describe an experiment to obtain a series of corresponding angles of incidence and reflection for rays of light reflected from the surface of a plane mirror. Indicate the relationship between these pairs of angles.

When a plane mirror is made of thick glass silvered on the back surface, it is found that an incident ray and the corresponding reflected ray do not meet at either surface of the glass. Explain with the aid of a diagram why this is so.

A lamp is placed in front of a thick glass mirror held vertically. Draw a diagram showing how more than one image of the lamp may be seen when viewed from one side.

Figure 6 University of London O Level Physics Paper 1, Summer 1972, Section B, Question B7

Dig into the background and it gets worse. The whole GCSE module was worth 60 marks. The pass mark for the module (grade C) was 23 out of 60. It is not just that the question is infantile by comparison to that asked in the O Level. Candidates can get over half the paper wrong and still get a grade C.

The situation in Biology is much the same. This is a question from the 2008 OCR Gateway Science Biology B paper (Higher Tier), in which, incidentally, the pass mark was 21 out of 60:

3 Kate is growing geraniums in her garden.

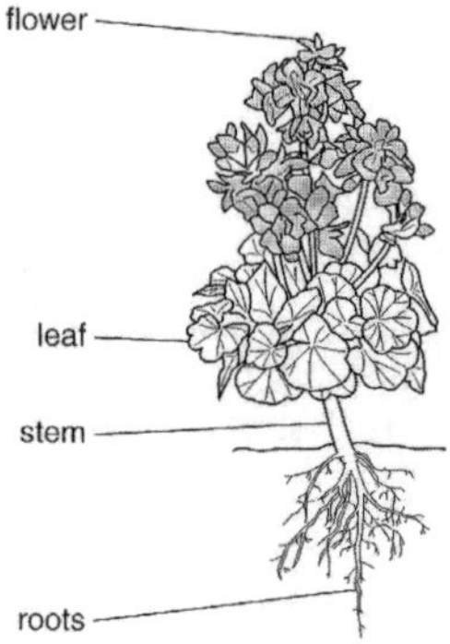

flower

leaf

stem

roots

(a) Geranium leaves are adapted for efficient photosynthesis.

Describe **two** ways leaves are adapted for efficient photosynthesis.

1 ....

....

2 ....

.... [2]

(b) Plants lose water from their leaves. This is called transpiration.

Describe how transpiration happens.

....

....

.... [2]

Figure 7 OCR GCSE Gateway Science Biology B, Unit 2 Modules B4 B5 B6 (Higher tier), June 2008, Question 3

Mr Knight might like to note that in the London O Level Biology paper candidates were asked:

> **3. What are the functions of the vascular tissues ('veins') in an herbaceous dicotyledon such as a buttercup? Describe an experiment that you could perform to demonstrate *one* of the functions you mention.**
>
> **With the *aid* of diagrams, compare the arrangement of vascular tissue in the stem and root of the herbaceous dicotyledon and briefly suggest a reason for the difference in arrangement.**

Figure 8 University of London O level Biology Paper 2, Summer 1972, Question 3

He might then like to comment on the relative 'scientific rigour' of the two questions and explain why the GCSE is pitiful in its demands when compared to the O Level.

More than a half of all pupils who take Chemistry GCSE are awarded an A or A* grade. The DCSF thinks we should celebrate this magnificent achievement and claims that 'standards in science have improved year on year thanks to ten years of sustained investment in teaching and the education system'.[11] The Royal Society of Chemistry disagrees. Having conducted an experiment in which 1,600 16-year-olds answered questions from O Level and GCSE questions set over the last fifty years, the Society is convinced that there 'has been a catastrophic slippage in school science standards'. The trial group scored an average of 35% on questions set today and 15% on questions set during the 1960s. My only surprise is that the latter figure is this high.

Greg Watson, you will remember, Chief Executive of the OCR, would have us believe that education and therefore examinations have progressed into the twenty-first century sunlight. GCSE examinations in Modern Foreign Languages (MFL) provide a good example of the progress he finds so captivating. The introduction of GCSE in 1988 brought about a revolution in MFL teaching. O Level examinations in MFL required candidates to have mastered a modicum of grammar and to be able to translate quite challenging pieces from, say, French into English and vice versa, with marks deducted for every mistake. What matters in the GCSE is the ability to communicate everyday information in a way that can be understood, with little regard for fluency or correctness. 'The important thing', candidates were told in the 2008 OCR GCSE German paper (Speaking Paper, Foundation and Higher Tier), 'is to convey the message.' And, in a similar vein, the Reading paper informed them that they did 'not have to write in full sentences' and that their 'answers [would] *not* be marked for the accuracy of the language' (my italics). (Don't worry, I had to read that last instruction twice, too.)

The rubric for the 1972 London French O Level stated: 'You must take special care to write correct, grammatical French which fully answers the question asked ... You should use a suitable tense of the verb, usually, but not always, that of the question.' This O Level, like every other MFL O Level of the time, involved: a translation from French into English, a translation from English into French, a composition in French, an aural comprehension test, and a dictation. The French composition question in 1972 was as follows:

5. Composition in French:

Write about 150 words on *one* of these subjects. Make your essay as correct and as interesting as you can. Choose a past tense, where required, suited to the composition you select, i.e. use *either* the Perfect (Passé Composé) *or* the Past Historic (Passé Simple, Passé Défini) as your main narrative tense. Check carefully everything you write.

(*a*) C'était, il y a quelques jours, l'anniversaire de votre mère. A cette occasion, vous avez pris l'initiative d'organiser une petite fête de famille. Racontez ce qui est arrivé.

(*b*) Votre frère aîné (ou sœur aînée) est momentanément éloigné(e) de la famille. Ecrivez-lui pour lui donner des nouvelles de la maison.

(*c*) En rangeant votre chambre, vous avez trouvé un de vos tout premiers jouets d'enfance. Décrivez-le. Quels souvenirs vous a-t-il rappelés?

(*d*) Racontez l'incident représenté par les images à la page 6.

(20 marks)

Figure 9 University of London O Level French, Summer 1972, Question 5

Today's GCSE does not require candidates to write a composition. There is a comprehension exercise of a kind. Here is an example from the 2008 OCR German paper:

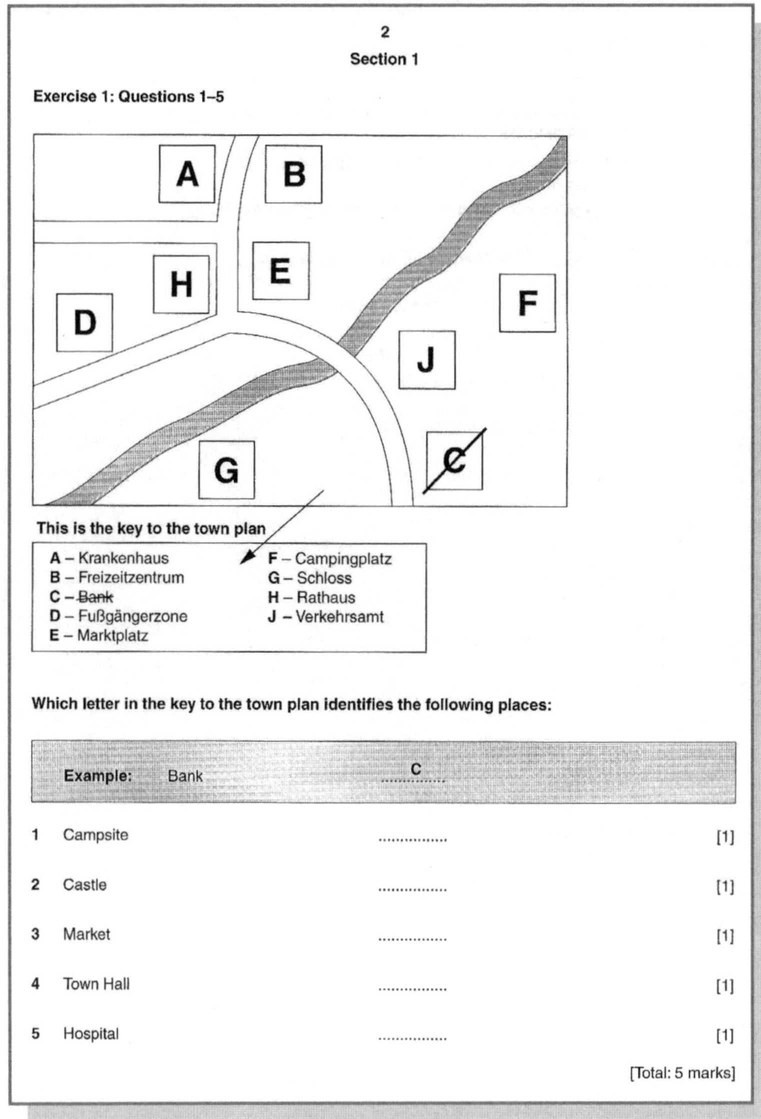

2

Section 1

Exercise 1: Questions 1–5

This is the key to the town plan

A – Krankenhaus	**F** – Campingplatz
B – Freizeitzentrum	**G** – Schloss
C – ~~Bank~~	**H** – Rathaus
D – Fußgängerzone	**J** – Verkehrsamt
E – Marktplatz	

Which letter in the key to the town plan identifies the following places:

Example:	Bank	C	
1	Campsite	....	[1]
2	Castle	....	[1]
3	Market	....	[1]
4	Town Hall	....	[1]
5	Hospital	....	[1]

[Total: 5 marks]

Figure 10 OCR GCSE German, Reading (Foundation tier), May 2008, Section 1, Exercise 1, Questions 1–5

I know no German, but had no difficulty in identifying two of the five answers. Neither, I imagine, did you. If we carried on through the paper we might well achieve our 40 per cent and walk away with our certificate of proficiency.

The point is, I hope, made. Finally, though, reflect for a moment on these Mathematics questions.

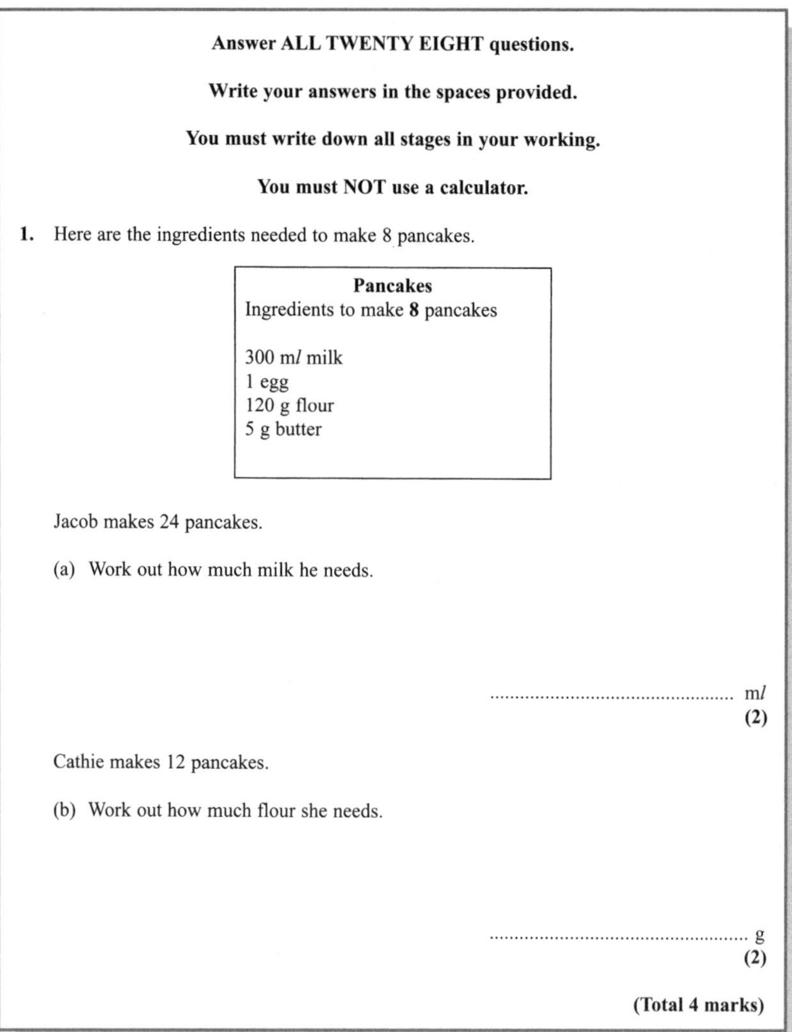

Answer ALL TWENTY EIGHT questions.

Write your answers in the spaces provided.

You must write down all stages in your working.

You must NOT use a calculator.

1. Here are the ingredients needed to make 8 pancakes.

Pancakes
Ingredients to make **8** pancakes

300 m*l* milk
1 egg
120 g flour
5 g butter

Jacob makes 24 pancakes.

(a) Work out how much milk he needs.

.... m*l*
(2)

Cathie makes 12 pancakes.

(b) Work out how much flour she needs.

.... g
(2)

(Total 4 marks)

Figure 11 Edexcel GCSE Mathematics A (Linear), Paper 3 (Non-calculator) (Higher tier), May 2008, Question 1

10. A garage sells British cars and foreign cars.
The ratio of the number of British cars sold to the number of foreign cars sold is 2 : 7

The garage sells 45 cars in one week.

(a) Work out the number of British cars the garage sold that week.

....
(2)

A car tyre costs £80 plus VAT at $17\frac{1}{2}\%$.

(b) Work out the total cost of the tyre.

£ ....
(3)

The value of a new car is £12 000
The value of the car depreciates by 20% per year.

(c) Work out the value of the car after 2 years.

£ ....
(3)

(Total 8 marks)

Figure 12 Edexcel GCSE Mathematics A (Linear), Paper 4 (With calculator) (Higher tier), June 2008, Question 10

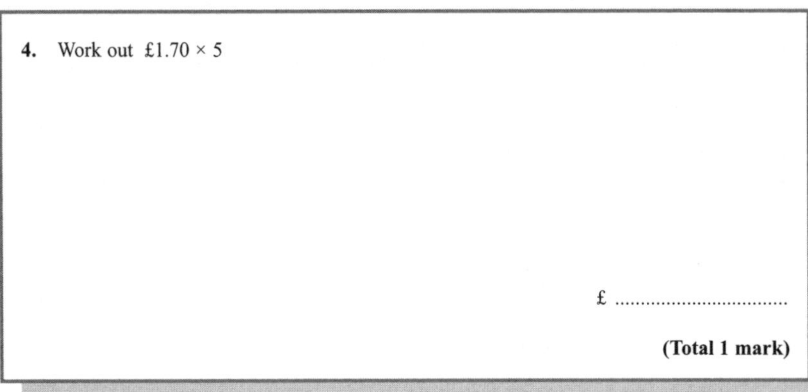

4. Work out £1.70 × 5

£ ....

(Total 1 mark)

Figure 13 Edexcel GCSE Mathematics A (Linear), Paper 2 (With calculator) (Foundation tier), June 2008, Question 4

I have, I hope, bolstered your mathematical confidence. Do not get too excited. Here is a question from a 1963 O Level mathematics paper:

> **(ii) A particle moves from rest in a straight line and after t seconds its velocity is $(3t^2 - 4t)$ feet per second. Calculate the distance which the particle travels in the interval of time from $t = 2$ to $t = 5$.**

Figure 14 University of London O level Pure Maths Paper 2, Syllabus B, 1963, Question 10(ii)[4]

Some students in some grammar and independent schools might understand that the concept of velocity can be represented by an algebraic expression and that integral calculus is the tool needed to solve the problem. Most would not know where to start.

A footnote

Last year, AQA, Britain's biggest examination board, admitted that, 'under pressure' from Ofqual, it had lowered the grade boundaries in science examinations to make the examination less difficult than it had been in previous years. Why? Because the pass mark AQA had set was higher than that set by the other two examination boards. One of these boards had awarded a C grade to candidates who got just 20 per cent of the questions correct. AQA had to be dragged into line so that its examinees were not disadvantaged. You could not have a clearer example of how central government influence can force standards down.

A Levels

Ten years ago, appearing before the House of Commons Education Select Committee, I said that the A Level examination was no longer fit for purpose. Too many candidates, even then, were achieving top grades and university tutors were complaining that an A grade told them very little about the real ability of the student. To my mind the answer was simple. We should make the examination harder so that fewer students were awarded top grades and more failed. The Committee disagreed. The Chairman, Barry Sheerman, who is, I believe, still in post, seemed particularly worried that in commenting on examination standards I was exceeding my brief as Chief Inspector. Other members of the Committee were horrified that I was calling into question the achievements of 'hard working' students and their dedicated teachers. It was, in short, good, knock-about comedy, but it left me fearful for the future of A Level. If the members of this Education Committee could not see what was blindingly obvious, what hope was there for an examination which had once had a world-wide reputation?

The answer, of course, was no hope whatsoever. Since then we have had 'Curriculum 2000', a Government initiative designed to make A Level subjects more accessible in order to encourage more students to stay on into the sixth form. The AS examination, which is taken at the end of the first year sixth, has been introduced. Syllabuses have been 'modularised' or divided into chunks which are assessed throughout the course. If a student does not like the mark they are awarded, then they can re-sit the test. Taken together, these developments have turned A Level study into a monotonous grind, and, in that any over-arching, synoptic work has been rendered difficult if not impossible to achieve within the limits of the modularised framework, helped to trivialise intellectual demand. Tightly defined 'specifications' have replaced the relative looseness of the old syllabus.

As Christopher Ray, the Headmaster of Manchester Grammar School puts it: 'An A Level syllabus for a given subject tended to allow scope for examiners to probe around as well as within the content set down' but 'a specification is much more prescriptive, specific, and therefore (in examining terms) limiting in character: farewell to general and flexible references to items such as "Momentum, elastic and inelastic collisions: formulae, applications and relevant experiments"; welcome to "the student shall re-call x, be aware that y and understand z".'[12]

The production of detailed mark schemes specifying the required answer has had, perhaps, an even more damaging impact on standards. Talk to any experienced sixth form teacher and they will tell you the same story of how their brightest students have been penalised for offering an individual argument that does not cover the required ground. Too often, moreover, the more demanding topics have been quietly removed from syllabuses. I had dinner recently with a Physics teacher from one of the most academically successful sixth form colleges in the country. He showed me the Joint Matriculation Board Physics A Level paper for 1991. The first question had a page and a half passage on Rheology (the study of the deformation and flow of matter). His current students, many of whom, of course, would achieve A grades, would, he said, 'have been completely floored by it'.

A conspiracy theorist would see these developments as a deliberate plot, driven by the desire to introduce a single 'Diploma for all', thus eliminating the dastardly divide between the vocational sheep and the academic goats. Secretary of State, Ed Balls, has certainly made it clear that he wants A Levels to wither on the vine so that his Diplomas, which are discussed in the next chapter, become the 'qualification of choice'. My own view is that this smacks a little too much of joined-up thinking. Better results each year, ministers no doubt reasoned, encouraged the electorate to believe that the policies they were pursuing were succeeding and that short-term electoral gain was more important than the destruction of what had once been a world-class qualification.

Now, when without radical political action it is too late, everyone is saying that something must be done. Even Isobel Nisbet, the acting Chief Executive of Ofqual, has acknowledged that there is a problem and that expectations may have to be raised to deal with the glut of A grades. Many headteachers, particularly in the independent sector, have voted with their feet and abandoned A Level in favour of either the International Baccalaureate (IB) or the Pre-U (see below). The two subjects I discuss below reveal why.

The University of London A Level English paper in 1974 involved eight and a half hours of examinations. Paper One, Chaucer and Shakespeare, asked candidates to translate some tricky passages of middle and Shakespearian English into modern English, to comment on stylistic features, and to answer questions on significant aspects of the content of the passages. They then had to write three essays on topics such as: '"It is impossible to identify the Criseyde of Books 4 and 5 with the Criseyde of Books 1–3. They are two different women." How far do you agree with this statement?' And '"Nobility in man is inextricably twined with baseness." To what degree is this the central theme of *Measure for Measure?*' Paper Two, Set Books, required four essays on texts such as: *Spenser: Selections*; *Seventeenth-Century Prose*; *Metaphysical Poets*; *Milton: Comus and Samson Agonistes*; *Gibbon: Autobiography*; *The Mill on the Floss*; *Bleak House*; *T.S. Eliot: Selected Poems*; and *The Secret Agent*. To give you a flavour of the questions, the two on Eliot, from which candidates had to choose one, were: '"Mr Eliot's poetry is the expression of a certain kind of unease." Judging from the poems in your selection, do you agree?' and 'To what extent is Eliot a personal poet?' Paper Three, Passages for Comprehension and Appreciation, involved comment on the opening paragraphs from two novels and a contemporary poem.

Turning to today's A Level and taking the Edexcel paper as our example, the first thing to note in the blurb for teachers are the Key Features the Board wishes to highlight. They are:

- Edexcel poetry anthology for use as an optional textbook;
- A wide range of contemporary set texts;
- Maximum permitted use of 'open text' examining;
- Maximum amount of optional coursework in AS and A2;
- Opportunity to study Shakespeare for coursework or examination;
- Opportunity for creative writing in coursework;
- INSET and teacher support materials.

Note the emphases: on contemporary set texts, as compared to the 1974 London paper, which attempted to introduce candidates to as wide a range of great English literature as possible; on 'open text' examining, in which candidates may take their texts into the examination and do not, therefore, have to memorise anything; on the scope for coursework, as an alternative to the traditional end-of-course examination when coursework is extremely difficult to authenticate; and on the opportunity for creative writing, which has nothing to do with the appreciation of English Literature.

Candidates have to study a minimum of eight texts. These must include three texts published before 1900. So five eighths of the examination can consist of twentieth-century texts. Specified texts include: Caryl Churchill's *Top Girls*;

The Best of Betjeman; The Penguin Book of American Verse; Captain Corelli's Mandolin; The Heinemann Book of Caribbean Poetry; and Timberlake Wertenbaker's *Our Country's Good*. There are some demanding pre-twentieth century texts, such as *The Merchant's Tale, Othello* and *The Return of the Native*, but I do not imagine that these are common choices. Questions are far from demanding. Here, as an example, is a question from the 2008 AS Drama and Poetry paper. Candidates, remember, have the texts they have studied with them.

> (b) 'Poets are nothing if not ambitious: they try to tell us what it is like to be human – both our good and our bad points.'
>
> In the light of this comment, examine the poetic ways in which the writers in this section of the anthology explore the idea of what it is to be human. You should refer to **at least two** poems of your choice covering **at least two** groups.

Figure 15 Edexcel GCE Advanced Subsidiary English Literature, Unit 1, Drama and Poetry, May 2008, Question 6(b)

I could not dream up a more vacuous question if I tried. It is an invitation to emote in a generalised way that makes no attempt to test the student's understanding of the actual words on the page.

Finally and briefly, Geography. First a couple of questions from a 1977 University of Cambridge A Level paper:

> **Large-scale international migrations have been responsible for great achievements, but have sometimes left a legacy of difficult problems. Discuss and illustrate this statement.**
>
> [...]
>
> **7 The preservation of soil fertility is an essential aim of good farming. How may this be achieved in two of the following types of farming: *(a)* shifting agriculture, *(b)* wet-rice agriculture, *(c)* mixed farming?**

Figure 16 University of Cambridge A level Geography Paper 3, June 1977, Section A, Question 1 and Section B, Question 7

To answer these questions you need considerable knowledge and the ability to think. Unit 5 in the AQA A Level paper for 2008, Challenge and Change in the Human Environment, demands neither knowledge nor intelligence. You might not have done the course, but I would be surprised if you could not answer this question:

3 RECREATION AND TOURISM

Total for this question: 15 marks

Study **Figure 3** which is a customer review of a visit to a theme park in France.

Figure 3

"You can drive up to the apartments nearby and unload your luggage. The place we had was good. We booked three bedrooms and also got a bathroom and another toilet in a little room near the door. All the cars have to go to the big car park and it's securely managed. Then there's the supermarket about a five minute drive away. It has a reasonable variety of items. There are also lots of restaurants and shops for you to eat at which are good. Without doubt though, the rides and other attractions were the best bits of the holiday. The swimming pool is great. There's a place where you can go outside with rapids, waterslides and whirlpools ... ."

3 (a) With the help of **Figure 3**, describe the advantages of theme parks for tourists.

....

....

....

....

....

....

....

....

(4 marks)

Figure 17 AQA A Level Geography (Specification A) Unit 5 Challenge and Change in the Human Environment, June 2008, Question 3

Nothing can be said in defence of this, though, if asked, Jim Knight would no doubt pop up, muster a few statistics, and try.

A second footnote

Robert Coe and Peter Tymms of Durham University's Curriculum, Evaluation and Management Centre have monitored A Level standards over the last twenty years. Each year they have compared students' A Level results to results scored in an aptitude test. A student with a particular score on the aptitude test achieved a grade C A Level in 1988. In 2008 a student with the same score would have achieved an A grade. In mathematics the grade increase was even higher. A student who gained a U (ungraded) in 1988 would have received a low B grade in 2008. Dr Coe was reported as saying: 'It was quite a surprise to see it so clearly. The scale of the difference is so big. At some point people must read what I and other people have written about it and it can't just keep going. Some robust mechanism will be put in place to stop the increase each year.'[13] That 'robust mechanism', don't laugh, is Ofqual.

Colin MacCabe, Professor of English at Exeter University, was a student with erstwhile Secretary of State for Education, Charles Clarke, in the early seventies. On Sunday, 22nd August 2004, the *Observer* published an open letter he had written to Clarke. Here are some extracts:

> When we were students together at Cambridge in the early Seventies I formed a high opinion of your political skills and judgement. You were able to stand up both to the university authorities and to the loony left, while pursuing principled reforms. If anybody had told me that in three decades you would be Minister of Education in a Labour government, I would have been delighted that our shared socialist goal of all being educated to the best of their ability was in the most capable of hands. Instead you are presiding over a potential catastrophe whereby soon anybody seeking the very highest level of undergraduate education will choose an American rather than a British university ...
>
> Nobody who teaches A-level or has anything to do with teaching first-year students has any doubt that A Levels have been dumbed down, to use the pejorative term, or democratised, to use a more positive description ...

In our day students doing arts subjects were marked on their ability to write essays. Grades were awarded on the basis of the candidate's ability to generate an argument in relation to a question. The writing of the essay has been the key intellectual form in undergraduate education for more than a century; excelling at A-level meant excelling in this form. All that went by the board when your predecessor, David Blunkett, brought in AS-levels, which are worth half an A-level and usually taken after one year in the sixth form. A-levels ceased to be an exam which tested students at the end of a two-year course and became two years of continuous assessment with students often taking their first module within three months of entering the sixth form. This huge increase in testing went together with a drastic change in assessment. Candidates were not now marked in relation to an overall view of their ability to mount and develop arguments, but in relation to their ability to demonstrate achievement against tightly defined assessment objectives. A-levels, once a test of general intellectual ability in relation to a particular subject, are now a tightly supervised procession through a series of targets …

I assume I would be wasting my breath appealing for the virtues of intellectual excellence for its own sake, or in stressing how crucial it is for a healthy society to develop independence of thought and judgement. While such appeals have political resonance in the United States and Europe, New Labour has erased them from the political debate.

Alternatives to A Level: the International Baccalaureate and the Pre-U

As I have said, increasing numbers of schools are abandoning A Levels in favour of the IB and the Pre-U. Does this mean that we should allow the A Level examination to slide quietly into oblivion? Most educationalists would be happy to help it on its way. They are wrong. Today's A Level is in a bad way; the principles upon which the traditional examination were based are as important as they ever were.

On the one hand, the buzzwords which resonate through every conference on the post-16 curriculum – 'breadth', 'relevance', 'accessibility', 'interdisciplinary', 'critical thinking', 'flexibility', 'stretch', 'coherence', 'innovation', and so on, ad nauseam; on the other, what I mean when I refer to the principles that underpinned the A Levels I studied in the 1960s: in a very unfashionable word, 'scholarship'.

Scholarship is so unfashionable a concept that, having racked my brains, I can think of only one headteacher who has in recent years celebrated its virtues in print. Last year, Christopher Ray, High Master of Manchester Grammar School, wrote:

> Even more alarming is the retreat from scholarship in schools, especially evident during the last forty to fifty years and if anything becoming more pronounced: this retreat is undermining the intellectual health of the nation. While we may be foolish to expect the pupils to achieve the depth and breadth of Mill, we should endeavour to put them on the right path. We should expect those pupils who are likely to go on to the serious study of a subject at university to be given excellent foundations for this. There is much talk of 'good learning' in schools but too often the learning is routine, repetitive, and trivial. Teachers are now required to give much time to and expend much energy on tasks unrelated to their subjects: many confess that they have only rarely read a scholarly work since leaving university – with a few admitting that 'never' would be more accurate than 'rarely'. Professional development for teachers is too often focused upon those aspects of their teaching lives which are not related directly to their subjects. The leadership of schools is too often entirely preoccupied with non-curricular matters. Under government welfare reforms, schools must now liaise closely with doctors, social services, youth offending teams and the police. The retreat from the academic domain let alone from genuine scholarship is now a depressing fact of school life.[14]

Examinations matter. With greater or lesser specificity, they define what has to be taught. More importantly, they determine expectations: expectations, obviously, of what students ought to achieve, but, more fundamentally, of what the educational enterprise should involve. Scholarship depends upon the student's willingness to submit himself to a body of knowledge. That willingness in turn depends upon a humility and patience, an ability, in Simone Weil's phrase, to 'attend'. The A Level English questions I quoted above encouraged scholarship in this sense. They could not be answered by a student who had not 'attended'. I believe that we need an academic qualification for academically gifted young people which is rooted in an understanding of what scholarship involves. I see no reason why the A Level could not once again be this examination. I think that the IB and the Pre-U are intellectually more demanding examinations than the A Level in its current debased state, but I worry at the extent to which they, too, have been infected by today's orthodoxies. Neither seems to me the ideal academic post-16 qualification.

The IB Diploma requires candidates to study six subjects from six subject groups (Language; Individuals and Societies; Mathematics and Computer Science; the Arts; Experimental Sciences; and a Second Language), to write an extended essay, to follow a Theory of Knowledge course, and to undertake a range of activities outside the classroom. These demands are obviously far broader than the traditional three subject A Level course. Does this mean that the IB is the better qualification? Only if you subscribe to the fashionable ideas that our students are allowed to specialise too early, that breadth can be expanded without compromising depth, and that what matters is not depth, or scholarship, but, to quote the IB Learner Profile, the development of 'internationally minded people who, recognising their common humanity and shared guardianship of the planet, help to create a better and more peaceful world'.

I have never understood why a 16-year-old who has passed a range of GCSEs in different subjects and who wants to specialise should not be allowed to do just that. I would have left school rather than continue with Mathematics. The moment when I learnt that I had scraped a grade 6 in my O Level is to this day one of the happiest of my life. If we worry about the substance of what today's 16-year-old knows, the problem is the poverty of the expectation of the GCSE, not the principle of specialisation post-16. Sixteen-year-olds who want to continue with a range of subjects should have the opportunity to maintain that broad curriculum, but why impose breadth on all as a point of dogmatic principle?

The broader the curriculum, the shallower it must be. In fact, if we focus on the teaching of the six IB subjects, it is clear that within these subjects breadth as well as depth has been compromised. It is then, of course, a matter of judgement and opinion as to whether this matters, and, if so, how much.

This judgement hinges on what we want the post-16 curriculum to achieve. I favour a range of post-16 qualifications because I recognise that different people will have different opinions and different students will have different aspirations. The IB mission statement is 'to develop enquiring, knowledgeable and caring young people who help to create a better and more peaceful world through intercultural understanding and respect'.[15] The IB curriculum may or may not deliver these aims. In that I do not think any curriculum can solve the miseries of man, I, personally, am deeply sceptical. But, so be it, that is my view. The point that does need making, however, is that if you are interested, as I am, in the virtues of scholarship, the traditional three subject A Level, with its disciplined focus on a limited body of knowledge, is likely to be a better route than the IB.

The Pre-U is less grandiose in its aspirations than the IB, but it is, nonetheless, a qualification that is tainted by many of the unexamined assumptions of the day. A publicity brochure tells us that it 'equips students with the skills they need to make a success of their studies at university' and that 'it is a solid and coherent grounding in specialist subjects at an appropriate level, and develops the ability to undertake independent and self-directed learning and to think laterally, critically and creatively'.[16] The emphasis on 'a solid and coherent grounding in specialist subjects' is absolutely right. But what, exactly, are the 'skills' that are needed to make a success of university study? Upon what does 'the ability to undertake independent and self-directed learning' depend? Why, moreover, is independent learning prized as it is? Because students see so little of their tutors at university? Or because we now value independence over the magic of a relationship with a tutor who can change the ground upon which the student stands? Is the ability to think 'laterally, critically and creatively' really the be all and end all of a university education? Does not an understanding of the body of knowledge matter at all?

It does and happily it is one of the five overarching aims for all Pre-U subjects. The five are:

- encouraging the development of well-informed, open- and independent-minded individuals;
- promoting deep understanding through subject specialisation, with a depth and rigour appropriate to progression to higher education;
- helping learners to acquire specific skills of problem-solving, critical thinking, creativity, team-working, independent learning and effective communication;
- recognising the wide range of individual talents and interests;
- promoting an international outlook and cross-cultural awareness.

But given such preoccupations as are evident in the other aims, it is perhaps not surprising that when we examine the subject syllabuses for the Pre-U they are not as demanding as we might have expected. Take my own subject, English. Candidates have to answer two questions for the Poetry and Prose paper, two (including one on Shakespeare) for the Drama paper, sit a Comment and Analysis paper and write a Personal Investigation on a topic such as 'The Gothic Novel'. The set texts are, for the most part, serious in a way the A Level texts are not, but this hardly amounts to a comprehensive introduction to the canon of English Literature. I can only conclude that the architects of the Pre-U do not think that this is the purpose of a sixth form course in English Literature, or, for that matter, any other subject. They are more interested in promoting what are known in the trade as 'the whole person aims' listed above and celebrating the possibilities of the Global Perspectives course and the Independent Research Report, two elements which can be added to the subject study to achieve a Pre-U Diploma.

Breadth, once again, rather than depth. An enthusiasm for independent thought and critical thinking, rather than a commitment to the virtues of scholarship. But if I were a headteacher, I would not hesitate: I would plump for the Pre-U over A Levels as they now are. That does not mean that A Levels as they once were should not be restored to their former, uncomplicated glory. They should, though the odds, educational and political, are stacked heavily against it ever happening.

Postscript

The Common Entrance Examination for Entrance to Public Schools on 25th February 1957 had this question:

7. A man uses 3 gallons of petrol for a journey of 78 miles in his car. How much petrol will he need for a journey of 130 miles at this rate ?

Figure 18 Common Entrance Examination, Arithmetic A, February 25th, 1957. Reproduced by permission of the Independent Schools Examinations Board ©

Today the arithmetic would have to be easier if it were a GCSE question, but there would be a sub question: 'How much should he be fined for using his car at all?' We deem the development of skills to be educationally more important than the acquisition of knowledge and the inculcation of politically correct attitudes to be more important than either. Our examinations reflect these shifts in educational thought. Examination results improve every year. It does not, I am afraid, mean that our children leave school knowing anything.

Chapter 2

Has Mr Balls Never Met Jimmy Shepherd?

> We have assumed that we could educate Jimmy Shepherd and make him a Shelley or an Isaac Newton. At the very least we were sure we could make him a highly intelligent being. And we're just beginning to find our mistake. We can't make a highly intelligent being out of Jimmy Shepherd. Why should we, if the Lord created him only moderately intelligent? Why do we want always to go one better than the Creator?[17]

WHY INDEED? D.H. Lawrence points out what in a less egalitarian and sentimental world would be obvious to all. Children are not equally intelligent, and some are not very intelligent at all. Why, he asks, pretend otherwise? And what are the consequences of this pretence? Ninety years after Lawrence wrote *The Education of the People* we have a Government convinced that its pursuit of equality will lead to a society in which everyone can succeed. The result, as Lawrence predicted, is an education system which 'turns out a lot of half-informed youth who despise the whole business of understanding and wisdom' and which is 'extravagantly expensive' to boot.

The pursuit of equality

A little earlier in his essay *The Education of the People*, Lawrence wrote, in a paragraph most twenty-first century teachers will find offensive, that:

> Every teacher knows that it is worse than useless trying to educate at least 50 per cent of his scholars. Worse than useless: it is dangerous; perilously dangerous. What is the result of it? Drag a lad who has no capacity for true learning or understanding through the processes of education, and what

> do you produce in him, in the end? A profound contempt for education, and for all educated people. It has meant nothing to him but irritation and disgust. And that which a man finds irritating and disgusting he finds odious and contemptible.[18]

I once quoted this passage at a conference when I was Chief Inspector. The then Secretary of State, David Blunkett, was deeply offended. Knowing Mr Blunkett, I can't say I was surprised, but there is no rational reason for anyone to take offence. Children are not equal. Physically they come in all shapes and sizes. Some can run fast; others can barely waddle. Some are intelligent and some are not very intelligent. Some have a capacity for academic education; many do not. What is surprising is that Blunkett and so many others find these obvious truths impossible to accept.

Nothing much, sadly, has changed since Blunkett moved on. Last summer it fell to Lord Adonis to defend the public examination system against anybody who dared to suggest that today's examinations were rather less challenging than those taken twenty, thirty years ago. If you have read the previous chapter, you will have come to your own conclusion as to who was telling the truth. Adonis said: 'It is class-based elitism that instinctively wants to ration success and cap the aspirations of the disadvantaged.' In his view there is 'no fixed pool of talent in society' and 'no genetic or moral reason why the whole of society should not succeed to the degree that the children of the professional classes do today, virtually all getting five or more good GCSEs and staying on in education beyond 16.'[19]

You do not have to know much about Lawrence's background to understand that his observations have nothing to with 'class-based elitism'. I agree with Adonis that there is no 'fixed pool of talent in society', but that does not mean, if we are defining 'talent' as he defines it (five good GCSEs), that everyone has the ability to succeed academically. He is right to want to raise the 'aspirations of the disadvantaged', or as I would prefer to put it, their actual achievements. His mistake is his utopian view of human potential.

It is educational romanticism, as Charles Murray, a leading social analyst and author of *The Bell Curve*, argued recently,[20] to pretend that intelligence is not to a significant extent genetically determined. Murray uses American data to show that schools can have only limited success in raising the academic ability of children, even in the early years, and that family background is by far the most important factor in determining student achievement, for reasons which are both genetic and environmental. I think Murray underestimates the impact that good teachers can have, but I agree with him that the American and, for that matter, the English research suggests that the goal of high academic achievement for all will never be achieved. It is hard, for example, to disregard American data that shows how intensive pre-school education for disadvantaged children can raise IQ scores in the short term, but that improvements fall off within three years to virtually nothing. It is even harder to deny, as Adonis and virtually everyone else nowadays does deny, that children of the professional classes benefit genetically and environmentally from the accident of their birth. Their mothers and fathers, as Murray argues, are likely to have high IQs and are more likely to read bedtime stories to their children and support them in their learning and development than are parents from lower social classes. Accept these empirical facts and the question becomes: what should Government do, not to level the playing field, which is an impossible aspiration, but to ensure that children who do not have academic talents can fulfil the talents they do have?

The response from many educationalists will be that children have different kinds of intelligence – eight different kinds according to the influential American psychologist, Howard Gardner. Some will be mathematically gifted, others will have advanced linguistic skills, others again creative talents. Gardner's followers argue that the problem with education as it is currently conceived is that we are preoccupied with linguistic and mathematical intelligence, and, as a consequence, do not value other intelligences properly. It is a nice idea if your main concern as a teacher is the self-esteem of your pupils, and you think, therefore, that every child needs to win some sort of prize, but is it true? In one sense, yes, obviously, because children are different. They will, indeed, have different talents. But some, sadly, like Jimmy Shepherd, are going to have very little talent for or interest in anything that goes on at school. It is not that they have talents that go unrecognised because their teachers are not interested in them; it is that, however watered down our concept of an academic education might be, they are talentless. In adult life they might prosper, better, perhaps, than their peers who succeeded in school, but that possibility is irrelevant. The point at issue is whether there are 'lads' who 'have no capacity' for 'true learning', and, if there are, whether it makes sense 'to drag them through the processes of education'.

I would not necessarily agree with Lawrence's statistic, though if I had to choose between his honesty and Mr Blair's political opportunism in suggesting that 50 per cent of 18–30-year-olds should go to university, it would be

Lawrence I would back. I know from my experience as a teacher and from the thousands of lessons I have watched as an inspector that the attempt to subject all pupils to the same, essentially academic, curriculum is both doomed to fail and dangerous. It is dangerous because, as Lawrence says, it causes those who fail to feel nothing but contempt for education, and, quite possibly, themselves; because it places the teacher in a hopeless and demoralising situation; and because the behaviour of those who have no interest in the lesson means that other pupils in the class do not make the progress they otherwise would. It is dangerous because, as Lawrence also pointed out, the contempt for education felt by those who have failed carries through into adult life with, I would suggest, obvious and disastrous social consequences. And, above all, it is dangerous because the assumption that everyone, given the opportunity, can succeed prevents us making any real progress towards the meritocracy which is our only real salvation.

In a meritocracy it is those with talent who, to state the obvious, succeed. Some will win big prizes; some small; some none at all. An education system based on the belief that everyone can make progress and win some sort of prize is profoundly unmeritocratic. It dumbs the prizes down, demotivates those who have genuine talent, and encourages false expectations in those who do not. None of which is good.

The egalitarian will reply that what matters is equality of opportunity, not outcome. This might be persuasive if there was a clear distinction between these two aspirations. There is not. If we want to equalise opportunities at a given point we have to equalise outcomes at that point. Opportunities would not otherwise be equal! In practice, a concern for the former leads inevitably to a preoccupation with the latter. Consider, for example, the extent to which, as I show in Chapters 4 and 5, the curriculum has been dumbed down in recent years. The ministers and educationalists who object so strongly to the observation that an academic education is not for everyone know that if everyone is to have an opportunity to succeed something has to give, and that something was not going to be their commitment to equality of opportunity. Every summer when the examination results are published ministers have to pretend that standards remain as high as they ever were. It is the penance they have to pay for their duplicity. Students whose expectations have been constrained by an impoverished curriculum pay, of course, in different and more fundamental ways.

Reflect, too, on the absurdity of an example Mr Balls might give of his commitment to achieving equality of opportunity: Strategic Objective 5 from the latest DCSF Corporate Plan argues for the creation of 'a qualifications system in which every young person can access a learning programme at the right level for them, in a style that suits them, no matter where they are in the country, and achieve a valuable qualification if they succeed'.

Such a system seems at first sight to command universal assent. Some of us might wonder about the practicalities of delivery, but, in principle, this must be good news, mustn't it? Jimmy Shepherd might have failed all the way along the line. It does not matter. Mr Balls is going to give him the opportunity to study exactly what he wants to study, 'in a style', whatever this means, 'that suits him', and the qualification he, hopefully, will be awarded will have real, practical value. Actually, it is nonsense. If Jimmy can't read, which he probably cannot, his aspirations are irrelevant. There will not be any courses he can 'access' and if he were to achieve a qualification it would be worthless in the job market. Unless, that is, Mr Balls is talking about teaching Jimmy to read, which would be a good, if somewhat belated, thing to do, but hardly an idea which justifies a brand spanking new DCSF objective to itself.

Mr Balls wants, to quote from his speech to the 2007 Labour party conference, to 'break down all the barriers to opportunity in Britain'. He talks of 'opportunity', but the implication of political rhetoric of this kind is that if the barriers were removed then 'no child would be left behind'. Everybody would be able to achieve. Quite what they might achieve is left vague, but outcomes, if not completely equal, would be a lot more equal than they are now. The problem is the barriers, not the abilities of the children who are, as some always must be, left behind. Neither is there any understanding that this move might have any negative consequences. The assumption is that we would simply have a fairer world. There is no recognition that the prizes might have to be diluted in order to ensure this more equitable distribution. Diluted they already are, and, if Mr Balls has his way, they are going to be diluted a lot more. It is, to repeat, outcomes rather than opportunities which are being equalised.

Last September saw the introduction of a new qualification for 14–18-year-olds: the Diploma. The Secretary of State wants this new Diploma to become 'the qualification of choice' and replace A Levels. By 2011 seventeen Diplomas will be up and running. 'They will provide a suitable offer for every young person,' he confidently asserts. Will they? Or is this one more experiment with young people's lives? A waste of millions of pounds of taxpayers' money and a further blow to social mobility?

The idea of the Diploma is rooted in the belief that, to quote 'Diploma Champion', Sir Mike Tomlinson, we must 'consign to history the artificial divide between academic and vocational subjects which does not make sense in today's world'.[21] As an ex-Chief Inspector of Schools who used to be a passionate supporter of the A Level examination, Sir Mike should know better. The divide is not artificial. However much the soggy egalitarians who dictate Government policy might prefer it otherwise, education and training are different activities. Education is an enterprise which has no external purpose; training involves the teaching of the specific knowledge and skills needed to perform a particular task. The logic of the distinction is clouded, of course, by the refusal of educationalists to accept that human beings differ in their abilities and aspirations. It is the 'artificial' divide between the academic sheep and the vocational goats that really upsets the great and the good of the educational world. The truth is that not everyone has the intellectual ability to study A Levels, even in their current debased form. A Levels, therefore, must be abolished. Mr Balls and his Diploma Champion want to believe that everyone is equal and that everyone can profitably follow one course.

They cannot. The Diploma will not challenge academic students and it will not motivate those who have been failed by the current predominantly academic curriculum.

The latter need a practical, job-specific training to give them a sense that study is worthwhile and that they might just succeed at something. The Diploma will not do this. It is explicitly not job-specific, but rather a general introduction to an area of employment. It asks students, to give a couple of examples from the Level One Engineering Diploma, 'to investigate the environmental impact of transport systems' or 'to investigate a range of renewable and non-renewable energy sources'.[22] They have struggled with such tasks in Geography for the last five years. Why are they going to be motivated now?

You only have to look at the structure of the Diploma to see why it will fail academic students. It is divided into four components: Principal Learning; Functional Skills; Personal, Learning and Thinking Skills; and Additional and Specialist Learning. Principal Learning is subject-specific learning. So when the Diplomas in Science and Mathematics, Humanities and Languages begin in 2011 this is the bit where students will learn their science and humanities and languages. But Principal Learning will only occupy 50 per cent of the teaching time and 'at least 50 per cent' of this teaching will be applied – 'i.e. practical learning, set in a work related context'.[23] This is fine, I suppose, if you want to study Herbal Medicine at the University of East London, but not so good if you have set your sights on Oxford and want to read a highly competitive subject like History.

Ministers are keen to tell us that over a hundred higher education institutions are enthusiastic about the Diploma. It is not difficult to guess which institutions are most enthusiastic. The silence from independent schools is pretty deafening. Indeed, as I explained in the previous chapter, the independent sector has developed its own examination, the pre-U, as a more intellectually rigorous alternative to A Level. And this, of course, is the tragedy. State schools are going to be cajoled into entering their students for the Diplomas. The independent sector will gravitate towards the pre-U or the International Baccalaureate. Top universities, keen to recruit students who have spent their time studying academic subjects rather than learning how 'to work in a team, think creatively, reflect on their own learning, and manage themselves', will opt for candidates from independent schools. Social mobility will decline yet further, and ministers in 2015 will be furrowing their brows and wondering why.

In addition, of course, there are the problems of implementation. I have talked to headteachers across the country about training and preparation for the Diploma. None has a good word to say. All worry about the practicalities of timetabling courses when students are moving between institutions. It will settle down. These experiments usually do, given enough extra cash to resolve the problems. Whether anybody will be better off is another matter. Why could not Mr Balls have toughened A Levels and developed proper vocational alternatives? Because he thinks everyone is equal and that education and training are the same thing. He ought to sack Sir Mike and appoint a Commonsense Champion.

The same assumption, that everybody would achieve if the 'barriers to opportunity' were torn down, explains the Government's determination to impose (see Chapter 7) strict admissions policies on all schools, so that working-class pupils can attend successful schools currently colonised by the middle class – or, put more honestly, the determination to find ways to spread the misery of disruptive pupils among all schools. Ministers purport to believe in the importance of enhancing parental choice, but they pursue policies which suggest that in reality they would like all pupils to attend exactly the same school and to be taught by teachers of identical competence. Will these policies ever deliver the holy egalitarian grail of equal outcomes? No, because some students are more able than others, and, as yet, the Government has not thought up a solution to this unfortunate fact of life. But, unless schools are able to cater for children with special educational needs, engage the often-neglected majority of average ability and stretch the most able students, Labour's efforts to level the playing field will result in a slide to the lowest common denominator. Anybody who thinks that good comprehensive schools have always managed to engage these different categories of pupil should reflect on the fact that one in seven pupils on the Government's Gifted and Talented programme last year failed to achieve five good GCSE grades.

Equality of opportunity has become an article of liberal faith: the acceptable face of socialism and an iconic commitment for Mr Cameron's revitalised Conservative party. Interviewed by Fraser Nelson in *The Spectator* magazine,[24] the Conservative spokesman on education, Michael Gove, said: 'If you are a progressive, you are angered by unmerited hierarchies, by establishments that block progress, by cartels and producer interests that stand in the way of people being able to author their own life stories.' Like Gove, I am a meritocrat. I, too, want bright students from disadvantaged homes to fulfil their potential at Oxbridge. But what does he mean by 'unmerited hierarchies' and 'establishments that block progress'? If he means the teacher unions, most university departments of education, many DCSF and Local Authority officials, then I am with him and come the next election I will drive the first bulldozer. Equally, however, he could be pointing the finger at grammar schools, at parents who choose to send their children to independent schools, at top universities, which, shame on them, continue to offer places to the best-qualified candidate irrespective of the school they attended. Does he not recognise that the 'life stories' we 'author' (to use his unfortunate phrase) have something to do with native intelligence? His words, read quickly, inspire a warm glow; when scrutinised, their vagueness is, if anything, sinister. Labour might be committed to equality of opportunity, he is telling us, but so too are the Conservatives. Show us a barrier and we will knock it down. I am reserving my applause until I know which barriers he has in mind.

If what we are talking about is a meritocratic drive to identify those who are capable of benefiting from a particular opportunity, then, yes, this is exactly what politicians should be doing. But, as we have seen, equality of opportunity can mean something very different: an onslaught, for example, on 'barriers' to opportunity such as academic examinations, independent schools, and selection at any stage in the system, even at entry to university. Indeed, interpreted in this second way, as nowadays it so often is, it should be an icon for a totalitarian rather than a progressive politician. A government that really wanted to achieve complete equality of opportunity would have to remove children from their families at birth, and, if it ever felt that it were safe to return them, it would have to take strenuous steps to prevent any parent helping their children in a way that other parents might not be able to help theirs. Those who would like to abolish independent schools because not all parents can afford the fees come, I suppose, close to this position. Most of us, happy though we are to bathe in the warm glow of words like 'equality', would probably not want to shut some of the finest schools in the world and deny parents the right to do what they think is right for their children.

The paradoxical result of the pursuit of equality of opportunity is that opportunity often becomes (see Chapter 7) less equal than it once was. The abolition of the grammar schools is the classic example of this. Grammar schools were abolished because they were thought to be middle-class institutions that condemned working-class children to a second-rate education. In fact, as Frank Musgrove has convincingly shown,[25] they were working-class institutions which gave thousands of disadvantaged children the opportunity to attend top universities. Social mobility has declined since the grammar schools were, in most Local Authorities, turned into comprehensive schools. The Government is, of course, vehemently opposed to selection, but, then, its ministers have probably not read Musgrove.

It is interesting, too, to reflect on the history of the Government's attempts to raise standards in literacy and numeracy. For Blair, this was, rightly, the number one goal, and some, though not nearly enough, progress was made during the first two Labour administrations. Then millennial zeal kicked in. Our children had to be the happiest in the world and England the best place in the world in which to grow up. I do not know what this means, and I am pretty confident nobody else does either. What is clear is that the more time teachers and politicians spend chasing utopian dreams, the less time and energy they will have to focus on goals, like universal literacy and numeracy, which could be achieved. If every child leaving primary school was reading to a reasonable standard, examination results in secondary schools would soar. Today's Jimmy Shepherds would be saved the daily humiliation of stumbling through a sentence or two while the rest of the class snigger. The country would save billions dealing with the social consequences of illiteracy. The best may not be the enemy of the good, but utopian fantasies like equality of opportunity certainly undermine progress on specific goals which might otherwise have been achieved.

I can only conclude that New Labour has neither the courage of its own political convictions nor the pragmatic good sense to focus on what is achievable. If Ministers really wanted to deliver on what they take to be the unfairness of elitism and privilege, they would follow the logic of their own instincts and abolish the grammar and independent schools. If they really wanted to make a difference, they would abandon the eclectic ambitions of the Children's Plan and focus on improving literacy and numeracy in primary schools and developing the vocational courses and qualifications non-academic students in secondary schools so desperately need.

The Children's Plan

But no, the Children's Plan will guide, if Labour remains in power, the next decade of education policy. It is a document of cosmic aspiration which pokes its nose into just about every aspect of a child's life. Jimmy Shepherd, poor lad, would have nowhere to hide. None of us have. Children, parents, teachers: Mr Balls has us all in his sights. He has escalated Mr Blair's promise to deliver 'a world class education system' into a pledge to make Britain the best country in the world in which to grow up. Forget schools, it is society now which is going to be transformed. Every child is about to realise his or her potential; every school is to become a great school. In reality a great deal of public money is going to be wasted, and little, I suspect, will be achieved, but, as a monument to a Government that has learnt nothing about the limitations of its own power and has forgotten all it once knew, which was not very much, about the nature of education, it deserves some detailed discussion.

The plan is based on five principles:

1 Government does not bring up children – parents do – so government needs to do more to back parents and families.

2 All children have the potential to succeed and should go as far as their talents can take them.

3 Children and young people need to enjoy their childhood as well as grow up prepared for adult life.

4 Services need to be shaped by and responsive to children, young people and families, not designed round professional boundaries.

5 It is always better to prevent failure than tackle a crisis later.

Fine, you might think: beyond the motherhood-and-apple-pie obviousness, there is little here to which anyone could object.

Consider, though, the assertion that because the Government does not bring up children it 'needs to do more to back parents and families'. Does it? Who says? Do you want access to an expert parent adviser? I guess most parents have from time to time wondered what the hell they should do with their children, but that does not mean that most think the state should stand ready to tell them what to do. The Government may need to do more to back inadequate parents, but, if this is what is meant, why not say it? Why suggest that every parent needs and wants to be dependent on the state?

Reflect, too, on principles two and three. Nobody can disagree with what is said because nothing is said. We all applaud the assertion that every child has potential, but what is going to be done to help, for example, Jimmy Shepherd realise his potential? Everything hinges on the force of 'enjoy' and 'prepared for adult life' – words that beg every question and contribute, therefore, nothing. And, yes, of course, the needs of the 'clients' are more important than the demarcation of professional boundaries, but this does not mean that the nature of schooling has to be redefined and a host of new roles created as the Children's Plan goes on to suggest. Would not a bit of old-fashioned communication do the trick with a great deal less upheaval? More fundamentally, should 'services ... be shaped by and responsive to children'? Is not this, in a nutshell, what is wrong with what Labour has done to education and society? We have a Children's Commissioner to champion children's rights; Ofsted is required to take into account the views of children on every inspection; and now, apparently, new legislation will require schools to take account of pupils' opinions on core policies including discipline, uniform and the curriculum. What about teachers telling children what they need to know and may not want to hear? What about the responsibility of the child to sit and listen? As for principle five, I suppose it is good that ministers have learnt something from their twelve years in office. I congratulate Mr Balls on his insight.

I dwell on the detail because I suspect that The Children's Plan, like most Government reports, was written on the assumption that very few people would ever try to read it and that those who did would very soon give up. Persevere, and the questions, as you can see, proliferate. The detail of what is actually going to be done is equally interesting.

In order to achieve Objective One (Secure the Wellbeing and Health of Young People and Children) £34m is to be spent to provide two expert parent advisers for each Local Authority. Setting aside the question of whether these expert advisers are a sensible addition to the state payroll and, indeed, the further question of the precise nature of their expertise, I wonder, given the number of parents in, say, Birmingham, how far their services are going to stretch. I wonder, too, whether every school really needs a 'Parent Support Adviser' and whether a 'Parents Panel' to advise Government on 'policies affecting children' is going to add much to the sum total of ministerial wisdom. The practical suggestion that families with disabled children need more financial support is more sensible, but the amount of money to be found is not specified, and, sadly, there are very few ideas of this kind that could make a real difference. Mr Balls appears to be more interested in grand promises to 'halve child poverty by 2010 and eradicate it by 2020'.[26] How he is going to do this remains a mystery.

Objective 2 (Safe and Sound) will fund 'a new home safety equipment scheme to prevent accidents to children in the home', commission a review on 'the impact of the commercial world on children's wellbeing', and publish Dr Tanya Byron's review of risks from the internet and video games.[27] It is pretty clear that all this is in response to alarmist stories in the press about the corruption of childhood. How it will restore innocence is another matter.

The key to achieving 'world class standards' in schools and 'closing the gap in educational achievement for disadvantaged children' is, according to the Children's Plan, 'partnership with parents'. I agree that it is a good thing for parents to be involved in their children's education; I know that the key to higher standards is better teaching. What worries me is the very obvious point that the more time teachers spend 'partnering' parents, the less time they have to teach. The announcement that the Government is 'to set out and consult on a new relation between parents and schools' does not, therefore, fill me with great enthusiasm.[28] Most of the examples of good 'partnering practice' presented to us already happen. I do not know of a secondary school which does not have 'personal tutors' for its pupils and most parents are already 'contacted' before their children start a new school. More typical of the Government, and more suspect, is the statement that schools must establish a 'Parents' Council' to ensure that 'parents' voices are heard within the school'. Just, I imagine, what most headteachers want. Is the £30m to be spent on helping 'parents and carers to learn with their children' going to achieve much either? Thirty million pounds is a lot of money, but spread across the country is not going to go very far, even if anyone had any real idea what was going to be done with it. Equally vague is the promise that the Government will 'build on' the £144m already allocated over the next three years to the Every Child a Reader and Every Child Counts projects. Why, many parents must be asking, are such initiatives needed when teachers are paid to teach children, whatever else they might be expected to do (which is now, admittedly quite a lot), to read and write? Why, too, is £25m needed for 'intensive one to one to catch up in the areas of writing children find difficult to master'? If teachers find these 'areas' difficult to teach then the Government should be helping them, not shutting the classroom door, at huge cost to the taxpayer, after the child has failed. Mr Balls seems to have forgotten (principle five) that it is better to prevent a failure than to have to tackle a crisis later.

These initiatives are quite clearly admissions of failure. The Government has not improved standards of classroom teaching in primary schools and is having, therefore, to introduce recovery schemes of one kind or another in an attempt to remedy things. Its decision, announced in the Children's Plan, to trial new 'stage not age' National Curriculum tests which, if successful, will replace the Key Stage tests at 11 and 14,* is another consequence of the same failure. The teacher unions have always hated these tests because they reveal the failure of individual schools. They are now revealing the failure of the Government's literacy and numeracy strategies and ministers have come to hate them too. So, the decision has been taken to end the embarrassment of having to explain the lack of progress every summer: children will take the tests whenever their teachers judge them to be ready and comparisons between and among schools and from year to year will become difficult if not impossible. In that Ofsted inspections now depend on test data, this decision means the end of school accountability, which is extremely bad news for any parent who wants to take a serious interest in their child's education.

Partnership with parents is the one key to achieving 'world class standards', 'system reform' is the other. Mr Balls wants, somewhat illogically, to create a 'system where all institutions are consistently achieving at the level of the best'. To do this he will spend £117m on supply cover so that the 'early years work force' can obtain more qualifications. How many qualifications adults working with two-year-olds actually need is not discussed. The assumption, as always with this Government, is that the more qualifications teachers have, the better they will teach. Sadly, the reverse in my experience is often the case. There might, I suppose, be somebody somewhere who feels he has learnt something from the

*The decision to abolish the Key Stage 3 tests was announced in the autumn of 2008.

NCSL course that is now mandatory if you want to become a headteacher in a state school, but they are few and far between. We can only hope, therefore, that a scheme to make 'teaching a Masters Level profession' (cost £44m) turns out to be of more practical use. I suspect it will be one more opportunity to brainwash the profession into a comatose acceptance of the 'personalisation agenda' and other articles of educational faith.

'Every secondary school', the Plan tells us, is to have 'specialist, trust or academy status'. There will be 230 Academies by 2010, 'on the road to 400'. And every school is going to have a business or university partner. 'Standards not structures' was the original New Labour cry, and it remains a mantra Mr Balls likes from time to time to mutter, but, as you can see, the obsession with structures continues. It is not (see Chapter 7) a programme that has delivered results, but it sounds purposeful and innovative and the Government is, in any case, too committed to re-think, so the re-labelling exercise continues.

Then, there is Objective 5 (Staying On) which details the Government's proud commitment to raising the school leaving age to 18. You might have thought that the need to find £31.5m 'to re-engage 16-year-olds who have dropped out', including 'financial incentives' (or bribes), coupled with the fact that secondary schools appear to find it increasingly difficult to stop 14–16-year-olds from bunking off, might have caused Mr Balls to question the wisdom of this particular commitment. It has not. In the face of mounting evidence that graduates are finding it harder and harder to obtain graduate status work and that the 'knowledge economy' might not require quite so many highly skilled workers as ministers have led us to think, Mr Balls continues to believe that Jimmy Shepherd and his mates need somehow to be cajoled into further and, better still, higher education.

But, if Jimmy had had the good fortune to be growing up in Mr Brown's Britain, my cynicism might be unwarranted, for, to quote Objective 6, he would be on the 'right track'. How could he not be? Mr Balls would have spent £160m improving 'the quality and range of places' for him to go and 'the things for him to do'. He would have benefitted from a 'national entitlement for all young people to participate in profitable activities'. And if he had at any time seemed likely to stray from the straight and narrow, an 'Acceptable Behaviour Contract' would soon have stopped any anti-social behaviour. Neither would Mr and Mrs Shepherd have got away with it. A 'youth alcohol plan to improve alcohol education and tackle parental alcohol misuse' would have rescued Mr Shepherd from the excesses of his local and installed him happily in a class for parents who want to learn how to learn with their children. Nobody can deny that the Children's Plan is inclusive or claim that Mr Balls is afraid of leading from the front. 'We will expect every school to be uncompromising in its ambitions for achievement, sitting at the heart of the community it serves,' he trumpets. Just like, a less humble minister would have added, the Government itself.

The extravagance of the expense

£50 million here, another £100 million there: it is easy to lose all sense of perspective. Lawrence condemned the 'system of education' as it was in 1919 as extravagantly expensive. Spending on state schools has now reached £77.4 billion a year, an increase of two thirds in real terms since 1997–8. Mr Brown is no doubt regretting his promise, but he has said that he will increase spending yet further until it matches levels found in the independent sector, so costs could rise significantly higher. Most teachers and, at least until recently, most parents would have approved of this increase in expenditure. Ministers, of course, are immensely proud of the fact that the nation's schools, after 'decades of underinvestment', are now better resourced. The question is: are standards higher because of this increased spending? Are they, one might reasonably ask, 66 per cent higher? The answer, as the previous chapter demonstrated, is that they are not. The examination statistics might look good, but that is because they have been fiddled. The cost of state education is now colossal, and, as the Public Accounts Committee recently concluded, a decade of over-investment has not resulted in a commensurate rise in standards.

If the initiatives which have been pursued since Labour came to power had been sensible, then the expense might be justifiable. They have not been sensible. Every penny wasted on some fanciful scheme could have been used to recruit more teachers, to buy more library books, or to lower taxation. It is worth, therefore, setting my analysis of the Children's Plan within the wider context of the Government's 'investment' in education since 1997.

Examples of wasteful spending are not hard to find. Over a billion pounds has been spent since 1997 on initiatives to counter truancy. Result: more children truant from school now than in 1997. Educational Maintenance Grants, which are paid to half a million teenagers from households with incomes of less than £30,810 a year, have cost the taxpayer a further billion. A recent survey of teachers in schools and colleges found that many students are turning up just to collect the grant. Half those surveyed said that the grants were being 'routinely abused'. Five hundred million pounds is being spent on Child Trust Funds to give every child £250 on their eighteenth birthday. DCSF expenditure on consultants and outside contractors has doubled in the last two years to £72m, a sum which would fund an extra 2,057 teachers.

The impact of these outside 'experts' is, to say the least, questionable. Last summer, 1.2 million children had to wait months for their SATS results after a series of mistakes by the Qualifications and Curriculum Authority (QCA) and its contractor ETS Europe. Another private firm employed by the DCSF failed to pay Education Maintenance Grants to 26,000 teenagers. Attempting to defend his department's extraordinary reliance on outside expertise, Schools Minister, Jim Knight, said that 'the most significant increase has been the need for external specialist support for our major delivery programmes, including the big expansion in Academies'. I was talking to a major sponsor of Academies recently. He told me that he had just sacked the consultants who were meant to be helping him. Their advice, he said, was useless.

It is hard, moreover, to justify the vast sums of money needed to employ the thousands of permanent staff employed by the DCSF and its many quangos. The QCA was originally responsible for the development of the National Curriculum, the management of the associated National Curriculum tests, and the monitoring of examination standards. A few years ago the decision was taken to contract the tests out to a private company. The monitoring of examination standards is now the job of a new organisation, Ofqual. When the Government wanted advice on the secondary curriculum and examinations, it ignored the QCA and turned to Sir Mike Tomlinson. When it turned its attention to the primary curriculum, ministers phoned up Sir Jim Rose. The Chief Executive of the QCA, Ken Boston, who had to resign in the light of the test debacle, was paid an annual salary of £328,000. The organisation's total budget for 2007–8 was £170m. The Secretary of State might just as well have poured this money down the nearest drain.

Looking back over the last 11 years, it is clear that many initiatives have failed because, like the majority of those listed in the Children's Plan, they were intrinsically silly. Education Action Zones, a flagship project of the late 1990s, are a good example. The basic idea was that partnerships between failing schools and local businesses in disadvantaged areas would invent new solutions to the problems under which the schools were sinking. In fact, as any headteacher who has turned round a failing school will tell you, what is needed is not new fangled ideas, but basic old-fashioned leadership and a relentless focus on behaviour. Other initiatives have ended in disaster because ministers and their civil servants neither planned nor delivered them efficiently. Individual Learning Accounts, which wasted millions of pounds of taxpayer's money because elementary safeguards against fraud were not taken, are typical.

The wisdom of humility

'The only wisdom we can hope to acquire', Eliot wrote, 'is the wisdom of humility.'[29] Mankind is not perfectible and ministers, however hyperactive they might be, are not omnipotent. Who does not want a society in which everyone has the opportunity to fulfil their potential? The question is how progress can be made towards that goal. My argument is that policy must be rooted in pragmatism, by which I mean three things.

First, that there are no quick fixes. Children from disadvantaged homes will achieve more if we can improve standards of teaching in the schools they attend. Rebranding schools; pouring money into initiatives designed to deal with symptoms rather than the root cause; attacking successful schools and universities for their supposed elitism: the story of the last 12 years is that none of this works. The only solution is the hard grind to turn round the failing school, to challenge low expectations, to refuse to accept the culture of resigned mediocrity that remains the norm in too many classrooms.

Second, the more utopian ministerial ambitions become, the less likely it is that we shall see the basic progress we need if children from disadvantaged homes are to be helped. Ministers should stop pretending that everybody has equal potential to achieve academically and waffling about making England the best place in the world to grow up and ensure that every child grows up literate, which, given good teaching, 95 per cent could.

Third, that the Government should restore academic rigour to courses which in the pursuit of equality have been dumbed down, and, simultaneously, develop curricula, and, better still, schools that offer all children the opportunity to realise their individual potential. The pretence to date, shared by the left, and, under Mr Cameron, the right, is that academic ability should not determine the education a child receives. It should. You may have found Lawrence's uncompromising comments on Jimmy Shepherd difficult to stomach, but the essence of his argument is irrefutable: children need different rather than equal opportunities. Like Lawrence, I think every child should have the chance to experience an academic liberal education to, perhaps, the age of 13 or 14. After that, again like Lawrence, I think it is 'useless, worse than useless' to pretend. The pretence that every child has academic potential has undermined academic standards and done nothing for those who are never going to achieve academically. Is it not time that we had a Government that accepted what all of us know? Fourteen-year-olds differ enormously in their abilities and aspirations. They need different opportunities. It is our responsibility as parents and teachers to know our children and to decide upon the education they need. Their needs are more important than the utopian dreams of politicians who have been bewitched by their own rhetoric.

Chapter 3

The Myth of the Knowledge Economy and the Death of Liberal Education

THE GOVERNMENT'S DETERMINATION to remove the educational barriers which, supposedly, prevent young people from disadvantaged backgrounds realising their potential, would in itself have sabotaged its attempts to reform state schools. Ministers, have not, however, wanted to leave anything to chance. They have pursued a parallel commitment to the myth that we now live in a 'knowledge economy' and that education, at every level from infant school to university, must be 're-engineered' so that the UK has the 'high skill' workforce it needs if it is to survive in increasingly global and competitive markets.

The myth of the knowledge economy

The strong version of the myth of the knowledge economy argues, as Charles Leadbeater puts it in his book, *Living on Thin Air*, that 'our children ... will make their livings through their creativity, ingenuity and imagination'.[30] In my view this is nonsense. Some of our children will, no doubt, lead entrepreneurial lives; the majority, sadly, will get up in the morning to do the kind of jobs most of us get up to do. The weak version wants us to believe that, at the very least, we are all going to be 'knowledge workers', dependent for our employability on the power of our brains and the sophistication of our skills. This, too, is nonsense.

Leadbeater and his fellow futurologists have jumped from two undeniable facts to an unwarranted conclusion. The facts are that computers have had a huge impact on how we live and work and that the development of information technology has created a new industry with job opportunities that did not exist twenty or thirty years ago. This does not mean that the nature of most people's daily employment has changed in a fundamental sense: an office worker using a computer is still doing office work. Neither does it mean, as Professor Alison Wolf rather pithily puts it in her seminal book on education, employability and the economy, *Does Education Matter?*, 'that we are all becoming computer programmers or biotechnology entrepreneurs'.[31]

Penrhyndeudraeth, near to where I live in Snowdonia, is, as the signs on the approach roads tell you, 'Wales's first networked village'. I sit half way up a mountain receiving emails from all over the world. Evidence, perhaps, for the reality of the knowledge economy? No, not really. The new technology means I can live where I want to live, but I earn my living through jobs which have existed down the years: I run a company, I write a column for *The Sunday Times*, and I teach at Buckingham University. I drove down our track this morning, passing a neighbour who was rounding up sheep and intercepting a delivery of wine. The farmer was on his quad bike and the deliveryman in his van, but, if mechanisation has made their jobs easier, it has not changed their essential nature. The bread I had bought in Penrhyndeudraeth had been baked locally. I popped in to see a carpenter about replacing a rotten window frame, and, trusting rather boldly to my own do-it-yourself skills, visited a builder's merchants to buy some planks to mend a collapsed garden bench. The carpenter's workshop looked as though it had not changed since the 1950s. The builder's merchant had computerised stock, but the stock was still building merchandise. Penrhyndeudraeth might be Wales's first networked village: it is also home to a good number of people whose work is in essence little different from that of their parents and grandparents.

How many biotechnology entrepreneurs do you know? How many teachers, social workers, care assistants? My guess is that there are and always will be significantly more people in the second group, and, reflecting on the fact that we are all getting older, my own piece of punditry would be to suggest that the knowledge economy, if it ever existed, is passé: we are moving rapidly into the 'caring for the elderly' economy. Whether we will ever escape from the 'jobs-that-have-been-created-in-the-public-sector' economy within which we now live depends on who wins the next election, and, if it is Mr Cameron, his willingness to challenge a dependency culture which could not be further from Mr Leadbeater's ideals of 'creativity, ingenuity and imagination'.

The obsession with skills and the expansion of further and higher education

The myth of the knowledge economy spawns the obsession with skills-based qualifications and the belief that our economic success depends upon the never-ending expansion of further and higher education. Is there, though, any evidence that the accumulation of qualifications makes anyone more efficient at their jobs? How many degrees do care workers, shop assistants, hotel receptionists, or, for that matter, teachers need? The Government might believe that because work is becoming more complex, the nation's prosperity depends upon its success in cajoling more and more people to stay in education for longer and longer, but is this another article of political faith that crumbles upon examination?

The answer to the third of these questions is that it is. Ministers seem to continue to be convinced that their policies are the right ones, or, if they do have private doubts, they cannot see how they can change direction. The Conservative party supports the decision to raise the school leaving age to 18, approves of the expansion of higher education, and appears to believe that there is a connection between post-16 education and our economic prosperity. This may be because Mr Cameron is as deluded as Mr Brown, or, to be more charitable, because he cannot decide how to resolve what has become a dilemma for politicians on the right and left: namely, that the electorate, understandably, given the evidence thus far, believes that more education means more money in their individual wage packet, but that the economic benefits do not justify the investment upon which the never-ending expansion of further and higher education depends. There is an argument that the tide is unstoppable. The economic case against expansion may be unanswerable, but the aspirations of the electorate are now undeniable. I do not think that the electorate is that stupid. Sooner or later, as student debt mounts and graduate unemployment rises, the penny will drop. Young people will realise that getting a job may be a smarter option than going to university.

This, however, is to move ahead too quickly. Post-16 staying on rates are, as Professor Wolf says in *Does Education Matter?*, increasing across the developed world for two reasons. The first is that it makes good economic sense to the individual student. Lord Dearing's Committee of Inquiry into Higher Education estimated a rate of return of between 11 and 14 per cent in real terms on a student's investment in a degree, and, though this rate is certain to diminish in the future as more people graduate, there is little reason to think that the figure has changed over the last ten years. The second is that there comes a point where many, perhaps most, young people come to the conclusion that they have no alternative but to continue in education. Everyone else is applying to go to university; employers are increasingly demanding degree-level qualifications for jobs which previously did not need A Levels: to opt out is just too risky.

Supporters of the expansion of post-16 educational opportunities argue that rates of remuneration reflect productivity. Graduates earn more than non-graduates and must, therefore, generate more wealth than non-graduate employees. If we are to remain competitive in an increasingly global economy, we have no alternative but to do what our competitors are doing and increase the number of graduates per head of population. This argument is then used to justify the cost to the state. Professor Wolf asks and answers the obvious, but crucial question: are people's wages an accurate measure of their productivity, and, therefore, because graduates earn more than non-graduates, of the importance of education to the economy? They are not. First, because earnings reflect natural ability as well as education; second, because rates of remuneration 'depend heavily on the ways in which a society is organised overall'.[32] On the latter point, she cites the example of the Kenyan bus driver who earns 13 times less than a German bus driver. Same job, different country. The Kenyan bus driver comes to Germany. Suddenly his wage shoots up 13 times. 'Did something magical occur,' she asks, 'as he stepped across the border, endowing him with a whole new set of skills?'

Like Professor Wolf, I find it 'difficult to construct a convincing argument that more sixth form qualifications and more degrees are needed so that people will be educated enough to stack shelves, swipe credit cards, or operate a cappuccino machine effectively'.[33] I find it even more difficult to understand how politicians have convinced themselves that the shelves will remain empty if billions are not spent on the expansion of post-16 education and training. The explanation is that they appear, on the one hand, to have swallowed the idea that such menial jobs are going to disappear from the knowledge economy; and, on the other, to have succumbed to their own rhetoric about the perfectibility of man: if everyone has infinite potential, nobody should be working in jobs that do not allow them to fulfil their potential.

The truth is that rates of remuneration do not reflect productivity and qualifications do not necessarily make anybody better at the job they do. Indeed, the frustration experienced by graduates who, unable to find graduate status employment, have to accept intellectually unchallenging work, may make them worse at the job than the employee who is less educated but more content. Why then are employers so keen on employing graduates? Sometimes, no doubt because the job is very demanding and the graduate has a very good degree from a very prestigious university. The employer knows that he is hiring someone with a first rate intellect, even if the specific knowledge and skills acquired during the degree are not particularly relevant to the job that has to be filled. More often than not, though, as Wolf suggests, it is because 'education today is a socially acceptable way of ranking people which most employers would find it hard to do without'.[34] It is, of course, true that education may be an indication of general intelligence in that the longer you spend in school, the more likely you are to have the kind of intelligence which school rewards and that a degree as a badge of long service may, therefore, tell the employer something useful. But with more and more young people staying in education for longer and longer, this argument becomes less compelling. Wolf raises, moreover, an interesting possibility. Suppose everyone left school at 15, or even 12, and took some sort of test that ranked them in terms of general ability. 'How much less productive would the economy and most of these people be? Conversely, is all the money poured into education and training beyond that point really having a substantial effect on the sorts of skills that people have, and their usefulness to employers?'[35]

At the very least, her analysis suggests that the Government ought to be asking itself such questions. The belief that increased education spending has fuelled growth in both developed and undeveloped countries deserves, she argues, a similarly sceptical examination. In 1980, Egypt was the 47th poorest country in the world. Fifteen years later, having expanded education provision at every level, it was the 48th poorest. It is a figure to hold in mind when South Korea, which over roughly the same period made a similar commitment to the expansion of education, is cited as an example of a country which made huge economic progress because it recognised that it needed to improve the education of its citizens. Investment in education may well be a necessary condition for economic growth; it is clearly not a sufficient condition. Was it, moreover, Korea's investment in education which explains its economic success or could its economic success have funded the expansion in education? Hong Kong had, as Wolf points out, 'nothing like the central direction and planning of education evident in Singapore or Korea, but its growth rate has been comparable'.[36] Switzerland was the richest developed country in the world in both 1980 and 1993, but spends relatively little on education, educating far fewer of its citizens to degree level than the OECD average. What, too, of America, a country which has an economy which was, until recently, the envy of the world and at the same time an education system at school level that is regarded as something of a joke?

Once asked, these questions are embarrassingly obvious. But the real embarrassment is that so few people want to ask them. To repeat my earlier question: how is it that ministers and educationalists have signed up to an orthodoxy that is so clearly so suspect? The sceptical answer is that the former believe that there are votes to be won in supporting it and the latter recognise, rightly, that it is a huge job creation scheme.

This is not to argue that education is irrelevant to economic success. No sensible person would. Equally, no sensible government would continue its unthinking expansion of post-16 education and training. Investment needs to be targeted on those aspects of the education service that do contribute: the teaching of literacy and numeracy in primary schools; the education of the intellectual elite, which is needed to drive the economy and, one might add, to govern the country; and, last, but not least, training in the skills that are in such woefully short supply.

The latter point is where I part company with Professor Wolf. She thinks that skills training is 'a great idea for other people's children'. She tells an accurate and deeply depressing story of how successive governments have failed to introduce vocational training initiatives into schools. Vocational courses are low status, she argues, and, therefore, an undesirable choice. 'Fine-tuning or kick-starting the economy via state-run vocational education is a misconceived endeavour, and it is time that governments recognised their inability to do anything of the sort.'[37] If she is questioning the ability of the state to run vocational courses, or, for that matter, courses of any kind, I would agree with her. But she appears to go further than this: she is dismissing vocational training as a viable option whoever is responsible for the courses.

Her conclusion would be valid if many sectors of the UK economy were not suffering from such serious skill shortages. But they are. The argument, moreover, that nobody will want to commit themselves to training schemes that lead to specific skills when jobs that use these skills may at some point in the future disappear seems to me fanciful. At what point is the construction industry going to decide that plumbers and bricklayers are redundant? Neither do I accept the claim that plumbing or any other craft involves a body of intellectual knowledge so demanding that it cannot be taught through schemes of vocational training linked to apprenticeships. In suggesting that it does, Alison Wolf seems to have forgotten her earlier, wry, but realistic, comment that people who serve cups of coffee do not need a degree to work the cappuccino machine.

Parity of esteem

At which point, such are the idiotic times in which we live, I must immediately confront the great god 'parity of esteem'. Am I suggesting that those of us who have degrees and, to pick a trade at random, write for newspapers, are superior to plumbers? Far from it. If a pipe bursts in the middle of the night, most of us would say that the plumber had the more useful skills. But judgements of this kind clearly depend upon the context, and I have never understood why so many educationalists try so hard to pretend that every trade and profession demands a comparable balance of knowledge and skill and is of equal value to the world. If pushed, and with the burst pipe mended, I would say that the genius of, say, Shakespeare, beats the genius of any plumber I am ever likely to encounter. There are, that is, values in my scheme of things beyond those of practicality and productivity. But we are talking about 14-year-old children, not geniuses, and all that matters in practice is that we recognise that different 14-year-olds have different abilities and aspirations and that we give them all as good a chance to succeed in their different ways as we can.

This silly debate about 'parity of esteem' is, in fact, one of the reasons why we still do not have decent vocational courses as an alternative pathway to the academic. Professor Wolf herself succumbs to what is a near universal malaise. 'Parity of esteem', she writes sardonically, 'is to be promoted by encouraging these young people who are failing academically to drop most of their ordinary GCSEs in favour of vocational courses from the age of fourteen onwards. This group is then expected to progress on to higher level apprenticeships or vocational A Levels.'[38] The latter expectation, itself an example of the Government's obsessive determination to insist that everyone is equal and can therefore be expected to achieve equal results (albeit by different routes), is indeed absurd. But why should 'young people who are failing academically' not be encouraged to drop courses they are going to fail? The question is whether we can offer them a worthwhile alternative. If we can, then these alternative courses will generate their own esteem. They will, if those responsible for their introduction have a modicum of common sense, be very different from academic courses, focusing on the tacit knowledge and skill upon which craft-based activities depend rather than the explicit intellectual understandings of GCSE, A Level and degree programmes. Thirty years ago A Levels were esteemed because students who achieved top grades won places at top universities. They led to prizes students valued, and were, therefore, valued in themselves. So, too, with vocational courses, which will be valued when, and only when, they are judged to be valuable by employers and by the young people who take them. Parity of esteem cannot be talked up by ministers or teachers. It cannot be secured by attempts to 'bridge the divide' between academic and vocational courses. Indeed, such attempts undermine what ought to be the difference between the two routes and, inevitably, create a watered down academic qualification that nobody, understandably, finds attractive.

As academic qualifications themselves become ever more watery and more graduates realise that their investment in three years of university 'education' is not going to secure them graduate-status work, vocational courses that have a distinct identity and a genuine currency in the real world will become increasingly attractive. The problem is essentially one of middle-class snobbery. It is educationalists and politicians, tortured by their egalitarian obsessions, who agonise over 'parity of esteem'. If my grandchildren turn out to be academically bright and decide to read, say, medieval history, at Cambridge, then that would be fine. I would encourage them every step along the road. But if they do not have that academic intelligence, then I would much prefer them to chose a vocational course than to waste their time pretending to study for a degree lacking in any intellectual rigour, leading nowhere anybody would want to be, and in which they would probably have no real interest anyway. Vocational courses are a great idea for anybody's children. The problem is that they have been sabotaged by woolly thinking, ministerial gullibility and white collar snobbery. Plus, of course, the miraculous ability of the bureaucrats to drown a good idea in bureaucratic detail.

My fear is that today's two-year-olds will not have any meaningful choice to make at 18. The conventional wisdom has always been that the English education system looks after academically gifted students very well, but fails the less able. Once, perhaps, this was true, but not, I suspect, for much longer, if it is now. The gap between the theorising of pundits like Charles Leadbeater and the actual needs of the British economy becomes ever more obvious. So, too, does the failure of vocational training initiatives, which might assuage the egalitarian guilt of policymakers and their advisers, but do nothing to meet the needs of real human beings and their potential employers. Sooner or later, reality will intrude and pressure from disgruntled students and increasingly desperate employers will lead to the creation of straightforward practical courses.

The death of liberal education

I am much less sanguine about the future of academic options. Over the last thirty years, A Levels (as I have shown in Chapter 1) have been relentlessly undermined. The new Diploma introduced into secondary schools last autumn will, ministers hope, kill off any examination aimed exclusively at academically more able students. Where are future generations of academic 18-year-olds going to find academic courses that engage their enthusiasms and challenge their intellects? The idea that students who have the necessary ability might read for a degree because they want to learn more about a subject they love has already been dismissed as an elitist and anachronistic embarrassment. Educationalists, employers, politicians all appear to agree that the current 'agenda' is what the country needs. Participation, that is, must be increased and access widened; courses rendered more relevant to the supposed needs of the economy; the walls of the ivory tower torn down once and for all. Nobody believes in universities as centres of liberal learning any more, and, if nobody cares, nothing is likely to change. Come 2025 our brightest two-year-olds may well find that there are very few institutions offering the academic courses they would have been able, in the past, to follow.

When I applied to university in the mid-1960s I did not give a moment's thought to my subsequent employment. Neither, with the exception of a handful of students who wanted to become doctors and accountants, did anybody else. There was no careers adviser at my grammar school. Our teachers simply assumed that we would choose the subject that interested us and spend three years learning more about it. Looking back, I am enormously grateful for the fact that I grew up at a time when education still mattered for its own sake.

The university I attended, Bristol, publishes a magazine called *Nonesuch*. I received the latest edition while writing this chapter. It was dedicated to 'Enterprise' and celebrated the way in which the university now helps its students to 'spot business opportunities'. Flicking through the pages, I read articles about 'How I became a Pie Shop Owner' and 'The Rubber Revolution', which detailed the plans of two ex-Bristol students 'to bring a conscience to the condom market'. It is not that I've anything against pies, or, indeed, ethical condoms. I am all for entrepreneurship and I appreciate how research in the sciences in particular may generate insights of huge practical significance. But a university magazine dedicated to business success? A Vice Chancellor who writes tritely that 'in recent years the University has taken to summing up its essential purposes in three words: learning, discovery and enterprise'?[39] In my time as a student at Bristol, the university did not feel it needed a mission statement, and its Vice Chancellor would not have dreamt of descending to this level of banality.

Back in 1992, polytechnics were transformed overnight into universities. Now universities pursue the ideals of 'enterprise' which once defined the polytechnics. We need 'enterprise' and we need polytechnics as they once were, but we need universities, too. The continuing existence of universities as institutions of liberal education depends, however, on the independence of mind of the men and women who lead them. Their fate is inevitable if their vice chancellors collude merrily with the ministers who have become their masters, sacrificing, in their eagerness to conform, the independence of the institutions they are paid to lead.

Most vice chancellors have probably never heard of the philosopher Michael Oakeshott. Few, certainly, seem to share his belief in 'the great and characteristic gift of the university ... the gift of an interval'. In his earliest essay on education, 'The Universities', published in 1949, Oakeshott wrote:

> Here was an opportunity to put aside the hot allegiances of youth without the necessity of acquiring new loyalties to take their place. Here was an interval in which a man might refuse to commit himself. Here was a break in the tyrannical course of irreparable human events; a period in which to look round upon the world without the sense of an enemy at one's back or the insistent pressure to make up one's mind; a moment in which one was relieved of the necessity of 'coming to terms with oneself' or of entering the fiercely trivial partisan struggles of the world outside; a moment in which to taste the mystery without the necessity of at once seeing a solution. ... One might, if one were so inclined, reduce this to a doctrine about

> the character of a university; one might call it the doctrine of the interim. But the doctrine would be no more than a brief expression of what it felt like to be an undergraduate on that first October morning. Almost overnight, a world of ungracious fact had melted into infinite possibility; we, who belonged to no 'leisured class', had been freed for a moment from the curse of Adam, the burdensome distinction between work and play. What opened before us was not a road but a boundless sea; and it was enough to stretch one's sails to the wind.[40]

Reading Oakeshott's words, I can hear the snort of ministerial disbelief. Neither, I suspect, is it just ministers and their obedient vice chancellors. We live in tough economic times. Many, perhaps most, taxpayers will, I suspect, dismiss Oakeshott's lyricism as *Brideshead Revisited* indulgence.

I can only say that I know exactly what he means, and that the experience he describes has nothing to do with the offensive and self-indulgent antics of the Bullingdon Club. I was an 18-year-old who wanted to spend three years of his life reading English literature. I had no idea where my studies would lead, and I did not care that I had no idea. It was enough 'on that first October morning' to walk down from Clifton through Victoria Square to the University Library at the top of Park Street and to revel in the fact that there were so many books I had not read. Looking back, I wish I had read more and read more seriously, but such regrets are, sadly, inevitable. Youth, as they say, is wasted on the young. The point is that I had the opportunity. It is an opportunity that most people would not want, and it is an opportunity that no government can afford to fund if 50 per cent of the population is to attend university. To which the obvious retort is that governments should not be spending taxpayers' money on opportunities people do not want and from which they are unlikely to benefit.

That benefit is, admittedly, not easy to define. It has nothing to do with enhancing 'skill sets' in the interest of employability and the country's economic competitiveness in 'an increasingly global economy'. It has nothing to do with the business of, to use Oakeshott's phrase 'coming to terms with ourselves'. It has nothing, in fact, to do with our 'selves' at all. The point, rather, is that a liberal education offers an escape from the confines of our 'selves'. 'What opened before us', Oakeshott wrote, 'was not a road but a boundless sea: and it was enough to stretch one's sails to the wind.' What matters is the 'boundlessness': the realisation that the 'opportunities' (that word which dominates all discussion of education) are endless. Without this sense of endlessness and a concomitant willingness to 'stretch one's sails to the wind' we are locked into a world of comfortable cliché and imprisoned within the limitations of our own experience. The gift of an interval is the gift of a life.

Some will reject these arguments as mystical claptrap; others will be worried about their elitist implications. My position is unashamedly elitist. The gift of an interval is not, for reasons explored in the previous chapter, for everybody. Why pretend otherwise? Why, except for reasons of socialist spite, deny the opportunity to those who can benefit? It worries me that poor state education continues to mean that some bright children from disadvantaged homes are denied the opportunity, but the problem here is not the supposedly elitist nature of serious academic study: it is the failure of the schools such children attend.

Oakeshott concentrates on the benefit to the individual. There is, however, a second argument in favour of liberal education which may convince readers who remain sceptical. This is that the intellectual and emotional benefits conferred by a liberal education are essential to the healthy functioning of a democracy.

Writing on de Tocqueville's *Democracy in America* in his classic book on higher education, *The Closing of the American Mind*, Allan Bloom states that: 'The great democratic danger, according to Tocqueville, is enslavement to public opinion.'[41] Every man in a democracy is free to come to his own conclusions and every man's conclusions are as valid as those of every other man. This would be fine if men were capable of coming to independent judgements. 'Some kind of authority', as Bloom puts it, 'is often necessary for most men and is necessary, at least sometimes, for all men.'[42] Access to traditional wisdom offers, paradoxically, the likelihood of greater independence of thought, because without it men will be dependent upon fashionable orthodoxies and the 'tyranny' of public opinion. Every man's decision might in principle be as important as every other man's, but political and social life demands consensus; which means that in most situations the will of the majority prevails. This, Bloom argues, is the most dangerous form of tyranny, 'not the kind that actively persecutes minorities, but the kind that breaks the inner will to resist because there is no qualified source of nonconforming principle and no sense of superior right'.[43]

Americans, Tocqueville observed, talk constantly about individual rights, but only rarely display independence of mind. He might have been writing about twenty-first century England. Very few people in the world of education are prepared to stand out against the prevailing consensus. In two decades of working with senior educationalists, I met half a dozen who questioned the anti-educational, egalitarian thrust of government policies. It was not that the rest had necessarily sniffed the political wind and had made their careerist choice: the majority had no sense of the limitations of such policies and no idea of how things might be different. In resigning as Chief Inspector, I myself succumbed to the tyranny of the majority. I knew I could not support Government policies. I knew, too, that the office of Chief Inspector is a Crown Appointment and thus independent of Government. But, in the end, I decided that Mr Blair and Mr Blunkett had been elected and I had not, so I had no option but to resign. I still wonder whether this was the right decision.

Neither, of course, is this 'monotony of thought' limited to the world of education. Our political leaders will not take any decision before the obligatory focus group has been consulted. Scientists who do not accept the consensus view on climate change are ostracised. As, indeed, are academics who are known to hold right-wing views. We live in a world in which the opinion of the majority dictates how, unless we are very stupid or very brave, we must think and therefore act. Why, after all, does the concept of 'elitism' attract such withering and universal opprobrium? Because the notion that some men might be more gifted than others leads to the unthinkable thought that some men's opinions are more valid than others. Which, despite every National Curriculum exhortation 'to think critically and creatively' is a thought no decent democrat, however hard he struggles, will ever be able to stomach.

For Bloom, the university 'is a place where inquiry and philosophical openness come in to their own. It is intended to encourage the non-instrumental use of reason for its own sake, to provide the atmosphere where the moral and physical superiority of the dominant will not intimidate philosophical doubt. And it preserves the treasury of great deeds, great men and great thoughts required to nourish that doubt.'[44] For Professor Eric Thomas, Vice Chancellor of the University of Bristol, and many of his peers, the university is an institution which encourages entrepreneurial zeal: the ability, for example, to spot the need for ethical condoms. On the one hand, 'great deeds, great men and great thoughts'; on the other a new pie shop to grace the high street. To put it thus is, I know, to exaggerate. We are not there yet. There are professors in our universities, just as there are teachers in our schools, who remained committed to the ideals of a liberal education. But the direction of travel is clear. The myth of the knowledge economy has swept Mr Blair and Mr Brown off their feet. Mr Cameron appears to be similarly bewitched. We need more skilled workers; the percentage of the population studying for degrees must be increased; access must, of course, be widened; the more obviously relevant the degree to the world of work the better: this is the cross party agenda for higher education. Readers who do not believe me should click on to the UCAS website and reflect on the weird and wonderful subjects now deemed to be worthy of inclusion in a university prospectus. And, meanwhile, the tyranny Bloom identified, the tyranny of the majority, tightens its grip on our democratic state. There is the occasional squeal of protest, but those in power cannot be bothered to listen. They have committed themselves to the myth, and they have no concept, it seems, of the importance of 'philosophical doubt'.

Chapter 4

The National Curriculum: A Desolation of Learning

> The curriculum should be treasured. There should be real pride in our curriculum: the learning that the nation has decided to set before its young. Teachers, parents, employers, the media and the public should all see the curriculum as something to embrace, support and celebrate. Most of all young people should relish the opportunity for discovery and achievement that the curriculum offers.
>
> Mick Waters, Director of Curriculum, QCA[45]

IN PRINCIPLE, I agree with Mr Waters that the National Curriculum should be accepted as an important and positive policy requirement, but life has taught me that the greater the need to talk something up the more likely it is that there is something to hide. We now have a new curriculum for Key Stages 3 and 4 and Sir Jim Rose is at the time of writing conducting a review of the primary curriculum. All change, once again. The new secondary curriculum is certainly different from earlier versions and the signs are that the primary curriculum will end up moving in a similar direction to the secondary. But, fundamentally, nothing is new. These latest developments in the National Curriculum have their roots in disagreements about the nature of education, and, therefore, the curriculum, which surfaced vigorously in the late 1980s and early 90s when the National Curriculum was first put together.

Subjects versus cross-curricular dimensions

I joined the National Curriculum Council, a predecessor body to today's Qualifications and Curriculum Authority, in 1990. The Council's remit from ministers was clear: to develop a subject-based national curriculum that defined the knowledge, understanding and skills to be taught in each subject. Most people, I imagine, if they ever thought about a national curriculum, would have agreed that this was a sensible approach. Most, I imagine, would still agree. There was, however, considerable opposition from, in particular, primary school teachers who did not like the idea of having to teach 'subjects'. 'We teach children', they would say, 'not subjects', though what they taught children I was never clear. Perhaps they were not, either. They simply wanted complete freedom to respond serendipitously to individual children and local circumstance. At secondary level, the argument was that cross-curricular 'themes' and 'skills' were more important than subjects, and, if the wretched curriculum had to be divided up into subjects, then every opportunity should be taken to highlight opportunities for the teaching of these 'themes' and 'skills'.

Initially, as we all know, the subject approach triumphed and cross-curricular odds and ends were packaged up into a small advisory section. Now, with the new secondary curriculum, the wheel has come full circle: they are centre stage. Subjects do remain, though a new subject 'Citizenship' has been added to the original ten statutory subjects and two new non-statutory Programmes of Study, 'Personal Wellbeing' and 'Economic Wellbeing and Financial Capability', have been added for schools to consider (and woe betide them if they have not implemented the requirements when the inspectors call). I will discuss the specific demands of these new 'subjects' later in this chapter. The obvious point to make now is that the more time which is given over to the teaching of Citizenship and Personal Wellbeing, the less time there is for Mathematics and History and Science.

In addition, heavy emphasis is placed on what are now called cross-curricular 'dimensions', such as cultural diversity, healthy lifestyles, community participation, enterprise, global dimension and sustainable development, technology and media, and creativity and thinking. A number of 'key skills', including 'functional' skills in English, mathematics and ICT and 'personal, learning and thinking skills', such as teamwork, creative thinking, reflective learning and self-management, have also been given a new importance. All this is set within a new statement of aims which asserts, somewhat ambitiously, that the curriculum should 'enable all young people to become: successful learners who enjoy learning, make progress and achieve; confident individuals who are able to live safe, healthy and fulfilling lives; and responsible citizens who make a positive contribution to society'.[46]

Aims

A discussion of this new curriculum should, logically, begin with these aims. 'It is important', we are told, 'to recognise a broad set of common purposes, values and aims that underpin the school curriculum and the work of schools.'[47] Why is it? The first version of the National Curriculum did not attempt to articulate a sense of the moral good upon which it was based. It assumed, rightly, in my view, that the programmes of study defining the knowledge to be taught in the ten subjects it encompassed needed no justification. Yes, other subjects, such as, for example, Drama, might have been included, but the subjects chosen reflected school timetables round the country. They were hardly controversial. Understanding and appreciation are better than ignorance and indifference. Full stop. What, after all, is there to say?

A great deal, if you believe John White, Emeritus Professor of Philosophy of Education at the Institute of Education in the University of London, and a Government adviser on the curriculum. White accepts that the subjects of the National Curriculum 'provide a comprehensive induction into the gamut of intellectual culture', but he is not very interested in 'intellectual culture'. In his view, subject disciplines are middle class constructs that working class children find alien. They were invented, he tells us, by 'eighteenth-century English Old Dissenters' and 'Scottish Presbyterians' who thought 'personal salvation' depended on one having 'a comprehensive grasp of the nature of God's world'.[48] The religious rationale for subjects having long disappeared, there is, he argues, no good reason for retaining them. Some pupils might find their intellectual delights exciting, but many do not, and, if the defence is that doing well in a traditional curriculum brings you a good job, Professor White, rightly, rejects this as an unacceptably utilitarian view of the curriculum.

He wants us to abandon a curriculum based on the 'introverted' aims of school subjects in favour of one rooted in 'whole person aims': a sense, that is, of 'the sort of person school learning is meant to foster'. The aims of the new secondary school curriculum could have been written by Professor White. Perhaps they were. 'Clear aims', the introduction to the statutory requirements tells us, 'that focus on the qualities and skills learners need to succeed in school and beyond should be the starting point for the curriculum'. Successful learners, confident individuals, responsible citizens: you could hardly have a brasher, less equivocal statement of purpose. There is no 'introverted' nonsense about the importance of particular subjects. No, this is big picture stuff, focusing on what really matters: the 'well-being' of the 'learner' and his or her subsequent contribution to society.

The trouble is, once you ask yourself what all this means, the warm glow very quickly starts to evaporate. Can the curriculum produce 'successful learners' who enjoy learning, make progress and achieve? No, of course it cannot. Good teachers can help the majority of their children to achieve, but, unless they are miracle workers, some of their pupils will, inevitably, fail. More fundamentally, should the curriculum seek to promote a love of learning? No, it should be a statement of the knowledge children need to be taught. What matters more than children's enjoyment of learning is their actual attainment: the knowledge they have mastered. The fact that this new National Curriculum focuses on the enjoyment of pupils rather than what they need to learn tells us all we need to know about the state of education in England today.

Second, while, of course, I accept that what happens to children at school can, for better or worse, affect their ability and confidence as adults, I do not think that schools, let alone what is, after all, no more than a number of printed pages, a National Curriculum, can deliver what, sadly, are not givens in human lives. Does anyone, other than Ed Balls and Mick Waters, believe that children leaving school in 2013 after five years of this magic elixir of a curriculum are necessarily going to live 'safe, healthy and fulfilling lives'? If the reference to safety is a gesture towards the danger of predatory paedophiles, then this is a curriculum which is contributing to our national paranoia about the safety of our children. If it is elevating safety to a universal human aspiration, then I would like to log a word or two about the importance of danger and risk. It helps, I know, not to stuff garbage into our mouths and too many of us drink too much, but our health in adult life depends more on the will of God than it does the lessons we sat through on Personal Wellbeing (more of which anon).

As for 'responsible citizens who make a positive contribution to society', I can only say that there is more than a whiff here of *1984*. You will conform. Your definition of 'responsible' might not be mine. Your sense of what constitutes a 'positive contribution to society' might be very different from mine. Hard luck, I am going to ensure through my new National Curriculum that everyone knows what is expected of them. So I imagine Mr Balls musing as he soaks in his bath, congratulating himself on the fact that he has finished off any possibility of the curriculum producing 'educated' citizens.

Cast your eye over the elaboration of these three aims printed on page 78[49] and ask yourself how you measure up. Are you creative and resourceful, a whiz at identifying and solving problems? Do you understand how you learn? Do you know about 'big ideas and events that shape our world' (whatever this might mean)? How is your sense of self-worth? Are you self-aware? Do you deal 'well' with your emotions? How are your healthy lifestyle choices? Do you understand your own and others' cultures and traditions, within (of course) the context of British heritage? Do you appreciate the benefits of diversity? Do you sustain and improve the environment, locally and globally?

Personally, I can only say that I hope your score was higher than mine. If I were at school today I would fail miserably. I do not know what half these statements mean, and, reflecting on the rest, I bow my head in shame. But this is the problem with 'whole person aims': what emerges is a statement of an ideal that is unrealisable in a fallen world. Remember Lawrence. Why when it comes to Jimmy Shepherd, or, for that matter, Chris Woodhead, do Messrs Balls and Waters think they can improve on the best that God can manage?

I have no answer to this question, but I do know that this new curriculum makes it harder for teachers to make the difference they can and should be making. Our schools are not very good at it, but there is no reason why 95 per cent of our children should not learn to read. There is no reason why 30 per cent of secondary school students should think, according to a recent survey, that Oliver Cromwell fought at the Battle of Hastings. A similar number could not name the century in which the First World War took place. This is one example from one subject, but there is, I am afraid, no reason to think that our children's ignorance is confined to matters of historical fact. Too many know precious little about anything. It is not their fault. I do not subscribe to the view, trotted out each summer to explain ever-improving examination grades, that every generation of students is brighter and more diligent than the one before, but neither do I think that each generation is more stupid. I do not blame teachers. They have to work with the curriculum and examination syllabuses they are given. Chapter 1 demonstrated how the intellectual demand of examinations has been lowered over the years. The analysis of the new curriculum which follows shows how knowledge has been marginalised to the point where ignorance is inevitable.

Turn over again to that set of aims which revealed your inadequacy as a human being. There is one reference to knowledge. 'Successful learners should know about big ideas and events that shape our world.' That is it. Subject-specific fact is, apparently, so unimportant that, other than this meaningless nod, it does not get a mention.

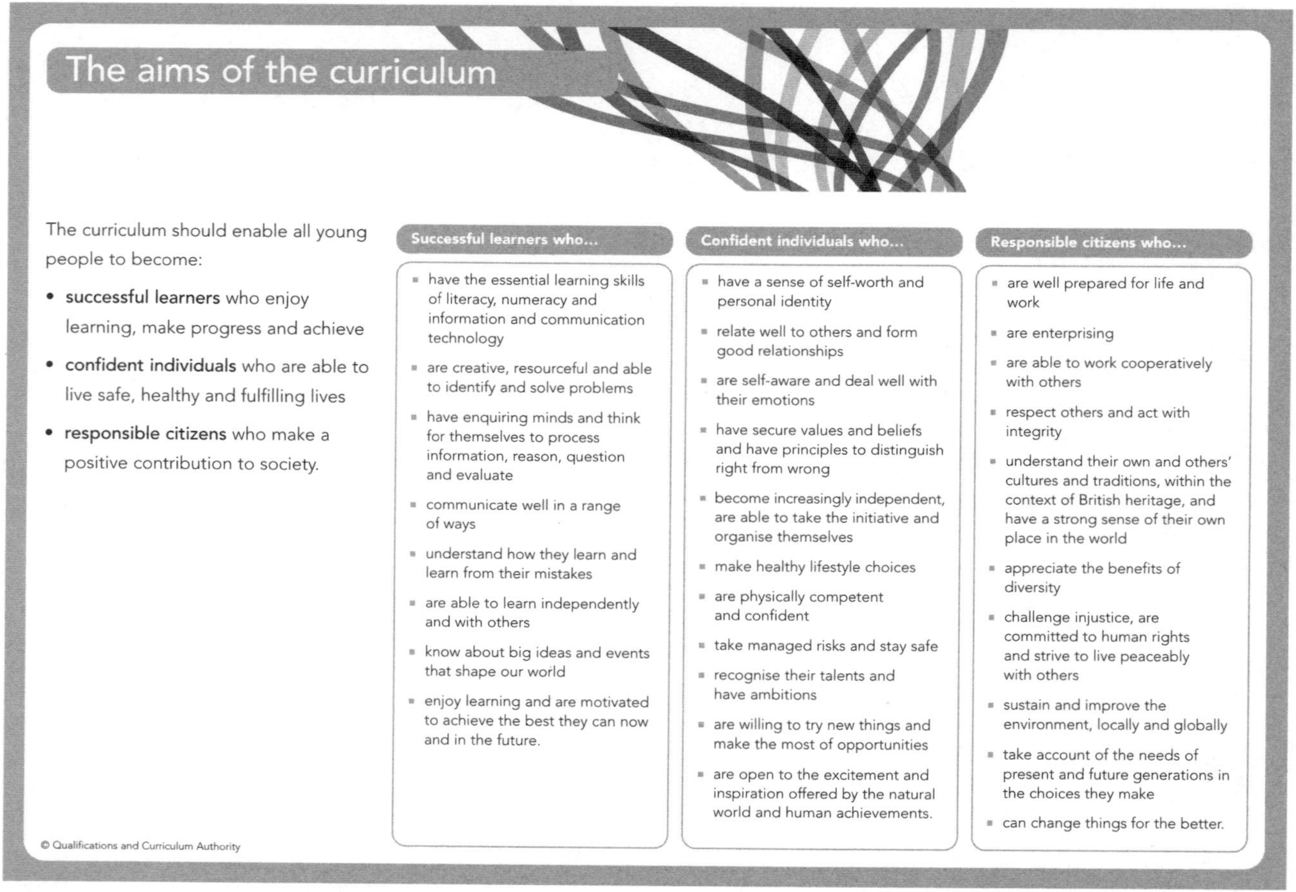

The aims of the curriculum

The curriculum should enable all young people to become:

- **successful learners** who enjoy learning, make progress and achieve
- **confident individuals** who are able to live safe, healthy and fulfilling lives
- **responsible citizens** who make a positive contribution to society.

Successful learners who…

- have the essential learning skills of literacy, numeracy and information and communication technology
- are creative, resourceful and able to identify and solve problems
- have enquiring minds and think for themselves to process information, reason, question and evaluate
- communicate well in a range of ways
- understand how they learn and learn from their mistakes
- are able to learn independently and with others
- know about big ideas and events that shape our world
- enjoy learning and are motivated to achieve the best they can now and in the future.

Confident individuals who…

- have a sense of self-worth and personal identity
- relate well to others and form good relationships
- are self-aware and deal well with their emotions
- have secure values and beliefs and have principles to distinguish right from wrong
- become increasingly independent, are able to take the initiative and organise themselves
- make healthy lifestyle choices
- are physically competent and confident
- take managed risks and stay safe
- recognise their talents and have ambitions
- are willing to try new things and make the most of opportunities
- are open to the excitement and inspiration offered by the natural world and human achievements.

Responsible citizens who…

- are well prepared for life and work
- are enterprising
- are able to work cooperatively with others
- respect others and act with integrity
- understand their own and others' cultures and traditions, within the context of British heritage, and have a strong sense of their own place in the world
- appreciate the benefits of diversity
- challenge injustice, are committed to human rights and strive to live peaceably with others
- sustain and improve the environment, locally and globally
- take account of the needs of present and future generations in the choices they make
- can change things for the better.

Figure 19 'The Aims of the Curriculum', © QCA

Skills and processes

Browse through the Programmes of Study for each subject[50] and you will soon see that what do matter in this new curriculum are the 'skills and processes' which are deemed crucial to progress in each subject. Here is another test. Read the lists of skills and processes printed below. They are taken from the requirements for three subjects. See if you can decide which each subject might be.

Subject 1:

- 'Taking risks and learning from mistakes'
- 'Analysing, designing, making, reflecting, evaluating'
- 'Developing their own views and expressing reasoned judgements'
- 'Use research and investigative skills'
- 'Reflect on and evaluate their own and others' work'
- 'Analyse, select and question critically'

Subject 2:

- 'Knowing and understanding what needs to be achieved, critically evaluating how well it has been achieved and finding ways to improve'
- 'Exploring and experimenting with techniques, tactics and compositional skills'
- 'Refine and adapt ideas and plans in response to changing circumstance'
- 'Analyse performances, identifying strengths and weaknesses'

Subject 3:

- 'Identify and investigate, individually and as part of a team … making and testing hypotheses'
- 'Reflect critically on questions or issues'
- 'Identify, select and use a range of sources'
- 'Evaluate the sources used in order to reach reasoned conclusions'

Subject 1 is Art and Design, Subject 2 Physical Education, Subject 3 History. There are clues, of course, obvious, no doubt, to the cognoscenti, but the essential point is, I hope, clear: the subject in the new National Curriculum has become the vehicle for the teaching of a set of skills deemed to be of vital importance if the learner is to progress in his or her learning. Indeed, the QCA congratulates itself on the commonality of these skills. They are seen as the DNA, or, to use a perhaps more appropriate metaphor, the concrete, which binds the subjects together and renders the curriculum more 'coherent'. What matters is the skill, not the subject: the latter is important now, if it is important at all, as a vehicle in which skills and, see below, dimensions, can be banged endlessly into the skulls of the learners who have the misfortune to be entering secondary school in September 2008.

Here is a quotation from a document called 'The role of functional English in supporting progression and success' published by the DCSF.[51] It purports to explain what 'functional skills' are, and, in failing, demonstrates something of the arcane world our teachers and the children they teach are now meant to inhabit.

'Functional skills are integral' to the 'movement from shallow to deep learning' because 'they require learners to internalise the skills they are developing so that they can draw on them to resolve a range of problems set against a tapestry of contexts'. Learners need to develop 'metacognitive strategies' that enable them to: 'know how to learn; identify a problem; analyse its components, and marshal resources appropriately; continually question methods and approaches; explain the process of learning to others; organise information and, through understanding, convert it to knowledge; know how and when to work on their own and in a team'.

A little of this, a very little, if we are talking about A Level students, is sensible. Sixth formers should learn how to define the problem they are thinking about, identify the premises of their arguments, marshal, if appropriate, empirical evidence, and learn how to move logically and persuasively to a conclusion. They should, though anyone who has marked A Level exam scripts will know that not every student has entirely mastered these sophisticated demands. Many have never learnt to spell, and, far from developing their own articulate argument, have difficulty re-hashing their teacher's notes. But, and this is my first objection, the authors of this nonsense are not talking about A Level students. They have 11–14-year-olds in their sights, children who may not be able to read and quite possibly think Oliver Cromwell fought the French. I worry too that teachers are being told 'to identify lesson objectives that are skills-focused and that are highlighted and explicitly threaded through a teaching sequence'.[52] Yes, when I taught English I wanted my children to learn how to spell and punctuate, but when I was teaching them, say, *Macbeth*, it was the magnificence of Shakespeare's play and the profundity of his insight into human emotion that preoccupied me in planning my lessons. The notion of using such a lesson to teach children 'how to learn' would have struck me then, as it does now, as a bizarre distraction from the true purposes of learning.

But the 'metacognitive skill' of learning 'how to learn' is now all the rage. The theory is that nobody needs to be taught anything any more. You can look up what you need to know on the web, and, in any case, by the time, so it is said, a fact is learnt, it will, such is the speed of intellectual discovery, be out of date. Neither proposition needs, I hope, much discussion. The more you know, the more useful the web is likely to be, and while, at the cutting edge of science, knowledge is being re-written, there is much in science and every other subject which remains constant and needs to be learnt.

What, moreover, is meant when we are told children need 'to know how to learn'? Human beings learn by listening to people who know more about the subject they are learning than they do themselves. They learn by reading and by exploring the limits of their understanding in writing. They learn by talking to other people who are at a similar stage in their understanding. They learn, if it is a practical subject, by doing. Do children need to be taught these obvious truths? And, if the retort is, as it will be, that this misses the point completely, and that the challenge is to help children become 'autonomous' in their learning skills so that 'they can make the transition from shallow to deep learning', then what, precisely, are the metacognitive strategies which need to be taught? Is it really sensible to encourage them to 'continually question methods and processes' and, presumably, facts, before they have the faintest understanding of what these methods and processes and facts involve and mean? Is the demand that they are taught when to work as a team anything more than a genuflexion to the demands of employers for more effective teamplayers? Do they need 'to explain the process of learning to others'? It does help on occasion to try to explain a new idea to other people, but this preoccupation with the process rather than the substance of learning is, to use John White's words, tediously introverted.

Learning how to learn is, after all, not very exciting. What is exciting is learning. By which I mean having your eyes opened to the mystery and magic of a world which as a child you know nothing about. That is what good teachers do. This is what schools are for. Or were, in the days before educationalists and politicians decided that children were being fed information to 'replicate' when they should, all on, of course, their autonomous own, be engaged in a process of 'deep learning' which enabled them 'to justify, explain, exemplify, apply, compare and contrast, contextualise and generalise'.[53] Functional skills stem, like so much else that is noxious in the world of modern education, from the cavalier dismissal of didactic teaching as a Gradgrindian anachronism. Some of my teachers at Wallington Grammar School in the 1950s and 60s fed me gobbets of information to regurgitate at appropriate moments. They were the inadequate and incompetent ones. The majority told me things I did not know and at the time often did not want to hear. They made me attend to, engage with, a world of learning which pushed back the limitations of my personal horizons and led to a sixth form in which our thoughts and arguments were very much part of the everyday fabric of every lesson.

Dimensions

Skills are one distraction; 'dimensions', the twenty-first century New Labour reincarnation of the cross-curricular themes I encountered in 1990, are another. These cross-curricular dimensions provide, the QCA tells us, 'important unifying areas of learning that help young people make sense of the world and give education relevance and authenticity. They reflect the major ideas and challenges that face individuals and society.'[54] This is an intensely revealing passage. I have never understood the argument that knowledge must be presented to children as a 'seamless web'. My own experience as a 'learner' is that I make connections between different areas of knowledge when my interest in something leads me to research something else. The discovery of links and influences is both fascinating in itself and, potentially at least, enriching of the original interest, but there has, it seems to me, to be a starting point. I am, therefore, less interested in the attempt to 'unify' areas of learning than I am in the development of a real understanding and appreciation of particular areas and subjects. The whole point of subjects is that they enable us to make sense of the world in which we live. Indeed, our understanding of the world depends upon our mastery of the different ways in which over the centuries men have organised their experience of it: by which I mean science, mathematics, history, literature and other subjects of the school curriculum. If 'relevance' means that what is taught should be immediately interesting to the young person, then the only riposte is that education should not be relevant. Schools exist to teach knowledge that would not be encountered elsewhere, or, at best, encountered in a fragmented and incoherent fashion. The more challenging and alien that knowledge, the more powerful the curriculum will be. Or, to put it a different way, the more immediate the 'relevance', the greater the danger of 'inauthenticity'.

An inauthentic curriculum is a curriculum that purports to achieve that which it cannot possibly deliver, which trades in populist and feel-good phrases that mean nothing, and which exploits anxiety about social concerns politicians have failed to resolve. This latest version of the National Curriculum is such a curriculum. At the heart of its inauthenticity lies its obsession with these so-called dimensions.

Click on the QCA website for guidance on the 'Global Dimension'[55] and you are confronted by the slogan 'Putting the world into world class education'. You are offered 'a clear definition' of the 'global dimension'. This supposed definition, amounts, however, to no more than a list, without any explanation of the terms used, of the 'concepts' which the 'global dimension' incorporates: 'global citizenship, conflict resolution, diversity, human rights, interdependence, social justice, sustainable development, values and perceptions'. Reading this, I am none the wiser. What is 'global citizenship'? What exactly is meant by 'interdependence' or 'social justice'? Taken together, these terms, plucked from the liberal ether, smack, just a little, to use one of the Government's favourite words, of an 'agenda'. It is an agenda *Guardian* readers might applaud, but not every parent of every child in a state secondary school reads *The Guardian*. The 'global dimension', the guidance trills, will enable 'learners' to 'deconstruct issues and events from a range of perspectives'. Somehow, I doubt it. The child who concludes that 'diversity' brings more problems than benefits or who questions the glib ideals of 'social justice' will, I predict, find himself or herself out on a pretty lonely limb. Equally dubious is the assertion that this dimension will 'help learners to participate in society as active and responsible citizens'. How exactly will it do this, and, as I have pointed out earlier, who will define the terms? Are Greenpeace activists, responsible eco-warriors, or criminals to be locked up? Is, moreover, the willingness 'to identify and challenge injustice, prejudice and discrimination' a teachable skill, as the QCA appears to believe or, as I think, a matter of courage, which is a function of character and, therefore, something that has to be taught by example?

The Government wants to believe it is a skill because the Government wants schools to solve insoluble problems that ministers find tricky. Would that lessons in global citizenship could prevent conflicts and help resolve any wars that did, by some mischance, happen to occur. Would that children could 'make their own distinctive contribution to global and local communities'. Local, maybe. The Physical Education curriculum requires them, after all, 'to work with others to organise, manage, officiate and run festivals, tournaments, competitions and events, both in school and the local community'.[56] It is true, of course, that the more such organising, managing and officiating they do, the less time they will have to do any physical education, but it is an example of local community involvement. Global involvement? Trickier, and I have yet to find much practical advice on how this might be done. Every subject, remember, is meant to contribute to the teaching of these elusive goals. Every subject teacher has to waste time pondering how he is going to restructure his lessons to conform to these new expectations. Time that would have been better spent thinking about his subject.

The Programmes of Study for History, Geography and Modern Foreign Languages provide clear examples of how such expectations distort the teaching of particular subjects.

Why is History important? Because, you might have thought, the story of our nation's history is a fascinating story which every child should be told. The new Programme of Study acknowledges this, commenting that the subject 'fires pupils' curiosity and imagination', but it then launches into a list of justifications designed to establish the 'relevance' of the past to our contemporary enthusiasms and obsessions. History is important because: 'it helps pupils to develop their own identities'; 'it encourages mutual understanding of the historic origins of our ethnic and cultural diversity'; it 'enhances employability' and 'develops an ability to take part in a democratic society'; and 'it helps pupils become confident and questioning individuals'. Oh, and somewhere in all this, pupils 'develop' (quite how, one wonders, given the overall emphasis on these preoccupations and the vagueness of the prescription when it comes to what actually has to be taught), a 'chronological overview'.

It is worth reflecting on how this 'chronological overview' defines the teaching of British history. We are told that: 'In order to give pupils a secure chronological framework, the choice of content should ensure that all pupils can identify and understand the major events, changes and developments in British, European and World history, covering at least the medieval, early modern, industrial and twentieth century periods.'[57] Note the 'at least', remember that the history teacher has no more than a period or two a week to meet these somewhat challenging requirements, and ask yourself how much detail of British history pupils are going be taught. The specification is as follows. They must be taught:

- the development of political power from the Middle Ages to the twentieth century, including changes in the relationship between rulers and ruled over time, the changing relationship between the crown and parliament, and the development of democracy;
- the different histories and changing relationships through time of the peoples of England, Ireland, Scotland and Wales;
- the impact through time of the movement and settlement of diverse peoples to, from and within the British Isles;

- the way in which the lives, beliefs, ideas and attitudes of people in Britain have changed over time and the factors – such as technology, economic development, war, religion and culture – that have driven these changes;
- the development of trade, colonisation, industrialisation and technology, the British Empire and its impact on different people in Britain and overseas, pre-colonial civilisations, the nature and effects of the slave trade, and resistance and decolonisation.

The preoccupations will, by now, be all too familiar. The 'settlement of diverse peoples' requirement is, for example, glossed in this way:

> The impact through time of the movement and settlement of diverse peoples to, from and within the British Isles includes: studying the wide cultural, social and ethnic diversity of Britain from the Middle Ages to the twentieth century and how this has helped shape Britain's identity and developing an understanding of the part played by internal and external migration in Britain's development, including the experience of key individuals. Examples should help pupils reach an informed understanding of, and respect for, their own and each other's identities. This can be linked with the study in citizenship of reasons for the recent migration to, from and within the UK.[58]

History has to be studied through the prism of political preoccupations. Everything has to be linked to what is deemed relevant to the pupil's experience and judged essential for the coherence of our diverse society.

I chose to study Geography at A Level because I was fascinated by the formation of landscapes I loved and wanted to learn more about places remote from my suburban childhood. Now I see that Geography earns its place in the National Curriculum because the subject 'inspires pupils to become global citizens by exploring their own place in the world, their values and their responsibilities to other people, to the environment and to the sustainability of the planet'.[59] To be fair, it is acknowledged that 'the study of geography stimulates an interest in and a sense of wonder about places', but the detail of the subsequent Programme of Study does not, to use the new geographer's favourite term, 'sustain' this admirable objective. One of the seven 'key concepts' concerns place; four (Interdependence; Physical and Human Processes; Environmental Interaction and

Sustainable Development; and Cultural Understanding and Diversity) develop the sustainability/global citizens theme. And, continuing in the same vein, when we come to 'Curriculum Opportunities' we learn that 'the curriculum should provide opportunities for pupils to participate in informed responsible action in relation to geographical issues that affect them and those around them'. This, an explanatory note tells us, is because such action helps pupils 'make informed and independent decisions and take action both at a personal level and as citizens in society'. Key geographical knowledge is subordinated, once again, to what politicians consider to be the issues of the moment.

So, too, with Modern Foreign Languages (MFL). Languages are now (in principle, at least) deemed to be an important part of the curriculum because they are part of 'the cultural diversity of our society' and because 'learning languages contributes to mutual understanding, a sense of global citizenship and personal fulfilment'.[60] One of the four 'key concepts' listed for the subject is 'intercultural understanding'. Pupils, that is, must be taught 'to appreciate the richness and diversity of other cultures' and 'to recognise that there are different ways of seeing the world and developing an international outlook'. The latter, according to the gloss provided by another explanatory note, means that teachers must ensure that their pupils understand that different peoples have different 'religious beliefs, social customs, traditions, values, attitudes to other countries and reactions to world events'. You will remember the infantile demand of the GCSE MFL examination papers discussed in Chapter 1. Now, you understand why. Missionaries for global understanding, MFL teachers have less time than they once did to teach vocabulary, grammar, and, the real reason, in my view, for studying a foreign language, its literature.

Pseudo-subjects

In itself this distortion of traditional National Curriculum subjects would be damaging enough. There is, however, a further problem. New Programmes of Study for Personal Wellbeing and Economic Wellbeing and Financial Capability have been added to Citizenship as 'subjects' which need to be fitted into the secondary school timetable. These two 'Wellbeings' are not, admittedly, statutory, but, as I commented earlier, the school that chooses to ignore the wisdom they encapsulate will, without doubt, incur the wrath of any inspector who chances to call. The National Curriculum text itself states coercively that 'schools *will wish* to plan use of the SEAL (Social and Emotional Aspects of Learning) material in their teaching of the Personal Wellbeing programme of study so that pupils have a coherent learning experience'.[61] My italics, but the threat will be clear to any headteacher, however independent-minded they might be.

I will return to the Personal and Economic Wellbeing and the SEAL 'materials', but let us begin with what is statutory: Citizenship. The first sentence of the first paragraph of the programme of study raises what for me is a fundamental problem. 'Education for citizenship equips young people with the knowledge, skills and understanding to play an effective role in public life.'[62] There are, in fact, many problems here, but the most fundamental is the ideal of citizenship which, without any discussion or explanation, is placed before us. 'Effective' for the Government means 'active', and its ideal of active citizenship goes far beyond the generally accepted idea that, if we can find a party which deserves our vote, we should vote in a general election.

There is the obvious fact that many of us cannot find a party deserving of our vote. Our enthusiasm for our democratic responsibilities has been squashed: by an incompetence which beggars belief and saps hope; by the self-seeking, patronising, short-termism of so many policy decisions; by the fact that in terms of policy there is, as they fight for supposed electoral advantage to claim the middle ground, so little difference between the three main political parties. I could continue, and so, no doubt, could you. This Citizenship curriculum is one more example of how the Government is dumping a problem on schools that it cannot itself solve, a problem in this case which it has itself created. My basic objection is, however, more fundamental. It is to the ideal upon which everything in this pseudo-subject is based.

I do not myself want to be an active citizen 'addressing' problems of 'social justice, human rights, community cohesion and global interdependence' and 'challenging injustice, inequalities and discrimination'.[63] A society, such as our own, which is obsessed with these huge abstractions is a society in deep trouble; and ministers who believe that citizens want to dedicate their lives to the promotion of equality and the celebration of diversity are living in cloud cuckoo land. It is not that I, and I suspect, the millions of citizens like me, are monsters of unfeeling egotism. It is simply that we do our best in our everyday interactions to render these bloodless ideals real, and that we continue, perhaps foolishly, to hope that one day we will have a Government that talks less about the amelioration of social injustice and achieves more.

If the ideal is deeply suspect, the expectations of what pupils are going to achieve are comic. 'Citizenship', the Programme of Study informs us, 'helps pupils make sense of the world today and equips them for the challenges and changes facing communities in the future'. Could you write a coherent essay on 'the changing nature of UK society, including the diversity of ideas, beliefs, cultures, identities, traditions, perspectives and values that are shared'? Neither could I. I would not do much better on 'the UK's relations with the European Union and the rest of Europe, the Commonwealth, the United Nations and the World as a global community'. I accept, of course, that I might know and understand less than a generation which will, no doubt, prove itself in GCSEs results to be more intelligent than any other previous generation. And I, of course, have not had the benefit of Citizenship lessons. Readers might, however, like to reflect on the following statement of what is expected from a gifted 14-year-old student of Citizenship.

> **Exceptional Performance:**
>
> Pupils use and apply what they have learnt about the origins and substance of different viewpoints to present coherent, perceptive and compelling arguments on a wide range of citizenship issues. They research complex issues, selecting appropriate methodologies and drawing on their own and others' experience of taking action. They assess and evaluate the validity of a wide range of viewpoints and evidence, synthesising them to draw clear conclusions. They take an overview of the key citizenship concepts of democracy, justice, rights and responsibilities, identities and diversity and make sophisticated observations relating to the connections between them. They take a leading role in defining, negotiating and undertaking courses of action with others to address citizenship issues and problems. They apply this practical understanding to analyse approaches citizens can take to improve society through individual and collective actions and democratic processes. They evaluate the impact and limitations of policies on communities (local to global) now and in the future and suggest alternatives. They debate challenging questions about the relationship between the UK and the wider world and the kind of society they as citizens would like to live in.[64]

How, again, did you do? Am I alone in my sense that whoever wrote this Citizenship curriculum has lost touch with reality and should be locked up?

Buried beneath the grandiose expectation, the jargon and the complexities is, of course, something very important: our children should learn that their actions affect other children and that they have, therefore, a responsibility to each other and the school they attend. Good schools, all schools, perhaps, with more or less effect, have recognised this. They have understood, too, that moral development is more a matter of caught behaviours than conceptual understandings. What happens in the everyday life of the classrooms and corridors of the school is more important, and always will be more important, than the formal 'teaching' of Citizenship lessons. Along with every other National Curriculum subject, Citizenship has 'key concepts'. These are 'democracy and justice', 'rights and responsibilities' and 'identities and diversities: living together in the United Kingdom'. The selection is both arbitrary and revealing, but the basic assumption is that if pupils are taught, for example, to 'understand and explore the roles of citizens and parliament in holding government and those in power to account', they will become better citizens. I doubt it. Some knowledge of how parliament works ought, of course, to be taught, and might occupy a lesson or two at the top end of secondary school. Essentially, however, good 'citizenship', whatever precisely we mean by this term, depends upon a sense of what is right and wrong, how oneself and others should behave. This is best developed through example and encouragement, not timetabled lessons.

Indeed, timetabled Citizenship lessons run two obvious risks. The first is that, despite the many references to pupils being encouraged to question and come to their own opinions, an agenda is imposed. Education, in other words, shades into indoctrination. I know from personal experience as an English teacher how difficult it is to sustain a role of neutral chairman in lessons where controversial issues are discussed. And, of course, the indoctrination may come from other pupils as well as the teacher. It takes a brave pupil to stand out against the majority view of his or her peers. The second risk is the mirror image of the first. It is that pupils who have neither the knowledge, nor the intelligence, nor the experience and maturity, to comment on what are extremely difficult moral and political questions are encouraged to question what others believe and to express their own worthless opinions. A sceptical intelligence may be the Socratic ideal, but the questioning of others is the easy part. Anybody, as Dr Johnson said, can be taught to ridicule patriotism. What is hard is the cultivation of a frame of mind that probes one's own dogmatism. 'This is fishy', Wittgenstein wrote year after year in the margins of the manuscript that was to become, when published after his death, the *Philosophical Investigations*. In his own lifetime he could never bring himself to send it to the printers. What seemed persuasive at the time of writing crumbled into confusion in the cold light of day. We might, as educators, do better if we did more to encourage a sense of humility in our students as they begin to engage with the complexities of life.

The introduction to the Personal Wellbeing Programme of Study admits that 'the world is full of complex and sometimes conflicting values'. We should, I suppose, welcome this unexpected honesty, for the National Curriculum as a whole is deeply committed to the belief that all will be well if our children can be indoctrinated into the simplistic certainties of the Government's utopian agenda. Personal Wellbeing is a subject which will help pupils 'explore' complex values and 'reflect on and clarify their own values and attitudes'. Where, though, is the 'teaching'? Some 'exploration', 'reflection' and 'clarification' is fine, but a pedagogic approach that abnegates responsibility for instruction and advocates 'values clarification' as the way to Personal Wellbeing is dangerously unbalanced. The assumption is that adolescents can think their way to personal salvation. No mention is made of the alternative view that adults have a responsibility to teach children what is right and what is wrong.

There is no explanation for this curious omission. Neither is there for the statement that: 'As pupils learn to recognise, develop and communicate their qualities, skills and attitudes, they build knowledge, confidence and esteem and make the most of their abilities.'[65] I would take precisely the opposite view: namely, that self-esteem develops through real achievements. As with so much else in the National Curriculum, a particular point of view is presented as a given. It amounts (see Chapter 6) to an insidious brainwashing of the teaching profession, and, in that the intended result is, presumably, that all teachers will share the same educational and, indeed, political values, torpedoes all talk of a diverse system of schools that allows parents a modicum of choice. Ironically, the spin accompanying this new curriculum is that it allows schools greater 'flexibility' so that they can 'personalise' learning to the 'needs' of their pupils. This is true in that the prescribed content in many subjects is now vague to the point of meaninglessness, but it ignores a more subtle form of prescription, which, ultimately, is far more damaging to both children and their teachers than the more detailed definition of content found in earlier versions of the National Curriculum.

The Personal Wellbeing programme of study refers teachers to the National Healthy Schools Programme (emotional health and wellbeing theme). This Programme 'requires' (note the verb and remember that Personal Wellbeing is meant to be a non-statutory part of the National Curriculum) schools to have 'clear, planned, opportunities for students to understand and explore feelings using appropriate learning and teaching styles'.[66] It makes positive reference to a further programme, Social and Emotional Aspects of Learning (SEAL) with the obvious expectation that secondary schools will use these materials.

Last September I was wandering idly through Ashburton, a pleasant little town on the southern fringes of Dartmoor. My eye was caught by an advertisement in a shop window for a three-day residential course in 'Kissing and Kicking'. Subtitled 'A Journey through Chaos, Passion and Vulnerability', it employed 'a range of creative approaches, including drama enactment, artwork, visualisation, movement, Gestalt, ritual and group process'. Just the thing, I thought, for everyone who believes the classroom should become a therapeutic workshop: just the thing for the SEAL enthusiasts! I made a mental note to call the current Permanent Secretary, David Bell, and strolled back to the car park.

The SEAL materials have been popular for some years now in primary schools, and I can see that they might have a place in reception classes. It is a sad fact of twenty-first century life that there are children who enter schools with few, if any, social skills. Some find speech, however minimal, difficult; many cannot sit still and listen or interact with other children in a remotely acceptable way. It makes sense, therefore, for their teachers to spend time helping them to reflect on their emotional experience in, say, starting school, making and falling out with friends, and bullying. It makes more sense, perhaps, for such children to be taught what constitutes unacceptable behaviour and what happens to them when they misbehave, but the group sessions that are advocated on the SEAL programme may make a valuable contribution to both emotional development and language acquisition.

It is the belief that this kind of activity should continue into the upper reaches of primary, and from September 2008, secondary schools, which worries me. I do not, of course, deny that older children can find it difficult to make a positive contribution to lessons. I think, though, that it is the teacher's job to deal with inappropriate behaviour. Children should be offered incentives to do better and clear deterrents to stiffen their will. They should not be given the opportunity to waste time on, for example, 'revisiting anger'. The 'intended teaching outcomes' for this particular session are that children come to understand: 'what my triggers are for anger; what happens when I get angry; what happens when I am overwhelmed by my feelings; some ways to calm myself down'.[67] Most children do not need this, and most teachers are not trained to help those who do.

SEAL and Personal Wellbeing generally is, obviously enough, another example of the belief that helping children to learn how to learn is more important than teaching them knowledge about the world in which they live. My alternative view is that the better teachers teach, the more children will learn, and the more they learn the better they will feel about themselves. The better they feel about themselves the less need there is for lessons dedicated to a dubious and perhaps dangerous scrutiny of emotions.

Do you want your nine or ten-year-old to spend time filling in rings of a circle with, from the centre, the names: of the people closest to you whom you love; of people you like a lot; of people you know quite well; and, the outer ring, people you know as acquaintances? I do not. I'd rather they were absorbed, to give an example of a lesson I observed recently in an independent school (which counts itself lucky to be independent) on the intricacies of the Battle of Hastings, learning about what went wrong for Harold and why. There is so much to learn that is so exciting, and the obsession with how we feel is so boring. I have talked to countless teachers who resent being forced to play games and trade confidences at in-service training sessions when they could have been learning something new from somebody who had something to say. Why, then, do they subject their children in the classroom, many with apparent enthusiasm, to similarly mindless games? Because, as I argue in Chapter 6, this is what they have been told to do.

Finally, there is Economic Wellbeing and Financial Capability. Financial Capability means 'learning how to manage money'. A short course for 14–15-year-olds on mortgages and overdrafts may be time well spent. But, ultimately, the ability to manage your money boils down to the ability to spend less than you earn. It is a matter, that is, of commonsense, or to put it biblically, the strength of character to resist temptation, not of knowledge or of any financial 'skill'. Economic Wellbeing amounts to getting a job that pays a decent wage. This is dressed up in sentence after sentence of waffle. 'Through their learning and experiences inside and outside school, pupils will', we are told, 'begin to understand the nature of the world of work, the diversity and function of business and its contribution to national prosperity.'[68] The Programme of Study will 'expand their horizons for action by challenging stereotyping, discrimination and other cultural and social barriers'.

They will 'build a positive and realistic view of their needs and capabilities … '. I simply do not know what these panglossian statements mean.

The requirement that pupils should 'identify the main qualities and skills needed to enter and thrive in the working world' is repeated at least three times.[69] They should, that is, be able to read and write, and, in addition, have mastered the 'soft skills' that the CBI and other employer organisations talk about so often. These 'soft skills' interest me. We went for a coffee last week and waited half an hour while the waitresses gossiped among themselves. The order was eventually taken with a grumpy indifference. The coffee, when it finally arrived, was lukewarm and tasteless. Needless to say, we will not be back.

'Soft skills', if this is what the girls serving in this café lacked, are clearly crucial to any business that depends upon interaction with customers, which is, of course, all businesses to a greater or lesser degree. At one level, therefore, I sympathised with the Director General of the CBI's recent plea that young people should understand the importance of getting to work on time. But then I noticed that he was talking about universities. Should universities be teaching their students how to get out of bed in the mornings? Should schools? Is getting up in the morning an example of the 'soft skills' employers prize and the Economic Wellbeing Programme of Study aims to teach? Have we really sunk this low?

The answer to this last question is that we have. Employers, educationalists, politicians: all agree that young people need to be taught that if you want a job you need to present yourself as positively as you can in the interview, that if you want to keep that job you cannot wander in half way through the morning, that if you are looking for promotion you need to show a bit of energy and initiative. Nobody asks what parents are doing. Nobody suggests that punctuality is a habit that is learnt. Nobody has any time for the commonsense approaches that when I was at school were simply taken for granted. Pupils who turn up late for school should be punished. Ditto if they drift, as so many do, carelessly into class, ten minutes after the lesson has started. Politeness is a habit, too. 'Communication skills', which I take to mean the ability to listen when somebody else is speaking and to reply with something more than a grunt, are, likewise, a habit. They are not skills at all and they do not need to be taught in a timetabled lesson which should be dedicated to something that is worth teaching and needs to be taught, like mathematics or music or geography.

The importance of knowledge

My objections to this new National Curriculum are, I hope, clear. In a sentence, those responsible for it are more interested in promulgating political views than they are in teaching academic knowledge. The key criterion in deciding what should be taught appears to be the 'relevance' of the topic to the child's interests as a child and to his or her responsibilities (though this is a word which is used infrequently) as an adult living in a 'diverse' society as a 'global citizen'; the underlying belief is that it is more important to teach children 'how to learn' than it is to open their eyes to the magic and mystery of the world that lies beyond their immediate experience. A curriculum that starts from the 'whole person' aim that children should become 'successful learners, confident individuals, and responsible citizens' is bound to result in a set of requirements that is anti-educational in these ways.

So much, to me, at least, is obvious. Why, though, do I think the mastery of different forms of knowledge important? Because the world is not a given: the world we experience is the world we perceive and our perceptions depend upon what we know.

To give a personal example, my experience of the Welsh mountains in which I live stems from my eyes and feet and lungs in the years when I used to struggle up a steep hillside. But, the more I have learnt about the geology and history and ecology of these mountains, the richer my experience of them has become. Take the deserted mining village in the upper reaches of Cwm Croesor. The first time I visited I saw ruins and rubble. Now, having read about the lives of the men who hewed slate out of the mountainside, the experience is different, and, I would argue, immeasurably richer. When in my teens I first visited the great cliff on the flanks of Snowdon, Clogwyn d'ur Arddu, I knew nothing about the climbers who had in their time stood, more often than not in the wind and the rain, gazing at the black precipice in front of them, wondering whether the routes they had traced with the eye of faith would in the event deliver sufficient holds to make an ascent possible. I became fascinated by that cliff, and at one time, knew every detail of every first ascent. Reading about the dramas and, at times, tragedies, talking to some of the people involved, did not necessarily improve my climbing. Too often the cliff appeared to steepen as the ghosts circled, and my resolve to climb would too easily evaporate into the mist. That, though, was a price, I felt, worth paying.

These are personal and perhaps trivial examples, but the basic point is vitally important in these anti-educational times: what we see depends on what we know; and the more we know, the richer our lives. 'The educational engagement is necessary', as Michael Oakeshott states, 'because nobody is born a human being, and because the quality of being human is not a latency which becomes an actuality in a process of "growth".'[70] If we deny our children the opportunity to participate in what Oakeshott calls 'the conversation of mankind', we deny them their humanity.

This is the crucial importance of the subject disciplines and the reason why the arguments of those who, for whatever reason, want to undermine the importance of subject knowledge need to be defeated. The most common objection to this concept of education is that it results in classrooms in which children are spoon-fed facts. I do not for one moment deny that there are such classrooms, but I blame the teachers who use the spoon, not the approach to education, which, in their laziness and incompetence, they bring in to disrepute. It is important, moreover, to note that the conversations of mankind involve forms of knowledge that have nothing to do with fact. Why should all children have the chance to experience great literature? Because, read attentively, poems and novels and plays quicken the pulse of our emotional life. 'Love', 'hate', 'jealousy', 'envy', 'anxiety', 'remorse': the words we use to define our feelings sink into the cliché of everyday use. We think we know what they mean, but we do not. As a consequence, our lives are deadened and diminished.

Take, for example, the unpacked complex of feelings which make up the unexamined cliché of 'self-esteem', promoted throughout this National Curriculum as the fundamental psychological good upon which successful learning depends. There is a pivotal line in *Macbeth* where Macbeth says 'to know my deed t'were best not know myself'. He cannot reconcile what he has done in murdering Duncan to his sense of himself as a human being incapable of such an action. And so, I would argue, is it for all of us. 'Self-esteem' is a fragile and complex emotional state, vulnerable, on the one hand, to the vagaries of fate and the weakness of the human will, and, on the other, such is the infinite capacity of human beings for self-delusion, to a collapse into the sticky mire of self-satisfaction. Trumpeted as it is throughout the National Curriculum, 'self-esteem' means nothing. Ponder Dorothea's infatuation for Casaubon or the crumbling of Lydgate's will as he convinces himself that marrying Rosamund is a sensible course of action. George Eliot cannot, sadly, teach us to love wisely, but she tells us more than we perhaps want to know about our willingness to love foolishly. Not every child will be able to read with sufficient attention to hear what is being said in the books they are taught, but all should have the chance to listen and to have their lives changed, if they are lucky, for ever.

I used the word 'attention' twice in the previous paragraph. 'By understanding', Geoffrey Hill wrote in *The Triumph of Love*, the poem from which the epigraph to this book is taken:

> ' ... I understand diligence
> and attention, appropriately understood
> as actuated self-knowledge, a daily acknowledgement
> of what is owed the dead'.

'Diligence and attention': how else are the 'forms of understanding upon which our humanity depends' to be understood? Through a 'personalised' curriculum, which subordinates the mastery of what is difficult to the whim of the individual student? Through programmes of study for the national curriculum subjects which have been bent to the political will? Through a pedagogy that encourages children to value their own opinions over the wisdom of the dead? Elsewhere in his poem, Hill refers to 'these strange children /pitiless in their ignorance and contempt'. England, he writes, has become a nation with 'many memorials but no memory'. He is referring specifically to the forgotten heroism of men who died in the Second World War, but his lament about memory, which is a powerful theme throughout the poem, is more general. These children value nothing because they know nothing. They have no sense of how our knowledge of ourselves depends, as Hill's wordplay points out, upon 'a daily acknowledgment /of what is owed the dead'. Neither do the ministers who are ultimately responsible for this strange new curriculum.

Like Hill, I believe that 'forms of understanding', such as history and mathematics and literature, are 'far from despicable'. I believe that the fulfilment of our potential as human beings depends on our struggle to engage with and understand these forms. I believe that knowledge and respect are to be preferred to ignorance and contempt. I do not believe that anything worth knowing can be known without diligence and attention.

But then, as Secretary of State, Ed Balls, said, I am out of step.

Chapter 5

The Flight from Knowledge: Sir Jim Rose's Interim Report on the Primary Curriculum

THIS CHAPTER, illogically, has to be a footnote to the last. For obvious reasons primary education ought to be the foundation upon which all subsequent learning is built. The Government should have reviewed the primary curriculum and then in the light of its conclusions decided how the secondary curriculum might best continue children's learning. In fact, the new secondary curriculum began to be taught in September 2008, and, at the time of writing, Sir Jim Rose's final report on his review of the primary curriculum has not been published. His Interim Report has, however, made specific recommendations which set the direction of travel. It is already very clear that Sir Jim is not going to fix anything. He has danced obediently to the Secretary of State's tune. He has listened attentively to primary headteachers who have never accepted a subject-based primary curriculum. If his recommendations are implemented, which they will be, primary education will return to its pre-National Curriculum, serendipitous state.

I ought, I suppose, to declare an interest, or, to put what I feel more honestly, a sense of betrayal. In 1992, Jim and I, with a professor of education called Robin Alexander, were asked by the then Secretary of State, Kenneth Clarke, who had been shocked by the teaching he observed on his visits to primary schools, to review the state of primary education. The paper we wrote, which, because it was published just before Christmas, became known as the 'Three Wise Men' report, began with the commonsense, but, in the world of education, highly controversial, premise that what mattered most in primary classrooms is the primary teacher: his knowledge of the subject he is teaching and his ability to communicate that knowledge to his class. We suggested that it might be a good idea if primary schools devoted less time to topic work (in which a theme such as 'chocolate' is used to explore the interdisciplinary links between subjects) and more to traditional subjects, such as history and geography. I then moved to Ofsted where Jim was the inspector responsible for primary education. We worked together on various publications and conferences designed to raise the profile of primary education and to challenge the discredited orthodoxies which continued to undermine standards in primary classrooms. We stood, if you like, shoulder to shoulder for the best part of a decade. I was never sure whether my other deputy, Sir Mike Tomlinson, knew what he really thought about anything. I believed that Jim did. It saddens me that, for whatever reason, he has decided that the time is right to change his mind so spectacularly.

A little context

When I talk of 'discredited orthodoxies' I am referring to a complex of beliefs rooted in the idea that everything important in primary education springs from some nebulous, mystical concept of 'the child' and that the systematic initiation of children into different bodies of knowledge inevitably drives a stake through the heart of the creative primary classroom. Those who worship at the shrine of 'the child' argue that the primary classroom should be a place of happy spontaneity in which teacher and child together explore experiences of mutual interest. Children, they suggest, should discover things for themselves rather than be told anything by their teachers. One to one, personalised conversations between the teacher and individual children are better, therefore, than whole class instruction in which the teacher explains things which, on a different view of education, it might be thought every child within the class needs to know.

This account is not a caricature. The famous first sentence of the Plowden Report ('At the heart of the educational process lies the child') may not have resulted in a wave of ultra-progressive child-centred teaching, but it did have a profound influence.[71] I think, for example, of the primary advisers I worked with in three different local education authorities in the 1980s and 90s. Most were enthusiastic advocates of the Plowden approach. They did not encourage their headteachers to develop a curriculum in which children engaged in a purposeful way with pre-determined subject knowledge. They dismissed whole class teaching as a didactic anachronism. Teachers who thought that instruction in phonic knowledge was important in the teaching of reading were criticised for encouraging their children to 'bark at phonemes' and dispatched to the outer professional darkness. These primary advisers were men and women whose convictions were genuine and deep. They damaged the education of generations of children.

My fellow wise men, Sir Jim Rose and Robin Alexander, have taken to saying that educationalists and commentators who write in this way impose a simplistic and unhelpful dichotomy on primary practice.* Good teachers, they like to argue, are neither traditionalist nor progressive. They will explain things when explanations are necessary and they will find opportunities for children to experience the excitement of discovering ideas and knowledge for themselves. They will plan meticulously so that insights from different subjects can be brought together to illuminate the child's experience. I do not disagree. This is indeed what good teachers do. The fact remains that everything that happens in a classroom is determined by the teacher's understanding of the educational enterprise. And, whatever Rose and Alexander might say, there are two fundamentally different views of this enterprise.

On the one hand, the emphasis on 'the child'; the insistence that everything must be 'relevant' to the child's experience and to the perceived needs of society; the argument that the teacher should be a 'mentor' or a 'coach' who 'facilitates' the growth of the child's understanding; the current obsession with 'personalisation'. On the other, the belief that a school is an institution in which children are initiated, by teachers who are authorities in their subjects, into a body of knowledge which has no immediate connection to their lives or necessary relevance to the problems of society. This body of knowledge needs no justification, no explanatory statement of aims or values. To allow children to remain ignorant of, say, literature, history or mathematics is to deny them the inheritance, as I argued in the previous chapter, upon which their humanity depends. The teacher's task is not to collude in the nonsense of personalisation. It is to encourage a willingness to submit to a body of knowledge which has, with patience and humility, to be

*'These perspectives helpfully counter a long-standing, worrying tendency in primary education where discussion about the curriculum is often mired by treating as polar opposites, things which should be complementary and together act to benefit children's learning, for example:
Subjects vs cross-curricular studies;

- Knowledge vs skills;
- Child-initiated learning through play vs teacher-directed learning;
- Formal vs informal classroom organisation; and
- Summative vs formative assessment.

The list is not exhaustive' (From Sir Jim Rose's 'The Independent Review of the Primary Curriculum: Interim Report, 2008'). Available at: www.dcsf.gov.uk/primarycurriculumreview/.

mastered. This willingness may not, of course, come willingly. The teacher may well have to bend the will of the child to his own stronger will.

Teachers cannot pick and choose between these two views. They cannot personalise their beliefs about what they are doing when they teach. The pretence that they can is a calculated deceit: a transparent attempt to capture the high moral ground of pragmatic, professional commonsense in order to demonise those who have attempted to clarify the obfuscation and to reassure those who worry about educational reports such as that Sir Jim Rose has just written. It is a lie.

What is education for? Kenneth Baker knew what he thought when he oversaw the introduction of the subject-based National Curriculum. Kenneth Clarke knew that that curriculum had not revolutionised the work of primary schools in the way Baker had hoped. Hence the Three Wise Men report with its emphasis on specialist subject teaching. Since Clarke, various Secretaries of State have tinkered, cutting content and softening prescription in order to placate teachers who complained that the National Curriculum is wrong in principle and in practice impossible to implement, but none has challenged the basic belief that primary school teachers should, one way or another, be teaching subject knowledge. Last January, Ed Balls, the latest politician to run the nation's schools, decided that more radical reform was needed. So he wrote to Sir Jim Rose setting out his expectations.[72]

Rose's remit

If Sir Jim had had any sense, he would have opened his rambling and contradictory remit letter and run a mile.

The first sentence of this letter refers, reassuringly, to the independence of the review. The third and fourth explain the limitations of this independence. Mr Balls wants Rose to deliver a curriculum which has 'the flexibility to personalise teaching and learning' in order to help achieve the 'ambitions' of the Children's Plan and the 'outcomes' of the Every Child Matters Agenda. This revised curriculum is, in other words, another piece in his political jigsaw. Sir Jim may be free to determine the means, but the ends have been spelt out for him. His job is to function as an educational technician and a political fig leaf. So much for his independence.

Primary school pupils, Balls states, must 'be introduced to a broad range of subjects'. But, because some primary schools have complained that 'the number of subjects and the amount of prescription in some of the current programmes of study restrict their flexibility' he wants Rose to consider whether 'pupils' interests may be better served by studying fewer subjects during primary education'. The hapless Sir Jim is required to square the circle and invent a curriculum that offers pupils 'a broad and balanced entitlement to learning' while simultaneously giving schools the greater flexibility they need if they are 'to meet pupils' individual needs and strengths'.

It gets worse. Balls wants the number of subjects to be reduced. He also wants a new subject, languages, to be added to the curriculum. He believes that 'personal development', whatever this might mean, 'should be a central aspect of the primary curriculum',[73] and, presumably, therefore, expects extra time to be found to deliver this enhanced responsibility. There is, of course, only one way in which these irreconcilable demands can be met. That is to cut down on the time given to traditional academic subjects, either by reducing the number of such subjects or by reducing the demands of each subject, or both. Neither Balls nor Rose admits to this, but, as we shall see, this is the solution Sir Jim has reached.

His Master's voice: Sir Jim's Interim Report[74]

The 20 provisional recommendations made in the Interim Report[75] can be divided into three categories: those that are unlikely to make much difference to anything; those that could have a negative impact; and those which, if implemented, would do serious damage. There are 13 recommendations in category one, 3 in category two and 4 in category three.

Recommendations 1, 2, 3 and 6 sit firmly in category one. Recommendation 1, that 'the National Curriculum should be retained as an entitlement for all children', will have surprised nobody, though in fact subsequent recommendations quietly torpedo any ideal of an entitlement to anything other than a solipsistic daydream. Recommendations 2, 3 and 6, that the curriculum should be reviewed regularly, that a statement of aims should be drawn up, and that 'the QCA should investigate whether it would help schools if the new primary curriculum were set out in three, two year phases', will waste a few million more pounds to no effect. It is, perhaps, sensible (Recommendation 8) to see 'whether some aspects of the Key Stage 3 curriculum for ICT would be more appropriately taught in Key Stage 2', though the second part of this recommendation, that the curriculum should ensure 'that by the end of Key Stage 2 children are able to select and apply ICT to advance their learning across the curriculum', betrays a dubious confidence in the power of ICT and a worrying failure to understand that the impact of the curriculum depends upon the skill of the teacher in interpreting the words on the page.

Recommendations 13, 14 and 15, which are intended to improve transition from one stage of a child's education to the next, are also part of this initial grouping. Thirteen proposes the publication of 'guidance' to help Key Stage 1 teachers build on the learning that has taken place in the EYFS. Fourteen suggests that Key Stage 1 teachers 'should be involved in the moderation of the Early years Foundation Stage Profile assessments ... to increase ... their confidence in the judgements of reception teachers'. This is a sensible idea in theory, but in practice, given that many reception teachers have themselves no confidence in these bureaucratic assessments, is unlikely to achieve very much. Fifteen is no more than a vague gesture of good intent: next time the National Strategies are reviewed 'curriculum continuity between Key Stage 2 and 3' should be 'strengthened'.

The five final recommendations in this category focus upon the introduction of language teaching into primary schools. Suffice to say that the problem here is, first, that 20 per cent of children in primary schools fail to master their own language, and, second, that children are not going to learn a foreign language if they are not taught by competent teachers. We do not have those teachers and Rose has nothing, unsurprisingly, to tell us about where they might be found. His suggestion (see below) that English as a subject should be subsumed into an 'area of learning' called 'English, communication and languages' is likely, moreover, to ensure that even more children leave primary school functionally illiterate.

I include Recommendations 11 and 12 in my second category because, as currently articulated, they are sufficiently vacuous as to be innocuous. If developed further, they could, however, have a negative impact on primary education. The first, Recommendation 11, states that 'the review will consider how best to support teachers and practitioners to provide effective play based learning'. Quite why is a mystery. Sir Jim himself says that 'pedagogical decisions' should be left to teachers. If, that is, a Key Stage 1 teacher thinks that standards in her classroom will rise if her children have 'more opportunities for exploratory play', then that is a matter for her judgement. The Children's Plan, which, as Sir Jim, declaring his independence, puts it, 'is the platform upon which this review is based', states, however, that 'many children would benefit from a more gradual shift from a play-based to a more formal classroom-based curriculum'.[76] He felt, I assume, a need to echo his master's voice. The danger is that this intrusion into pedagogy will leave children who are ready to be challenged by more formal teaching languishing in the sand pit.

Recommendation 12 ('The QCA and the National Strategies should support schools to implement the principles of personalised learning') is problematic for similar reasons. I discuss the silliness of 'the personalisation agenda' elsewhere in this book. The key point to make here is that the decision to personalise or not to personalise learning is a matter for the individual school and individual teachers. Again, I imagine Sir Jim felt obliged to endorse a ministerial fad. I have no idea how, in a review that sets out to reduce prescription, he justifies what amounts to prescriptive meddling in an issue which has nothing to do with the National Curriculum. The good news, however, is that he can find nothing to say about personalisation beyond the fact that teachers need to recognise 'the varying degrees of confidence and independence' young children 'exhibit'. The truth, of course, is that there is little more that can be said.

Also in this category is Recommendation 7:

> Primary schools must continue to give priority to literacy and numeracy, while making sure that serious attention is paid to developing spoken language intensively as an attribute in its own right and essential for the development of reading and writing. In so doing, attention should be given to building the vocabulary which is germane to each subject and area of learning, and realising the potential of the visual and performing arts, especially of role play and drama, for young children's language development.

Ed Balls' remit letter asked Sir Jim to find ways 'to enable schools to strengthen their focus on raising standards in reading, writing and numeracy'.[77] Like much else in this letter, the wording is odd. What does 'strengthen their focus' mean? Spend more time on? Be more effective at? Or what? We know from inspection evidence that time is not the issue in raising standards in basic skills. It is, as common sense would suggest, how teachers use the time available to them that matters. We know, too, all we need to know about the best ways to teach children to read and add up. The problem is that too many teachers remain committed to other, less effective methods. If I had been, God forbid, in Sir Jim's shoes, I would have proposed that the programmes of study for English and mathematics be re-written in order to cut out material that conflicts with the approaches laid out in the national literacy and numeracy strategies. I would have 'strengthened the focus' of the National Curriculum. Sir Jim has chosen instead to undermine the identities of English and mathematics as separate subjects; to remove content and prescription from other subjects in an attempt, I presume, to find time (which is not needed); and, ignoring his own recognition that 'pedagogical decisions' should be left to teachers, to offer pedagogic advice on how English should be taught.

That advice, moreover, is worrying. 'Discussion', he says, 'of reading, writing and numeracy in primary education sometimes fails to recognise the fundamental importance of children's spoken communication.'[78] I agree that talking and listening are important skills. This is what Douglas Barnes and others were saying in the 1970s.[79] I worry, though, at the timing of Rose's message. As he, more than anyone, knows, the battle to introduce phonics is far from won and this new enthusiasm for spoken communication, though educationally valid, could prove to be a very unhelpful distraction. Less educationally valid, and equally unhelpful, is his statement that 'the concept of literacy' needs to be 'broadened so that the values, for example, of scientific, technological, mathematical and economic 'literacy' are recognised by society and schools to a far greater extent than ever before'.[80] What is he talking about? He argues, rightly, that 'the central importance of literacy, generally understood as the ability to read and write, is undeniable' and then stresses the importance of these other pseudo-literacies. This section of his report is a recipe, at best, for confusion. It could exacerbate what is already an educational disaster.

The final recommendation in this second category is number 10: that all children should start school in the term following their fourth birthday. This is perverse. Sir Jim acknowledges that many parents would like their children to start school, as they do in many continental countries, much later than they currently do in England. His response is to propose that the age of entry should be lowered by a year and that the DCSF should do more to persuade parents to stop making a fuss. Despite the fact that these suggestions are based on some pretty inconclusive research, the state, once again, it seems, purports to know best.

None of the above really matters. I discuss these various recommendations because I think that the Secretary of State and Sir Jim Rose should be held to account for the shoddiness of their thinking, but, with the possible exception of Recommendation 10, I do not believe that our children's lives are going to be much affected by them. Recommendations 4, 5 and 9, to which I will now turn, are different. If implemented, they will do real damage.

Taking Recommendation 9 first, the Secretary of State's remit letter[81] states that the review should 'develop a more integrated and simpler framework for the personal skills which all pupils should develop through their schooling'. For once, Sir Jim does not nod obediently. He makes the obvious but very important point: 'For young children, of course, the way they are treated and the examples they are set by their peers and by adults are almost certainly the strongest influences on how they will treat others, their environment, and develop respect for themselves.' The only word I would quarrel with is 'almost'. There is no need, Sir Jim says, for a 'framework', a formal curriculum with timetabled lessons on, to quote the examples he gives, 'teamwork skills and conflict resolution, empathy and tolerance, respect for others and the environment; and self-respect and confidence'. Of course, there isn't. But Sir Jim has a remit to fulfil, and a Secretary of State to please, so he gathers his wits and changes tack, telling us that in order 'to make sure that these and other personal qualities are well supported ... many primary schools also make good use of guidance such as that of the popular SEAL programme'. As I argued in Chapter 4, the popularity of this programme says more about the gullibility of the teachers who use it than it does about the educational good sense of the SEAL materials. Self-respect and confidence grow when challenges are mastered, when, for example, a child learns to read. The more lessons dedicated to confidence-building, or conflict resolution, or whatever, the less time there is to teach reading. The calculation necessary to reach this conclusion is not difficult, but it appears to be beyond the arithmetical powers of both the Secretary of State and Sir Jim Rose.

I say 'appears' because the truth is that Ed Balls, and, it seems, Sir Jim in his latest incarnation, are more interested in the inculcation of personal 'qualities' and 'skills' than they are in the transmission of subject knowledge. We are back with the clash of views about the educational enterprise that I discussed earlier in this chapter. This review is firmly in what, to annoy Sir Jim and Robin Alexander, I am going to call the progressive camp. Parents and teachers who take a different, more traditionalist view should study Rose's proposals with great care.

The current primary curriculum requires schools to teach children ten subjects: Art and Design, Design and Technology, English, Geography, History, ICT, Mathematics, Music, Physical Education and Science. Rose wants these ten subjects to be subsumed into six Areas of Learning. Nowhere in his Report does he offer a definition of an Area of Learning, but the six areas he proposes are: Understanding English, communication and languages; Mathematical understanding; Scientific and technological understanding; Human, social and environmental understanding; Understanding physical health and well-being; and Understanding the arts and design.

Recommendation 5 proposes that:

> The Qualifications and Curriculum Authority (QCA) should work with relevant leading authorities, such as, subject organisations, the Royal Society, heads and teachers to validate essential knowledge, skills, understanding and attitudes in each of the proposed six areas of learning, and organise them into manageable programmes of learning.

Rose insists in the text of his Report that a move to Areas of Learning would not result in 'key ideas currently brigaded in subjects' being 'downgraded or lost'.[82] His intention is 'to embed and intensify these ideas to better effect in cross-curricular studies and, where appropriate, provide opportunities to teach them directly as unmissable knowledge and skills'. These statements raise, however, more questions than they answer. First, the verb 'brigaded' suggests that key ideas or knowledge can be transferred in an arbitrary way from one subject discipline to another. This is not true. A work of literature can be read for all sorts of extraneous reasons, but, if the reason for reading it is to appreciate it as literature, it must be studied as a work of literature. The concept of 'literature' cannot be 'brigaded' according to the whim of the curriculum theorist. Second, the adjective 'key' in 'key ideas' is a very weaselly word. What is of subordinate importance to Rose may be of major significance to me. Thirdly, I do not understand the verbs 'embed' or 'intensify'. Embed in what, and to what effect? How can the experience of reading a work of literature be 'intensified' through cross-curricular study? Fourthly, I note and am worried by the, again weaselly, word 'appropriate' in the reference to the teaching of some knowledge and skills as a separate subject. Who is to determine what is and what is not 'appropriate'?

An earlier paragraph of the report offers a different, and somewhat contradictory account of the proposed move to Areas of Learning. Rose writes:

> There will be times when it is right to marshal worthwhile content into well-planned, cross-curricular studies. This is not

> only because it helps children to better understand ideas about such important matters as: sustainable development, financial capability, and health and safety, but also because it provides ample opportunity for them to use and apply what they have best learned from discrete teaching.[83]

So the area of learning is better than the subject because the area of learning is the better vehicle for teaching issues such as financial capability and health and safety. We can only conclude that Rose, like his Secretary of State, believes such issues to be more important than the teaching of traditional subject knowledge. The 'use and apply' argument is a longstanding enthusiasm of the progressive educator. It is not enough to study, reflect and understand; that understanding has to be consolidated through the application of ideas to real-life situations. In some cases this may be sensible; in many it is not. But, even if we agree that every child must have every possible opportunity to use and apply everything he learns, why does a cross-curricular area of learning offer more such opportunities than a single subject? It does not, and Rose does not explain why it should. He is grasping at straws.

In fact, of course, this issue of cross-curricularity is a red herring from the point of view of how the National Curriculum should be structured. Rose admits as much in his fourth recommendation. 'Given the excellent examples of both witnessed by the Review, neither discrete subject teaching nor cross-curricular studies must disappear from primary schools.' But why would they disappear? Schools have freedom to organise the curriculum as they wish. The present National Curriculum is subject-based. The review has witnessed 'excellent' cross-curricular teaching. Why has Sir Jim proposed a move to cross-curricular areas of learning, with all the disruption this will involve, when cross-curricularity is already flourishing?

There is one plausible answer to this question. Areas of learning follow naturally from the Early Years Foundation Stage (EYFS) 'areas of learning and development' and are a way, therefore, of meeting the Secretary of State's requirement that Rose should 'strengthen continuity' between the EYFS and Key Stage 1. Indeed, his remit letter went further. 'You will also want', the Secretary of State wrote to Rose, 'to consider whether some aspects of the EYFS should be extended into the primary curriculum. This might include, for example, placing emphasis on the full range of areas of learning and development contained in the EYFS, including social and emotional areas of development, and widening the curriculum opportunities for child-centred and play-based activities.'[84] Rose, ever obedient, has built each of these hints into his recommendations.

Balls clearly wanted to placate that considerable body of professional and lay opinion which believes formal education should be delayed. He had, no doubt, at least one eye on Professor Alexander's review of primary education which was due to publish its final report in the spring of 2009.[85] Rose, however, was meant to be offering independent advice. He should have paused before swallowing the Secretary of State's bait.

I have no doubt that some five-year-olds are not ready for 'big school'. The question is whether the needs of this minority should dictate the challenges that, through the National Curriculum, are offered to the majority. There is no point in a National Curriculum that does not challenge. If Sir Jim, or anyone else, can prove that children make more progress when less is expected of them, I would agree that the intellectual and pedagogic demands of Key Stage 1 should be delayed. In the absence of such proof, I think that his proposals will frustrate the education of thousands of children who would otherwise have responded positively to new challenges. I do not, therefore, find the argument that areas of learning are justified by the need to bridge the gap between the EYFS and Key Stage 1 convincing.

Rose is, in any case, proposing that his areas of learning should apply across the whole of primary education, so, even if accepted, the continuity argument provides at best a partial defence. His problem is that there he has no other justification for what on logical as well as logistical grounds is an indefensible proposal.

The logical point is this. Rose wants us to believe that 'rich cross-curricular studies ... make connections between subjects and encourage children to apply what they have learnt in one subject to others, thus reinforcing learning and deepening their understanding'.[86] Fine, but the specific subject knowledge has to be mastered before the connections can be made. Rose, to repeat, declares that 'no key ideas currently brigaded in subjects should be downplayed or lost', but I do not believe him. He has, for a start, to deliver on the Secretary of State's requirement that content and prescription are reduced. His areas of learning will result in less knowledge being taught and that which is taught being taught inefficiently because teachers will be trying to forge links between bodies of knowledge which have not been properly understood. There is no reason, moreover, why teachers who teach subjects as discrete bodies of knowledge cannot make links between these subjects if they think that this will help their pupils' understanding. There is no need, that is, for areas of learning. There is no need either, the logistical point, to impose this huge upheaval on primary education. A sensible primary review would have strengthened the demands of the separate subjects and left the organisation of the curriculum to the individual school.

Sir Jim failed miserably when he tried to explain his proposals on publication day. He was interviewed, for example, by Jeremy Vine, who confessed that he had tried to read the Interim Report, but did not understand a word. He was none the wiser when Sir Jim had offered his on-air gloss.[87] The report itself abandons words to take refuge in a diagram:

Figure 20 The Aims of the new Primary Curriculum, © HMSO

This diagram is meant to 'illustrate' how 'the three curriculum aims, together with literacy, numeracy, ICT and personal development, will be at the heart of the curriculum and secured through each area of learning'.[88] Note that at the 'heart' of this curriculum lie three vacuous aims that no teacher, let alone curriculum, can guarantee to deliver. Note, too, that the areas of learning exist to 'secure' the equally vacuous 'skills for learning and life' and 'personal development' rather than as identities in their own right. But, above all, reflect on the challenge of implementing the curriculum portrayed in this diagram. Schools are expected to consider how everything they do contributes to the development of their pupils in terms of responsible citizenship and the other politically determined aspirations. They then have to interpret the skills circle, deciding how each skill is 'embedded' in each subject and/or area of learning. Then, finally, they will have to master the 'programme' setting out 'the essential knowledge, skills, understanding and attitudes that we want children to acquire' which is going to be written for each area of learning. This will involve deciding which bodies of knowledge are to be taught as discrete subjects and which tackled through cross-curricular topics. Personally, I would rather teachers spent their time thinking about how they might make their history or art lessons more exciting.

There is one further point to make about this review. I have already commented on the absurdity of a remit letter which celebrates the breadth of the curriculum while asking for content and prescription to be cut. Teachers have, of course, demanded that content and prescription be reduced since the National Curriculum was first introduced. They disliked the division of the curriculum into subjects, the emphasis on knowledge within the programmes of study, and the fact that they were being told what to do. Sir Jim takes, of course, these laments at face value. 'The fact', he rather touchingly writes, 'that the remit letter for this review requests that: "the content of the programmes of study should be reviewed, reducing prescription where possible" suggests that we have yet to achieve the right balance between central prescription and flexibility for schools to localise at least some of the curriculum.'[89] Of course, if the Secretary of State asks for something to be done, that something must need doing.

It would have been better if Sir Jim had remembered his independence and thought about these issues. The National (note the adjective) Curriculum was introduced because Parliament thought that the eccentricity of local provision in schools across the country was unacceptable. Why should children growing up in Penzance experience a different curriculum to those growing up in Penrith? The body of knowledge, understanding and skill which has to be mastered when a child studies science is the same irrespective of where that child may live. Neither do I believe that local circumstance dictates a local curriculum. To a very limited extent it may, but we live, as we tell ourselves endlessly, in a globalised world. The children who are growing up in Penzance may as adults move to Penrith, or, perhaps, even, to Peking. Teachers already have, moreover, very considerable freedom as to how they manage what Sir Jim calls 'curriculum-related activities'. All of the following are, as he says, 'within the control of schools':

> teaching methods and pedagogy; teaching content additional to the statutory curriculum; how the curriculum is organised and described, for example, as subjects, topics or themes; the distribution of the curriculum across each Key Stage; the daily timetable; the teaching hours per week; the time allocated to each subject and the length of each lesson; the organisation of teaching groups; how the curriculum caters for inclusion and differentiation; and, resources for learning.

This is the view of the man he appointed to advise on the reduction of prescription. Is the National Curriculum really the straightjacket the Secretary of State believes it to be?

There is an argument that a National Curriculum, any national curriculum, embodies a particular set of educational beliefs and militates, therefore, against a proper diversity of educational provision, but this is a different argument. The accepted wisdom that schools need greater flexibility to match learning to local circumstance needs to be challenged. Sir Jim himself demonstrates this when he writes: 'These programmes [which set out the essential knowledge, skills, understanding and attitudes we want children to acquire between the ages of 5 and 11] must be flexible and limit prescription while being sufficiently specific and clear for schools to plan and adapt content to make the best of their own localities without being too parochial.'[90] To my mind, the nervous equivocation of the qualifying clauses says it all. We have reached a stage where there is no political confidence in the concept of a national curriculum, but we are trying to pretend otherwise. The National Curriculum has to be national. This means that a very significant body of content must be prescribed in very significant detail. If we find this level of prescription unacceptable and want schools to have the freedom to determine their own curriculum, then we should give them that freedom. The current pretence that we can have it both ways is untenable.

Conclusion

The only conclusion that can be reached is that this review has been botched. At best, it is a fudge that fails to tackle any of the real problems in primary education; at worst, its enthusiasm for complicated models of cross-curricular organisation will do very considerable and long-lasting harm. I blame Sir Jim for his lack of courage and his shallowness of thought, but, ultimately, of course, the responsibility is the Government's. In many ways, the failure of this review is a case study in why so little progress has been made in raising standards since 1997.

There is, first, the way ministers have so willingly colluded with the views of supposed experts in the education establishment. Nobody at the DCSF seems to have asked the very obvious questions about overload and prescription I have just raised. Teachers have complained, so ministers believe that there must be a problem. Teachers do not like subjects, so areas of learning must be preferable. This is a repeat of what has happened with regard to inspection and the National Curriculum tests. When I was Chief Inspector the unions did everything in their power to replace external school inspection with a system of school self-evaluation. Their motives were transparent. We now have an inspection methodology which relies upon school self-evaluation. Ministers, and, of course, Ofsted, pretend that the new approach is just as rigorous as the old. It is not. The Key Stage 1 tests were introduced to give parents information about whether the school their children attended or might attend was successful in teaching the basic skills. These tests are now marked internally and are, therefore, worthless. The Key Stage 3 tests have been abolished. It is highly likely that the Key Stage 2 tests are to be replaced by some form of assessment that does not provide firm data on how each individual school is performing. Again, the official line is that accountability is as robust as it ever was. Again, it is a lie. Ministers have capitulated to the demands of the educational establishment.

They tend, moreover, to be equally influenced by swings in public opinion. I accept that politics is the art of the possible, but public service reform will not happen without a genuine determination to do what has to be done. To quote Robin Alexander, who is leading the Cambridge Review of Primary Education funded by the Esme Fairbairn Foundation, there is

> a widespread concern that many primary-aged children are under excessive pressure: inside school from an over-crowded curriculum, a high-stakes national testing regime and the backwash of teachers' anxieties about league tables, inspection and the public and somewhat punitive character of school accountability; outside school from the degrading of children's values and aspirations by consumerism, the cult of celebrity and pressure to grow up, or, indeed, adopt the trappings of adolescence, too soon.[91]

A more cynical commentator might conclude that Rose's review was established to take the sting out of Alexander's analysis of what is thought to have gone wrong with state education and childhood generally. The Children's Plan is after all committed to making England the best place in the world to grow up. If Rose can reassure the electorate that the primary curriculum will be less demanding, more child-centred, less crowded with demanding academic subjects, then this, ministers might reason, would be a good thing.

Whether these proposals are a good thing for children is, of course, another matter. The death of Victoria Climbie and the public outcry that followed prompted a massive reorganisation of local authority responsibilities. It was argued that the problem was the lack of co-ordination between the services involved. Local Education Authorities became Local Authorities and Directors of Education became Directors of Children's Services. Now, with the death of Baby P in 2008, we learn that this reorganisation has achieved nothing. Communication remains problematic. It is, predictably, hard to find candidates for these new Children's Services jobs who have front-line personal experience of both education and social work. The merger has, moreover, resulted, again predictably, in a loss of focus on education. Exactly the same points can be made about Ofsted's expanded brief. The education inspectorate is now responsible for children's social services. Its reports on the contribution local authorities are making to school improvement are not worth the paper on which they are written. Neither, it seems, are the reports on children's social services. A year before Baby P's death Haringey's services were judged to be 'good'. A re-inspection after the tragedy apparently uncovered problems so acute that the report could not be published. The Government's desire to be seen to be doing something coupled with its enthusiasm for root and branch upheaval has not always resulted in sensible reform.

The review exemplifies a third and more fundamental weakness. The secondary curriculum, discussed in the previous chapter, is, to put it charitably, less interested in education as the transmission of worthwhile knowledge than it is in the inculcation of skills and attitudes that are deemed to be vital to our economic and social good. Rose's recommendations reflect a similar failure to understand the nature of the educational enterprise. His areas of learning, remember, exist to 'secure' the 'personal skills' he and his ministers place at the heart of the curriculum. He accepts without question the need to jettison 'content', which is, of course, a different word for knowledge. He embraces the fantasy that a curriculum can produce 'responsible citizens' and never for a moment worries about how easy it is for such an aim to result in lessons which have more to do with propaganda than education. The fantasy appeals because it appears to offer the Government a lever to pull. Instruct schools to teach lessons designed to counter childhood obesity or global warming or political apathy and, hey presto, the problem is solved. It is not, of course. Teachers cannot solve deep-seated social ills, and should not be expected to try. Their job is to teach children worthwhile knowledge, and, in that understanding is preferable to ignorance, there is some reason to hope that a society in which citizens have been educated is likely to be a better society than one in which nobody knows anything. The attempt to use schools for direct political ends results in the destruction of the very thing that could have made a difference.

Other chapters of this book describe other instances of this same irritable and ignorant political impatience. The expansion of higher education is one; the constant fiddling with school admissions policies another. In each case the result is the same: excellence is threatened by politicians who do not understand the difference between social engineering and education. Sir Jim's recommendations for a new primary curriculum will deepen the divide between the state and the independent sector. Parents who can afford to pay the fees will send their children to schools that offer a proper education. These children will grow into the students who win the places at Oxbridge and other top universities. It is not so much an example of the law of unintended consequences as the failure to appreciate what ought to have been blindingly obvious.

Chapter 6

The Thought World

Norman Hale

As I STARTED to write this chapter, the phone rang. It was Paul Angus, a teacher at Milbourne Lodge Preparatory School in Esher. 'Had I heard', he asked, 'that Norman Hale had died?' I put the phone down and sat for a while gazing out of the window, wondering what power had led Paul to phone at the precise moment when I was about to describe the various ways in which the Government has lobotomised the teaching profession.

Norman Hale was a legendary figure in the world of independent education. He started Milbourne Lodge in 1948 and retired fifty odd years later at the age of 80, the longest serving headmaster in the country by a decade or two. He had no truck with progressive educational thinking and he ran Milbourne as a personal fiefdom, delighting, for example, in the fact that the school was expelled from the Independent Association of Preparatory Schools after he had told some inspectors he did not respect to go and bother someone else. His own teaching and that of the equally independent-minded staff he appointed was as brilliant as it was, by today's grey standards, eccentric. Milbourne's pupils, as his obituary in *The Times* noted, 'have won more than a hundred scholarships to Eton and Winchester alone, with many others gaining scholarships to Ampleforth, St Paul's, Charterhouse, Wellington, Rugby, Westminster and Marlborough'. To stand in the hall at Milbourne and to look up at the boards listing these scholarships is to realise that you are in a very special school.

I met Norman once in early 2007. He and his wife Stassy had contacted Cognita, the education company I chair, to see if we might be interested in buying Milbourne. Needless to say, we were. Discussions were proceeding smoothly when Ofsted published a damning inspection report on the school. The school had, it seemed, ignored just about every regulation in the book, and, worse still, it was employing traditional teaching methods to achieve dangerously high academic standards. My colleagues had a moment of anxiety. Were we, they asked, about to acquire a failing school? My reaction was to laugh. I would have been amazed if Norman Hale had given a moment's thought to pettifogging regulatory demands, and I was not in the least surprised that Ofsted's inspectors had once again paraded their progressive educational prejudices. The report said more about the madness of the educational world in which we live than it did the quality of education at Milbourne.

The fact remains that if Cognita had not taken responsibility for the school it would probably have been shut by DCSF bureaucrats more interested in regulatory compliance than fifty years of superb educational achievement. And Norman himself, if he were starting out today, would have found himself very much up against it. Every year the regulations multiply, the educational orthodoxies harden. He would never, of course, have wanted to work in a state school. It nonetheless saddens me that nowadays he would never be allowed to. His independence of mind and spirit made him one of the greatest headmasters of his era, and that, of course, is the problem: the world of state education does not value individual thought. Indeed, it exerts every possible pressure to secure the greatest possible conformity to the Government's vision of what schools should be doing.

Teachers in state schools are required by law to follow the National Curriculum. Anyone who has read the previous chapters will know what this means. Trainee teachers have to enrol on a course that meets the approval of the Training and Development Agency. The grip of this agency on university departments of education has to be felt to be believed. National Strategies for Literacy, Numeracy and Key Stage 3 hammer the required messages home. If you want to become a headteacher in a state school you must waste a year of your life studying for what is known as the National Professional Qualification in Headship. Needless to say, this qualification does not devote a great deal of time to the core purpose of any school: raising educational standards. It is more interested in vision statements and moral purpose, community cohesion and personalised learning. Then there is the Specialist Schools and Academies Trust, an organisation dedicated to ensuring that no headteacher strays from the Government's desired path. Ofsted inspectors wait on the sidelines ready to pounce on anyone reckless enough to think for themselves. Ministers know best. Maverick headteachers like Norman Hale have no place in our schools.

The fact that I personally do not think that ministers know best is neither here nor there. The tragedy is what this Government has done to the teaching profession. Teachers and headteachers should not be programmed to parrot the Government's message. As professionals, they should think for themselves, and, since education is a contested concept, if they were permitted to think they would reach different conclusions. Parents would then have a genuine choice between schools offering a genuinely different ethos. The days of the bog standard comprehensive school would be over. Forget the specialist schools and the Academies, which I discuss in Chapter 7. The truth is that while some of these newly labelled institutions are certainly more effective than others they are essentially the same. Their heads and teachers dance to an identical tune. Ministers might talk of a new era of 'earned autonomy' in which successful schools are allowed to make their own decisions. It is a lie, just as the rhetoric of parental choice is a lie. Teachers today are programmed into a robotic conformity, and parents have, therefore, no choice. Worse still, children are increasingly unlikely to be taught by men and women whose maverick genius inspires a real love of learning. I do not use the word tragedy lightly.

The Training and Development Agency

The Teacher Training Agency, as it was then called, was set up in 1994. Ministers thought that teacher training institutions were hotbeds of progressive educational thought, and responsible, therefore, for many of the failures in the nation's schools. Then, as now, generalisations are suspect, but there was more than a grain of truth in this anxiety. The late Baroness Blatch used to say that if the Conservatives had started their educational reforms with a real attack on the training institutions, they would have made real progress. Logically, she was right. There is not much point in reforming the curriculum if new teachers are being trained, as in some institutions they were, to undermine it. Now, the curriculum conforms to the orthodoxies promoted by the training institutions and the Teacher Training Agency, which has become the Training and Development Agency (TDA), works with higher education lecturers to implement a commonly agreed agenda. There are, inevitably, spats over inspection and bureaucracy, but fundamental conflict over the nature of the educational enterprise is a thing of the past. All is sweetness and light.

Is this a good thing? Yes, if you believe that all teachers need to be initiated into the Government's 'agenda'; no, if you are sceptical of that agenda and want tomorrow's teachers to come to their own individual judgements about the nature of their work and the purpose of schooling. New teachers have to prove they are competent to be awarded what is known as Qualified Teacher Status (QTS). The TDA lists the professional standards that have to be met.[92] It also defines standards to be achieved at other staging posts in a teacher's career. So we have 'core', 'post-threshold', 'advanced skills teacher', and 'excellent teacher' standards, all described with bureaucratic exactitude by the TDA and all highly significant for any teacher who wants to progress in his or her career. These standards reflect, moreover, the TDA's on-message priorities. This is an organisation which, according to its Corporate Plan, has a 'critical role in achieving the priorities of the Children's Plan' and which aims to 'ensure that the key outcomes of the Every Child Matters agenda are embedded' in all its work.[93] In other words, an organisation which exists to ensure that nobody can become a teacher or be promoted as a teacher if they do not dance to the Government's tune.

Somewhat immodestly, the TDA declares that its QTS standards will 'help to promote the highest professional standards for all entrants to the teaching profession'.[94] Disingenuously, it asserts that these standards 'do not set a curriculum'. They are, it is true, more a syllabus than a curriculum, but, just as topics on an examination syllabus drive the detail of the curriculum offered in a school, so these standards define what happens in training courses. No training institution can ignore the TDA standards if it wishes to remain in business.

I help to run a PGCE course at the University of Buckingham. Our students are already teaching at independent schools which are highly unlikely ever to have anything to do with the Government's new Diplomas. In April 2008 we received a letter from the TDA informing us that 'the TDA intends ... to ensure that there is adequate scope and capacity within secondary ITT to cover all the Diploma lines by 2010–2011'.[95] Fair enough, I thought, the Diplomas, whatever my view of them, are a significant development, and some training institutions might well be interested in preparing their students to teach them. The letter, however, continued: 'From 2007 all secondary trainee teachers training to teach at KS4 or post-16 ... must demonstrate an appropriate level and range of knowledge and understanding of the new Diploma courses.' 'Appropriate' means that, among many other things, they need to have demonstrated their ability 'to prepare, deliver and assess teaching sessions which embed functional skills' and which 'support the development of personal, learning and thinking skills'. I am prepared to concede that an hour's lecture on the

Diplomas and the skills they are meant to develop might be a good thing in that it would give me an opportunity to open my students' eyes to the lack of thinking skills the Diplomas demonstrate and, in so doing, to make my own little contribution to high professional standards. I do not think that teacher training institutions should have to equip their students to deal with courses that the institution deems to be undesirable educationally and which are irrelevant to the needs of the students.

The 33 standards are a testament to the grinding inclusiveness of the bureaucratic mind.[96] I once asked a number of headteachers I admired to tell me the qualities they looked for in appointing teachers to their schools. There was a clear consensus: a passionate enthusiasm for their subject; high expectations of their pupils; and, obviously enough, a mastery of the craft of the classroom.

Passion and enthusiasm do not feature in the TDA's standards. There are a couple of references to the need for 'secure' subject knowledge, but 'secure' here means something the bureaucrats like to call 'pedagogic knowledge'. This is 'knowledge which demonstrably enables trainees to plan and deliver the subject effectively, deal with pupils questions and common misconceptions, and monitor, assess and report on the progress of pupils in the subject. This is the knowledge required to teach the subject effectively and to secure learning.'[97] It is, apparently, different to and more important than knowledge of the subject, though I have to confess that I have never really understood the distinction.

What is clear is that we have headteachers, on the one hand, who want to employ teachers who can communicate their knowledge about, say, Shakespeare, with passion and enthusiasm, and, on the other, TDA officials, reflecting the orthodoxies of the education establishment, who are more interested in the 'pedagogic knowledge' which is apparently necessary if teachers are to plan and, vile word, 'deliver' effective lessons.

The one reference to the importance of 'high expectations' is also odd. It reads: 'Have high expectations of children and young people including a commitment to ensuring that they can achieve their full educational potential and to establishing fair, respectful, trusting, supportive and constructive relationships with them.' This seems to me to be saying that prospective teachers must have high expectations of themselves. Indeed they should, but my heads were interested in teachers who thought that their children could do more than the children themselves believed. While, moreover, fairness, as every pupil will tell you, is essential in any teacher, the adjectives which follow say more about the panglossian frame of mind of the bureaucrats than it does their depth of classroom experience.

Turning to the craft of the classroom, the standards tell us that prospective teachers must 'have a knowledge and understanding of a range of teaching, learning and behaviour management strategies and know how to use and adapt them, including how to personalise learning and to provide opportunities for all learners to achieve their potential'. 'Personalisation', the Government's latest fad to raise standards, makes an unwelcome, but, in that ministers are determined to ensure that every member of the teaching profession has been inculcated into its enthusiasms, inevitable, appearance. More generally, I am struck by the disconnect between the grey abstraction of these words and the conversations of real teachers as I remember them from my days as a teacher and as an inspector visiting schools. The TDA's new entrant to the profession is a man or woman who can 'design effective learning sequences within lessons and across a series of lessons'; who 'takes practical account of diversity and promotes equality and inclusion'; who has 'the ability to manage the learning of individuals, groups and whole classes, modifying their teaching to suit the stage of the lesson'; who, in other words, is a bloodless, passionless technocrat, expert at identifying a problem in the classroom and selecting the appropriate 'strategy' from his pre-programmed 'range' to deal with it. That is not how I see teaching, and it is not the kind of teacher I want to encourage as a teacher trainer.

I have, however, no choice. If my students are to become qualified teachers, they have to show that they are at least competent in each of the TDA's 33 standards, and, if Buckingham wants to continue to train students who may at some stage of their careers teach in state schools, it has to do what the TDA tells it to do.

The National College of School Leadership

The total budget for the National College of School Leadership (NCSL) in 2008–9 was £110.6m. As Chief Inspector, I was involved in initial thinking about the College. In that the headteacher is so obviously the key to raising standards in a school, I liked the idea of a college where heads and aspirant heads could meet to think about what leadership in a school means. I wanted to find ways to move discussion beyond the platitudes that so often constrain thinking about leadership, to encourage people to be honest about themselves and their schools, to reflect on the challenges they faced in working with staff to improve teaching, and, crucially, to explore their individual thinking about the nature of the educational enterprise.

In the event, the College has become an institution dedicated to promoting the Government agenda. The first goal set out in its Corporate Plan[98] is 'to develop provision for school leaders. Our work here will reflect the priorities set out in the Children's Plan.' Why? I can see that new headteachers need to know what the Children's Plan says, but I do not think it should be the starting point for the College's work and I would have hoped that the aim throughout would be to generate a critical engagement with the Plan's 'priorities'. This is not how Steve Mumby, the College's Chief Executive, and his Board see their responsibilities. The challenge for them is to 'equip current and future leaders to meet the demands of a dynamic policy environment'.[99] This means tell them what they have to do to implement Every Child Matters and the '11–19 reform agenda'. Elsewhere in the Corporate Plan it states that the College 'will work to ensure that understanding of the 14–19 reform is embedded in the NCSL's core programme', and, on the personalisation of learning, that the College 'has been working in partnership with SSAT, QCA, TDA, Becta and Ofsted to develop a joined up approach. We have developed a framework for the leadership of personalised learning.'[100] Should Government policy be taken as an unquestionable given? Should the NCSL be focusing so enthusiastically on the Government message? Am I on my own in finding the declaration that the College 'will work with the TDA and build on successful pathfinder work to identify and support those leaders who have yet to engage in the ECM and extended schools agenda' rather sinister? You may not want our support, but we know where you are and you are going to get it.

The programme the College runs for aspirant heads, the National Professional Qualification for Headship, is equally prescriptive in its preoccupations. At the end of the course, trainees meet up at a hotel for, as an accompanying think piece puts it, '48 hours of intense experience'.[101] This residential ignores the here and now, the challenges and opportunities headteachers face today, in favour of a vision of 'the school of the future', though delegates are warned to be wary of the concept of a 'school' for 'the very use of the word can limit our thinking to what we understand goes with a school' and 'in the future such a concept may become rapidly outdated'. How, these poor unfortunates are asked, can 'we plan an education for a world which will be different from that which we know and may involve concepts with which we are not yet familiar?' The short answer is that we cannot and that it is a waste of valuable time, which could be spent reflecting on leadership, to try. But those responsible for this 'intense experience' have clearly been seduced by the punditry of the futurologists. Like so many others, they believe all that is said about 'the knowledge economy' and are totally committed to the challenge of wholesale innovation. 'Change', the think piece article trumpets, 'will be ongoing and, as a leader, you will be at the forefront of leading and managing the change so that the staff and stakeholders but may take advantage of the opportunities which become available on behalf of the pupils (are not held back)'. I have typed this sentence as it was published. The question which follows is 'What might this mean?' I have no idea, but I do know what it reveals. This is a public body, funded to the tune of £100m, responsible for determining the headteachers of the future. Delegates who fail this course cannot apply for headships. Prose as slipshod as this demonstrates not simply a failure to think. It suggests a failure to care which amounts to an unpardonable arrogance. The schools of the future may well be different from the schools of today, but those who lead them will still, I would suggest, need to take responsibility for what they say and do.

This preparatory paper then describes the various 'developments' delegates should be reflecting upon. It is a revealing, if entirely predictable, list: the central importance of 'a truly personalised learning agenda'; 'changes in society and to the nature of work'; the ever-increasing potential of technology; the exciting prospect of community schools, open '24/7', which address 'the needs of individuals, families and groups in a holistic way'; the huge advantages of 'collaboration across schools'; the recognition that 'all staff are leaders' and that 'leadership patterns' must be 'distributed'. Each of these 'developments' is presented with a breathless enthusiasm. 'Philosophically', delegates are rather bizarrely asked, 'can you afford not to work in collaboration?' There is, needless to say, no mention of the headteacher's core responsibility to improve standards of teaching and, therefore, pupil learning. The NCSL would no doubt argue that this crucial duty is implicit in each of these developments. If so, it is buried so deep that I missed it.

There are teachers in our schools contemplating headship who remain committed to the idea of a school that pupils attend for a set number of hours each day, who are not convinced that everything has to be 're-engineered', who are deeply suspicious of faddish orthodoxies such as 'personalisation'. How should such men and women respond to this coercive agenda? Do they smile sweetly and pass the course? Or do they challenge everything put before them? It is a test, I suppose, of the political skills every headteacher needs to learn, but it is a dilemma they should not have to face in a training course.

The Specialist Schools and Academies Trust

The Specialist Schools and Academies Trust (SSAT) is a Government-funded organisation which has become very much more influential over the last few years. In 2007–08 its total budget of £61.8m included a £38.1m grant from the Government. This grant, in a rare outbreak of intelligent prudence, is to be reduced to £18.8m in 2008–09. 2,400 of the nation's 4,000 secondary schools are now members. Its mission is 'to give practical support to the transformation of secondary education in England by building and enabling a world class network of innovative, high performing secondary schools in partnership with business and the wider community'.[102] Does secondary education need 'transforming'? Yes, if this means raising standards dramatically; no, if, as the use of the word 'innovative' suggests, the preoccupation, as with the National College, is with the 'school of the future'.

Every year the SSAT runs a major conference, which is now attended by some 1,500 headteachers. In 2008 the theme was 'Redesigning Schooling'. Here are three sessions taken from the programme: 'The Deeps in Action: The Co-Construction Imperative: Improving Tomorrow's Leaders'; 'Student Voice as a Strategy for Transformation'; and 'Pedagogies of Contingency and Transformation'. If, reading the above, you feel a degree of mystification, do not worry. I have spent the last forty years working in education, and I do not know what they mean either. To check that senility had not set in, I phoned half a dozen headteachers at some of the most academically successful grammar and independent schools in the country to ask what they thought. There was in each case a long silence. One said he felt queasy; another asked whether the conference had been sponsored by a millennial sect.

In crucial respects, the SSAT is a millennial sect. It quite clearly thinks it has special access to divine educational wisdom, and it brooks no disagreements. Delegates (or should I say disciples?) to the conference are immersed from dawn to dusk in the 'personalisation' agenda. You only have to look at the list of keynote speakers to understand the intensity (or lop-sidedness) of the vision. Professor David Hargreaves, the Associate Director of Research and Development at the SSAT, who has written, at last count, a dozen pamphlets on 'personalisation' for the Trust; Robert Hill, who was Blair's adviser on health and local government during Labour's first term and a special adviser to Charles Clarke from 2002–05; 'world leader on innovation and creativity in organisations', Charles Leadbeater, a senior research associate at the left of centre think tank, Demos; 'innovator, author and consultant', Sir Ken Robinson, who 'shows organisations and governments throughout the world why and how to promote a culture of creativity and innovation'; and Professor Michael Fielding from the Institute of Education, who is 'in the process of creating a Centre for Radical State Education'. This is not so much a professional conference as an evangelical crusade, and a party political crusade at that – Sir Michael Barber, who once headed Tony Blair's Delivery Unit, and Matthew Taylor, who was Blair's chief adviser on political strategy, are also in the line up.

It is the lop-sidedness that worries me most about these different organisations: the fact that they are promoting the Government's agenda with such vigour. Other views on education and schools are simply ignored. There is an obvious parallel with the latest version of the National Curriculum, which does not appear to envisage that there might be legitimate objections to the idea of, say, active citizenship, which now permeates virtually every subject. I want children and their teachers to think, to come to their own conclusions, and this means that both must be exposed to a variety of opinion.

I would, I hope, make this point if I were more sympathetic to the ideas the SSAT is trying to promote. The fact that these ideas amount, in my view, to at best a massive distraction and at worst a very serious threat to our children's education adds, I must admit, to my disquiet.

Two years ago Professor Hargreaves wrote a pamphlet for the SSAT called 'A New Shape for Schooling.'[103] In his opening paragraphs he made an analogy between 'the change from mass production to mass customisation' in the world of commerce and the move from a mass produced education service to one that is personalised.[104] If you believe, as I believe and many teachers and parents believe, that the purpose of education is to initiate the young into bodies of knowledge such as History or Physics and that this process of initiation necessarily involves the student submitting himself or herself to the knowledge to be mastered, the analogy is ridiculous. Sitting down to learn French grammar is very different to sitting down to choose the make, specification and colour of your new mobile phone. Professor Hargreaves, who, as this pamphlet makes clear, has a somewhat idiosyncratic view of what education ought to involve, does not understand this difference.

Before she took up her current appointment as Chief Inspector of Schools, Christine Gilbert chaired a task force on personalised learning. She summarised the thinking of this group in a lecture she gave to the 2007 SSAT conference: 'Personalising learning means taking a highly structured approach to each child and young person's learning in order that all are able to progress, achieve and participate.' I wince at the on-message, New Labour 'participate', but, in essence, I agree. This is what good teachers have always done: know the strengths and weaknesses of their pupils and do their damnedest to help them make progress. Hargreaves, who, if anyone, is the intellectual architect of personalisation, goes far further.

At the heart of his 'newly shaped school' lies something called 'co-construction'. Co-construction is rooted in what are known as 'constructivist' approaches to learning. He writes:

> On this view students (like all human beings) are constantly in search of meaning and use their prior knowledge and experience to make sense of what is presented to them as new or unfamiliar, as is the case with much of the school's formal curriculum. The learner is neither an empty vessel into which teachers can pour the curriculum, nor the tabula rasa implicit in the now rather discredited behaviourist approaches to learning and teaching. Knowledge is not directly transferred to students through teaching, which is an intervention into a continuous process of the student's knowledge-building activities.[105]

This is suspect in two ways. First, because in forty years I have never met a teacher who thinks that the curriculum can be 'poured' into the 'empty vessel' of the child. Teachers know that the progress their pupils make depends upon the skill they have as teachers. Second, while it is true that we have as learners 'to make sense' of new knowledge, this does not mean that we are 'knowledge constructors'. We make sense of new knowledge when, as I argued above, we submit ourselves, with due humility, to whatever it is we are trying to understand, not when we manipulate and distort new knowledge into something that sits comfortably with our prior experience.

Hargreaves wants, however, to move beyond these half truths of constructivism. His emphasis is 'less on the teacher having to take account of the learner as knowledge constructor and more on the need for the teacher to treat the learner as an active partner in the jointly constructed activity of learning-and-teaching'. And he proposes that 'personalisation involves various forms of co-construction over every aspect of schooling, not just learning itself'.

These propositions are elaborated in terms of the four 'deeps': deep learning, deep experience, deep support and deep leadership.

In 'deep learning' students 'articulate their needs, problems and preferences in an invited conversation with the teacher'. Who issues the invitation is unclear from Hargreaves' exposition, but he is adamant that 'learners play an active role in shaping how the teacher teaches as much as how they themselves learn'. If this means that the teacher responds to the particular needs of individual pupils, then it is simple common sense. If Hargreaves is suggesting that the lunatics should take over the asylum, then he himself should be locked up. But this is the problem with so much of what is written about 'personalisation'. Is it common sense or nonsense? Take Hargreaves' comments on assessment. Students, he says, should 'begin to internalise the teacher's notion of a quality performance or standard, and the criteria for assessing the extent to which that standard is reached in any particular performance'. I agree: the comments a teacher makes on a student's work should help that student understand what is good and bad in what he has done and what more needs to be done to improve. Does this mean that assessment is 'an arena for co-construction'? For Hargreaves, yes. 'Students', he suggests, 'may well play a role in influencing the nature of these criteria and how they are applied'. That spelling and punctuation are important? That verbs in French have to agree with the subject? That you either know your tables or you do not? These criteria are non-negotiable. They are dictated by the subject matter and they are no more open to 'influence' by the teacher than they are the pupil.

Deep learning, Hargreaves tells us, has three 'gateways': 'assessment for learning', 'student voice', and 'learning to learn'. Note that the student has a voice, but the teacher does not. Indeed, personalisation means jettisoning the concept of a teacher in favour of that of an educator. The educator, when personalisation is well developed, is:

> a person who is passionate about learning, for self and for students, a skilled mentor and coach, committed to the

> co-construction of all aspects of schooling; who views students as partners in the creation of, and access to, data about their learning and achievement to assist in their progression; who is an expert in a relevant domain but who knows that forging the conditions of successful learning is not simply a matter of telling; who strives to engage students to generate the motivation that underpins true learning; who recognises that student needs are complex and variable and so personalisation entails drawing on a wide range of human and material resources to support learning; and who constantly relishes the changing responsibilities of a leader in education and of the need to redesign our educational institutions.

The learner is:

> an articulate, autonomous but collaborative learner, with high metacognitive control and the generic skills of learning, gained through engaging educational experiences with enriched opportunities and challenges, and supported by various people, materials and ICT linked to general well-being but crucially focused on learning, in schools whose culture and structures sustain the continuous co-construction of education through shared leadership.

There are common-sense truths in each of these statements. Teachers must, for example, be expert in (and I would add passionate about) the subjects they teach; students should be offered engaging and challenging educational experiences. Neither condition is met in many schools. I agree with Hargreaves completely: secondary schools fail an unacceptably high percentage of their pupils. Will, however, these new definitions help? I am prepared to suspend my disbelief about the utopianism of the tone. These are, after all, statements of how, in Hargreaves' view, it should be. I do not, however, find it helpful to abandon the idea of a teacher for that of a 'mentor or coach', and, for the reasons I set out in Chapter 4, I am unpersuaded by references to 'high meta-cognitive control and the generic skills of learning'.

Neither do I think (Hargreaves' second 'deep') that 'students must play a role in co-constructing the curriculum'. He tries, as advocates of radical reform often do, to head off the opposition by stating that 'this does not deny that schools should offer a pre-existing body of knowledge – subjects, disciplines – inherited from the past'. But actually he wants, in pursuit of 'deep experience', to abandon the subject in favour of the project, and the more open-ended the project the better. You either believe in the curriculum as a body of knowledge that children go to school to learn or you think that as active participants in their own learning they should have maximum freedom to decide what and how they study.

The third 'deep', 'deep support', focuses on 'the crucial importance of mentoring and coaching' to personalised learning, and, ignoring the crucial importance of the teacher as an authority in his or her subject, emphasises the contribution 'learning conversations' between students and students and other adults can make to learning. Again, up to a point I agree. Such conversations can be helpful, but to suggest that they are more important than a good teacher teaching well sidelines the one hope we have to improve state schooling.

'Deep leadership', the fourth deep, deals with the ways in which leadership is conceptualised and implemented to ensure 'full personalisation'. Predictably 'the notion of students as leaders is essential to this'. I sense that by this stage in his pamphlet Hargreaves himself is beginning to wonder. How else do you explain these two sentences which are more or less consecutive? 'A school culture underpinned by co-construction promotes co-leadership' and 'Deep leadership is crucially about creating and sustaining co-construction in the school'. Which is the chicken and which is the egg? What, more fundamentally, does any of it mean? A leader is in charge. He or she sets the agenda, inspires others, monitors progress, and deals with those who cannot or will not perform. Students cannot, in any meaningful sense of the term, be leaders.

My mistake, perhaps, is to expect any of this to mean anything. As I said, the SSAT has become a millennial sect. Professor Hargreaves is its Chief Priest. He writes that:

> It is deep leadership that creates the culture of personalisation grounded in co-construction. In such a culture the leaders can undertake the re-design of schooling to establish and embed both the deep experience that engages students in learning and the deep support which underpins it. And the outcome is deep learning through personalisation.

There are many Widemerpools in the upper echelons of education, but there is only one Dr Trelawney. Dr Trelawney was the 'high priest, if not actually messiah' of a 'peculiar, religious, philosophical – some said – magical' cult in Anthony Powell's *A Dance to the Music of Time*. 'The Essence of the All is the Godhead of the True', he would intone to his followers, who, in their turn, would declaim 'The Vision of Visions heals the Blindness of Sight'. It is wonderful, isn't it, the way life imitates art?

Ofsted

I began this chapter with a lament for the death of Norman Hale and the values he exemplified so powerfully. I will end it with some comments on the report Ofsted wrote on his school, Milbourne Lodge, in July 2007. In that Cognita now owns Milbourne some readers may feel that I have an axe to grind. I do, but not as the Chairman of Cognita. My colleagues have rectified the compliance failings which so exercised the inspector, and the school has moved on. My emotional involvement is as an ex-Chief Inspector of Schools. I spent six years of my life fighting to establish Ofsted as an inspectorate that reported objectively on the strengths and failings of the schools it inspected. It saddens and angers me to read a report that says more about the prejudices of the inspector than it does the quality of the school. And these prejudices are, of course, the fashionable nostra promoted by the Government and dear to the hearts of the great and the good in the education establishment. Ofsted has become part of that establishment, arguably the most lethal part, because headteachers know that if their teaching does not conform, their schools will be criticised and possibly failed.

Remember: Milbourne's reputation in the world of independent schools is second to none. Last year, the year following the inspection that identified so many grievous failings, five pupils won scholarships to Winchester and Eton. Few other preparatory schools, if any, rivalled this achievement. The report appears to recognise the school's successes: 'Pupils', it states, 'achieve very high standards of academic work and some achieve national success in sport.'[106] And, later: 'Good teaching helps them to attain very high standards, as is evidenced by their success in public school entrance examinations and scholarships.'[107] Neither is the success limited to academic subjects, for the inspector acknowledges that 'the quality of their art work is exceptionally high with many pupils winning awards in national competitions'. And, finally, we are told that 'the pupils are polite, articulate, self-assured and well motivated to learn'.[108]

The school, nonetheless, was judged to provide only a 'satisfactory' standard of education. 'Satisfactory' in Ofsted speak means 'not good enough'. The message is that there are significant issues which need to be addressed. So what were these significant issues? In part they were regulatory. I discuss these criticisms below. They annoy me as much as they annoyed Norman Hale, but I cannot blame Ofsted for them. The Government has decided that schools should be trapped in a web of regulation and Ofsted has been told to ensure that everybody does what they are expected to do. I can blame Ofsted, however, for the subtext which lurks beneath the explicit comments on the quality of education. Consider: 'The staff and proprietors are passionate in their commitment to pupils' academic attainment and achieve their primary aim of facilitating entry to public schools at the age of 13.'[109] When I first read this I paused on the word 'primary'. Was this, I asked myself, a simple statement of fact? Or was there a, perhaps unconscious, note of disdain, a hint that schools should have aims beyond the academic, beyond the goal of gaining entry to Eton and Winchester, that they should be promoting, I don't know, 'community cohesion' or 'active citizenship' or whatever? Then, I thought, that this was silly, that I was being paranoiac, and, dismissing my doubts, I read on.

My sense of the inspector's underlying hostility returned, however, when I came, pretty soon after, to this sentence: 'The school provides a traditional, classical education with an emphasis on English, mathematics and Latin and fulfils its main purpose of enabling pupils to work through the required programmes for examinations.' It is, in other words, nothing more than a boring old crammer, a school that no parent in their right mind would want their child to attend. If you consider this to be an over-reaction, reflect on the sentence which follows the one I have just quoted: 'This works well to impart knowledge but does not provide sufficient opportunities for pupils to apply skills or develop analytical and creative thought.' A little knowledge of the scholarship papers set by Eton and Winchester might have helped the inspector avoid this stupid comment. But she, of course, was on automatic pilot, parroting the clichés that crop up in every other Ofsted report. 'Knowledge' is bad, 'imparting' knowledge worse; 'applied skills' are good and 'analytic and creative thought' is, of course, best of all.

Here are three quotations taken from what were at the time of writing the three schools with reports at the top of the Ofsted website. The words vary, but the message is the same.

> Teaching is no better than satisfactory because there is generally little variety in teaching approaches and not enough opportunity for students to undertake challenging, independent work' (Kingsbrook School, Milton Keynes).
>
> Students do not always take an active role in lessons as they are not given enough opportunities to take responsibility for their own learning through independent research, discussion or group work (Darlaston Community Science College, Wednesbury).
>
> Teaching is sometimes over-directed and prevents greater involvement of students (St Thomas More Catholic School, Willenhall).

The first Cognita school to be inspected by Ofsted, Akeley Wood Senior School, drew exactly the same criticism. There was, we were told, too much didactic teaching. My response was to say that if there was poor didactic teaching then I would very much like to hear about it, but that I expected our teachers to teach and was not very interested in an analysis of teaching and learning based on the assumption that pupils should be working independently. The lead inspector huffed and puffed, but had no reply. He could not, I think, understand why anybody would challenge what for him was an unquestionable pedagogic truth, or, for that matter, why a school might complain when inspectors impose their own educational views on what its teachers and parents see as good practice.

When inspectors trail their ideological baggage, inspection becomes enforcement. The education offered at Milbourne Lodge did not conform to what is thought by those in power to be good practice and the school was, therefore, bound to be savaged by Ofsted. Equally inevitable was the long list of areas in which the school failed to comply with Government regulations.[110] It had no curriculum policy; no policies (note the plural) 'to safeguard and promote the welfare of children … in compliance with DCSF guidance Safeguarding children and safer recruitment in education (2007) (paragraph 3(2)(b)'; no policy 'relating to the health and safety of pupils on activities outside the school which has regard to DCSF guidance 'Health and safety of pupils on educational visits (reference HSPV2) (paragraph 3(2)(c)'; no policy 'to promote good behaviour'; no policy on 'first aid', and so on. The list of policies Milbourne did not have occupies in fact two pages of the text of a seven page report. Ofsted may have been told to report on compliance issues, but it does not really matter whether a minister or the Chief Inspector is responsible for this nonsense. Everything has to be written down, every box has to be ticked. Enormous amounts of time are wasted in schools, state and independent, on what is a useless, cover-my-backside industry. Yes, of course, teachers need to know what they are going to teach when they enter a classroom. Does this mean that schools need 'curriculum policies supported by appropriate plans and schemes of work'? I used to say when I was Chief Inspector that more often than not there was an inverse correlation between the volume of paperwork the school offered the inspectors and the quality of the teaching observed when the inspectors finally made it into the classroom.

Conclusion

It is the hypocrisy which in the end angers me most. This is a government which pontificates endlessly about the importance of thinking skills. Not content with celebrating teaching as 'a graduate profession', it now proposes that every teacher should have a post-graduate degree. It nonetheless treats its teachers as though they were dim-witted infants who need to be told exactly what to do. It is a government which congratulates itself on liberating the National Curriculum and therefore teachers from the prescription of earlier versions of the programmes of study. In fact the prescription now, which amounts to the imposition of a utilitarian and politicised view of what should be taught, and, indeed, how it should be taught, is far more constraining than anything that went before. It is a government which prides itself on encouraging 'diversity' and promoting parental choice. How can teachers develop their independence and schools their individual ethos when these different agencies attempt to imprison every member of the profession in a very particular and, in my view, deeply corrupt, view of education?

Chapter 7

The Failure to Re-Invent the Comprehensive School

Grammar schools: some historical context

IN 1979 THE SOCIOLOGIST Frank Musgrove wrote in his beautifully astringent book, *School and the Social Order*: 'The English working class has been betrayed twice in my lifetime: first in the General Strike of 1926 and then forty years later when the grammar schools "went comprehensive".' He continued: 'The Labour Party did not abolish the great Public Schools, the obvious strongholds of upper-class privilege; with unbelievable perversity they extinguished the only serious hope of working class parity ... the upper classes kept their Public Schools, the working class lost theirs.'[111]

Twenty years later, the old Etonians in David Cameron's shadow cabinet are, in public at least, as critical of upper class privilege as the most unreconstructed of Gordon Brown's backbenchers. Social justice is the key goal for all three political parties. And no politician, with the exception of the courageous Graham Brady, who resigned from his shadow ministerial post in 2007 in order to be able to speak out against Cameron's decision to embrace comprehensive education, has a good word to say for grammar schools.

Driven by an excess of modernising zeal and an over-reliance on the suspect wisdom of the ubiquitous focus group, the Conservative U-turn will prove, I suspect, to have been a temporary blip. Conservatives do not (see Chapter 9) believe that all men are equal and they are sceptical of the utopian dreams that inspire comprehensive education. Amazing though it may seem today, Labour, too, was once a meritocratic party. Ellen Wilkinson and George Tomlinson, ministers for education in the post-war Labour government, defended selection. In the 1964 election campaign Harold Wilson declared himself in favour of grammar schools for all. His logic, as Musgrove notes, was faulty, but his instinct was right. So, too, was that of Tony Blair, though in this area of public policy, as in so many others, he lacked the political will to embark on the radical reform he knew to be necessary. Mr Brown will never question his party's commitment to the comprehensive ideal; a subsequent, less ideological Labour prime minister might.

I do not, therefore, subscribe to the view that the principle of selective education is dead. The fact remains that today's politicians and educationalists would like it to be. Why?

The political decision in 1965 to introduce comprehensive education was driven by three arguments: that clever working class children found it difficult, if not impossible, to win places in grammar schools; that if they did get in they failed academically; and that selective education had done nothing for social mobility. Frank Musgrove's chapter on selective education in *School and the Social Order* systematically demolishes each of these assertions.[112]

Grammar schools may now be colonised by the middle classes. In the 1940s and 50s they were working class institutions. Musgrove examines historical data, studies of particular grammar schools in south west Hertfordshire, Middlesborough and Manchester, and national surveys, to show that by 1953, 'using a very stringent definition of working class as manual workers', 'two-thirds of grammar school pupils were working class'.[113] His analysis of A Level examination results for 1960–1 school leavers challenges the conclusion of the Robbins Committee[114] that 'working class children are progressively less successful than children of the same 11+ grading in other social groups'.[115] The figures are as follows: 65% of the children of skilled manual workers got at least two A Level passes, 64% of the children of clerical workers, and 67% of the children of professional and managerial workers. The children of unskilled workers did do less well, with only 56% achieving two A Levels, but this statistic says more, as he suggests, about the relative intelligence of these children than it does the failure of the grammar school as an institution – relative, that is, to social class, which I argue is a factor that cannot be denied in any assessment of the goals of the educational enterprise. It is hard, reading Musgrove, to understand why the 'potent and mischievous myth' of the failure of working class children in grammar schools took such hold. Then, as now, I suppose, there were academic careers to build and anti-elitist prejudices to justify.

It is quite clear, moreover, that grammar schools made a very impressive contribution to social mobility. Anthony Sampson points out in *The New Anatomy of Britain*[116] that 4 out of 21 heads of major civil service departments in the early 1970s went to 'Clarendon' schools (Eton, Harrow, Charterhouse and

St Paul's). Seventeen were ex-grammar school pupils. The Head of the Civil Service, Sir William Armstrong, whose father was an officer in the Salvation Army, went to Bec School; Sir Douglas Allen, Head of the Treasury, whose father had been killed in the First World War and who had been brought up in some poverty, went to my own school, Wallington Grammar; and Sir Philip Allen, Head of the Home Office, went to King Edward the VII School in Sheffield. But, as Musgrove says, the impact of grammar schools on social mobility is perhaps most evident when we look at men in mid-career. In 1967, for example, only 7% of Admirals had been educated in grammar schools, but when we move down the ranks to lieutenants nearly 60% were grammar school educated as opposed to 30% at public schools.

Sampson thought that the public schools would only survive if they became more like grammar schools. Michael McCrum, then head of Eton, agreed with him. Public schools had become less dominant and their influence, he thought, was set to decline still further. It has not, of course, happened. The majority of grammar schools were closed down, and, at a stroke, the competition was removed.

Secondary education in 2009: the common school

So much for historical fact. What, though, of the contemporary debate about secondary education and selection in particular? The battle lines are for the moment non-political. Labour and Conservative policy alike supports comprehensive education and the development of different sorts of comprehensive school – specialist schools, National Challenge Schools, City Academies, and so on. On the left, a good number of people like, for example, Fiona Millar, fear that such initiatives will water down the purity of the original comprehensive ideal. On the right, there are those who are committed to the concept of selective education and who view the development of specialist schools and Academies as an attempt to modernise the bog standard comprehensive which is bound to fail. Deckchairs, if you like, on the Titanic. Faith schools attract the wrath of the left for much the same reasons as grammar schools. And, to complete the turbulent picture, controversy rages over admissions policies. Should admissions be a lottery as, in part at least, they are in Brighton? Do faith schools flout the rules, as Ed Balls alleged in 2008? Should all schools be forced to take quotas of children from different social backgrounds and ability? The basic problem, of course, is one of supply and demand. We do not have enough good secondary schools. Those that are good are desperately oversubscribed, and parents whose children are turned away are naturally aggrieved.

A recently published essay by a long-standing advocate of comprehensive education, Richard Pring, summarises the case for 'the common school'.[117] With a degree of intellectual honesty that is rare in these debates, this essay sets out the objections critics might make. Personally, I think Pring is of the devil's party without knowing it, and I shall argue that the subtext of his argument amounts to an explanation of why schools which select their pupils on grounds of academic ability or religious affiliation make a positive contribution to social cohesion and social mobility.

Pring states that 'the basis of selection at the age of eleven was flawed' and that once this was understood the move to the comprehensive school was inevitable.[118] It was not, of course. A new and better method of selection could, in theory at least, have been developed and selective education retained. His argument is that psychological research in the fifties showed that the 'so-called fixed intelligence', which the tests were meant to measure, 'could be unfixed by preparation for the tests'.[119] The 'fixedness' or otherwise of intelligence is, in fact, a red herring. What matters is, first, the pupil's potential for serious academic work as demonstrated by his achievements in his primary school, and, second, the possibility of transfer from the secondary modern school to the grammar, or vice versa, if a mistake was made. The claim that it is possible to prepare for the tests is equally irrelevant. It is possible to prepare for every examination ever invented. But it is the implication here that is significant. Certain children, middle-class children, Pring is hinting, will be better prepared, by their parents and their teachers, than working class children, who do not have the good fortune to live in homes filled with books and whose teachers are less aspirational and, possibly, less competent. Adam Swift, who has written recently on the hypocrisy of parents who send their children to private and/or selective schools, puts the point explicitly and with righteous indignation: 'Selection by ability becomes, to a great extent, selection by social class.'[120]

At first sight Swift's indignation is justified. As he points out, ten times fewer children claim free school meals in grammar than in comprehensive schools. In that the percentage of children taking 'free school meals' is the generally accepted index of social disadvantage, this seems to clinch the point. Not, however, if we remember, the distinction Musgrove drew between the skilled and the unskilled working class. The free school meal statistic may well show that very few children from the latter class win places in grammar schools.

Grammar school pupils from skilled working class families may not need to claim free meals. Swift's sneer is premature. He may have a valid point, but he has not dug deep enough into the data to justify his disdain.

If the problem is the under-representation of children from the most socially disadvantaged families, then we should keep that problem in perspective. I have long felt that grammar schools should do more to identify and support bright children from homes and schools where the local grammar school is not the traditional option. Whatever the exact proportion of children from different classes, grammar schools are almost certainly more middle class institutions now than they were in the mid-twentieth century. It is easy to see why: the number of grammar schools has shrunk, so competition for places has become more intense. Partly because of the success of grammar schools when grammar schools existed in any numbers, many skilled working class families have become middle class. The make-up of the most socially disadvantaged groups has, moreover, changed in that there is less family stability. Qualifications, for better or worse, have become more important in the job market. The priority successive governments have given education may not have done a great deal to raise standards of educational achievement, but it has certainly focused the minds of parents from all classes, and perhaps, in particular, the middle classes, on the importance of the school their child attends. Middle class elbows are probably sharper than they once were, and it is quite likely that they are deployed more frequently. So grammar schools should do more. Equally and crucially, primary schools located in disadvantaged areas need to raise their aspirations. In Northern Ireland, which still, just, has a system of selective education, the 11+ rate varies dramatically from area to area. A remarkable 95% of children from the seven primary schools in the affluent Malone Road win grammar school places. The figures for Shankhill and New Lodge are 25% and 21% respectively. But, and it is a very big but, a great deal depends upon the quality of teaching in the individual school. One primary school in Northern Ireland with disadvantaged children achieved a 30% 11+ pass rate last year; 75% of the children from another school serving a similarly disadvantaged community passed the test.

We must never succumb to the bleak determinism that lurks behind so much of the debate about social class and education. There will always (remember D.H. Lawrence) be exceptionally bright children growing up in exceptionally difficult circumstances. Their teachers have a huge responsibility. But, equally, we must never climb on to the egalitarian bandwagon and pretend that educational achievement has nothing to do with social class. Musgrove wrote about the problems posed by children from unskilled working class families. The term used today is socially disadvantaged, or, more controversially, the 'underclass'. Much money has been spent, but very little has been done for such children since Musgrove wrote his book in the late 1970s. I return to their fate, which affects us all, later in this chapter. The point I want to make here, however, is that glib, anti-elitist talk about the grammar school as a middle class institution does nothing for the bright child from a disadvantaged background. It has led to a situation in which bright children from all classes have fewer opportunities to develop their academic potential. It is a twenty-first century manifestation of the old socialist dictum: unless everyone can have it, nobody shall.

All of which will grate with Richard Pring, and, indeed, Adam Swift. I see education as the pursuit of intellectual excellence. Pring's starting point is that the 'fundamental purpose' of 'formal education' is to prepare 'the next generation to live harmoniously together'. Swift, likewise. He writes: 'Selection is socially divisive, inimical to the value of community. Even if (selection) procedures were perfect ... segregating children of different abilities into different kinds of school would undermine the sense of a common culture and shared experience.'[121] If children of different abilities attend different schools, they will learn different things and emerge 'as different kinds of people with little or nothing in common'.[122] If they attend the same school, they will, conversely, share the same experiences and be initiated into a common culture.

The question is whether there is any such thing as a common culture. Children of different abilities and from different backgrounds who attend the same school do not share the same experiences. In the early 1970s I was teaching in a Gloucestershire comprehensive school. I taught two fourth year classes, a top and a bottom set. One girl in the top set was reading John Fowles's novel, *The Magus*. Most of the pupils in the remedial bottom set could not read at all. The two groups did not, unsurprisingly, have a great deal to say to each other in the playground. The curriculum they followed was, necessarily, different; their friends were different; their interests were different. They might just as well have attended different schools.

Pring tells us that the comprehensive school

> would seek to do three things: first, to understand and respect the different cultural traditions that the young people bring with them into school; second to reconcile those cultural differences, which, if ignored, fragment the wider community so that it is no community at all; third, to connect

> those with the more universal cultural traditions and achievements of the arts, crafts, sciences and humanities – what Dewey refers to as the "accumulated wisdom of the race" – through which their own ways of thinking and doing might be illuminated.[123]

If the idea of a 'common culture' equates to Dewey's 'accumulated wisdom of the race', then I understand what Pring means by the phrase. I do not, however, think that schools should seek to 'connect' this wisdom to the cultural experience of the young. Nor do I think that the point is to 'illuminate' that experience. It is, rather, to show the young what is possible: to open their eyes to different ways of thinking and feeling and seeing. Late in his essay, Pring quotes Jacob Neusner approvingly:

> Civilisation hangs suspended, from generation to generation, by the gossamer thread of memory. If only one cohort of mothers and fathers fails to convey to its children what it has learned from its parents, then the great chain of learning and wisdom snaps. If the guardians of human knowledge stumble only one time, in their fall collapses the whole edifice of knowledge and understanding (Neusner, 1993).[124]

Precisely: schools exist to preserve 'the great chain of learning and wisdom'. Pring apparently accepts this, but he cannot admit that 'the great chain' is, to quote his own words, 'objectively superior' to the 'gang culture' or 'slum culture' or 'teenage culture' students may live within outside school. Neither can he admit what is obvious to any teacher: some students will find it easier to understand the knowledge encapsulated in 'the great chain' than others. He prefers to follow Dewey in believing that all students can develop a real understanding of 'the accumulated wisdom of the race', though, as we have seen, he is less interested in the 'understanding' of the knowledge than he is in the 'illumination' of the student's experience. The slow, necessarily halting mastery of a body of knowledge alien to the experience and interest of the student has no place in Pring's scheme. To Pring's mind intellectual illumination is some kind of road to Damascus conversion in which the student's culture is 'understood and respected' while at the same time, implausibly and illogically, changed for ever.

In short, he seems to me to be trying to have it both ways. The culture of the street gang is inferior to the 'accumulated wisdom of the race'. You either recognise this or you adopt a position that is both relativistic and profoundly anti-educational. Pring tries to suggest that he is simply saying that nobody is in possession of the whole truth, that wisdom evolves, and that we must, therefore, be open to new and different experiences. Some kinds of understanding do, indeed, evolve, but I do not think that the teenagers who stab each other to death on London streets have a great deal to offer to 'the great chain'. Neither, I suspect, deep down, does Pring.

He is more open about a second weakness in his defence of the common school.

> On the one hand, the common school seeks to create a common culture whereby people are able to live within the same community ... On the other hand, the common school brings together people from different communities, maintained through different cultural traditions that are central to their sense of identity and that embody distinctive visions of the life worth living. How is it possible to reconcile these two – creating a common culture while respecting and supporting the distinctive cultures within the school community?[125]

The short answer, obviously enough, is that it is not, and Pring's attempt to free himself from the trap that his own honesty has sprung once again does not work. Diversity, he says, is a good. The whole, when every individual, whatever their cultural background, has become an accepted member of the society, is better than the sum of the parts. Perhaps, but this does not necessarily mean that we have a 'common culture'. The society may simply be wise enough to tolerate and maybe enjoy cultural difference. Again, I think Pring knows that what he wants to believe does not add up. 'Can there be a common culture in any meaningful sense?' he asks in a rather desperate way.[126]And he answers his own question: 'The aims and values and understandings' that might 'underpin' a common culture seem, he admits, to be 'vacuous'. His problem is that 'the moral and educational values that shape our lives are embodied in concrete situations, in specific institutions, in particular practices which have been handed down through the generations'.

This, of course, is why the different faith traditions argue that their children should be educated in schools that reflect the values of their faith. Given the 'vacuity' of the ideal of a common culture and the implausibility of the idea that the comprehensive school can be a community which brings children of different intelligence and from different backgrounds together in a meaningful way, this is a sensible enough aspiration. More controversial, perhaps, is the argument that children educated within the specific certainties of a particular faith tradition will be able to make a more positive contribution to the wider, pluralist community than those educated within the mishmash of competing belief and non-belief of a 'common culture'. Pring advances, however, no evidence or argument against the claim, and neither can I.

In the penultimate paragraph of his essay, he in fact underlines the good sense of those who support faith schools with the statement (admittedly prefaced by the phrase 'it is argued') that: 'To enforce a common schooling with a distinctive ethos, perhaps inimical to that of the contributing cultures is a form of centralisation that is indefensible'.[127] It is indefensible because, on the one hand, 'it assumes a central or government wisdom ... that is unfounded'; on the other; because 'that wisdom is necessarily to be found in complex traditions that embody a distinctive view of what it means to be human and to be so more fully'. He is stuck, as he himself admits, in an 'impasse' and his attempt to break free can only be called a cop out. The Government wants all secondary schools to develop partnerships in which schools will work together to deliver 'the range of experiences' which should be open to young people. Hey presto, the problem is solved. Faith schools and selective schools can continue to exist because their pupils will be freed from time to time to mix with other pupils. All is for the best in the best of all possible worlds.

I have discussed Richard Pring's essay at some length because his arguments illustrate the weakness of the pro-comprehensive position in such an illuminating way. There is no plausible case to be made against selective or faith schools on grounds of social cohesion.

The academic success of selective education

The evidence, on the other hand, for the academic success of selective schools is very strong. I do not simply mean that grammar schools achieve in absolute terms better results than non-selective schools. They do, of course, and opponents of grammar schools retort, understandably, that, given the ability of their pupils, they should. The statistics are, nonetheless, worth pondering. Of the 184,000 pupils who took A levels at schools in England in 2008, 66% were at comprehensives and 12% at grammar schools. However, of those who achieved three A grades, 36% were at comprehensives and 21% were at grammars.[128] And, as other research has shown, the performance gap in the grammar schools' favour is even wider when the three A grades are confined to languages, Maths and Science.[129] It is not surprising given such statistics that research undertaken for the Sutton Trust found that 21 of the 100 schools with the highest admission rates to Oxbridge were grammar schools; 78 were independent; and only one comprehensive featured.[130] Grammar schools might educate some of the most academically able students in the country, but their success in realising the potential of these students is remarkable.

A recent report by the Centre for Evaluation and Monitoring at Durham University published by the Sutton Trust, concluded that they are similarly successful at GCSE: pupils at grammar schools do better than pupils of similar ability at non-selective schools, achieving, on average, up to three-quarters of a GCSE grade higher per subject.[131] Earlier studies, reviewed by the researchers, came to the same conclusion. The report also noted that, even when adjustments have been made for the tendency of more able pupils in any school to be entered for more demanding subjects, grammar school pupils are entered for more challenging subjects than pupils at other schools.

The relatively recent introduction of 'value added' measurement as a means of comparing schools has so far worked to the disadvantage of selective schools. Before the now very sophisticated model of Contextual Value Added (CVA) was developed by the DCSF, a school's position in the league tables needed to be understood in terms of the population it served, whether an affluent or a socially deprived area, and the nature of the school, whether selective, comprehensive or secondary modern. Now all of these factors, and more, are taken into account in advance. Each student's results are 'contextualised',* and each school has a CVA calculation, which determines the standard its students need to achieve in order to be judged to be adding the required amount of value-added. The most significant factors in CVA are prior attainment, both the pupils' average point score at the previous Key Stage and the variability in that point score. Almost all grammar schools will, by definition, have a high average prior attainment and low range of prior attainment at Key Stage 2 among their pupils, as a result of which they are expected to add at least half a level more in each Key Stage 3

*According to a paper produced for the SHA Education Committee in December 2005, 'When is an exam grade not an exam grade?', 'a female Chinese student with level 5s at KS2 who went on to gain 8 A grades at GCSE would be shown to under-perform by at least one GCSE grade. However, a white male who joined the school after September and had a postcode that had been targeted by the DFES would have the equivalent of two GCSE 'C' grades added to their score before they sat a single examination.'

test over and above schools with a 'normal' CVA profile.** Despite that, and the fact that the 'ceiling' of level 7 in the tests in English and Mathematics makes this very difficult to achieve as an average, selective schools do achieve strong value added. Well over two thirds of pupils (over 90% in the highest achieving schools) achieve a level 7 or better, moving them into the top 10% of the cohort. The 'ceiling effect' is, however, a greater obstacle in value added from Key Stage 3 to Key Stage 4: the expected performance of each pupil in Key Stage 4 is recalculated on the basis of their achievement in the Key Stage 3 tests. Some of these pupils in selective schools are now in the top 1% of the cohort at Key Stage 3 and, just to maintain this standard, would have to achieve the top 1% of the cohort in GCSE grades. Because the A* grade represents a ceiling of GCSE achievement (and for CVA purposes they are capped at 8 GCSEs), the best these pupils can do is break even: it is impossible for them to 'add value'.[132]

The one area of the UK which, for the moment at least, has a fully selective education system is Northern Ireland. In the 2008 examinations, more than a third of Northern Ireland entries (35.4%) were awarded A grades at A Level compared to 25.6% in England.[133] At GCSE, 26.4% achieved A or A* grades, compared to the overall figure of 20.7% for the whole of the UK. Northern Ireland students were also ahead on A* to C grades, achieving 74.5% compared to an overall 65.7%.[134]

Opponents of selection will argue, however, that the success of grammar school pupils is achieved at the expense of the failure of the children who attend secondary modern schools. 62,279 pupils attended grammar schools in Northern Ireland in 2007/08 compared to 85,663 in other secondary schools.[135] The examination results for Northern Ireland state secondary schools in 2007 (64.7% of pupils achieved 5 A*–C GCSEs) were, however, 2.7% better absolutely than the results for England (62%).[136] In 2000, pupils in Northern Ireland schools were ahead of pupils in England at Key Stage 3 in both English and Mathematics by about 18 months of progress. A detailed study of test and examination results for different types of school published by Dr John Marks in 2000 showed that secondary modern school pupils in England achieve Key Stage 3 results that are only very slightly below comprehensive school pupils: the differences in the average standard reached in English equates to about two months of progress and in Mathematics about seven months.[137] At GCSE, secondary modern schools' results in English and

**Pupils achieving level 5 at the end of Key Stage 2 are in the top 20 per cent of the national cohort.

Mathematics are on average better than those for about 900 comprehensive schools, or one third of the total. A higher number of students achieve 5A*–C grades at GCSE in secondary modern schools than do students in 700 comprehensive schools.

Dr Marks went on to compare the performance of groups of Local Education Authorities in England. In 1998 those authorities with a wholly selective system achieved 51.5% A*–C GCSEs. Those with a wholly comprehensive system achieved 43.5%. Those with groups of or individual grammar schools were somewhere in between. The results of these various studies led him to conclude that selection is better for all pupils and not just those selected to attend grammar schools.

The performance of schools in Kent, which has 33 grammar schools, 21 comprehensives and 48 secondary moderns, on 5 A*–C GCSEs in 2004, was 96.8% grammar, 48.4% comprehensive and 36.5% secondary modern. Bristol, which is wholly comprehensive, had an average performance from 2001 to 2004 below that of the national secondary modern schools. The Bristol figures were 31.8% (2001) and 35.1% (2004) pupils with 5+ GCSE grades A*–C. The comparable national secondary modern figures were 32.8% in 1999 and 42.3% in 2004.[138]

Ministers used to talk about 'evidence-based policy making'. It depended on whether the evidence fitted the policies they wished to pursue.

Faith schools: a footnote

Tony Blair wanted more faith schools to be established. He encouraged independent faith schools to seek state funding and voluntary aided status and was happy for the churches, and individuals like Sir Peter Vardy, to set up Academies with a religious ethos. Speaking, however, to the House of Commons Children, Schools and Families Select Committee, Secretary of State Ed Balls signalled a slackening of enthusiasm which might amount to a change in policy. 'In some local communities', he said:

> there is support for faith schools, in some there are schools moving from the independent sector to the state. Other communities are clear that faith schools aren't the right schools for their communities. It is up to the local community to decide what it wants. We're not leading a drive for more faith schools.[139]

Given his attacks on the supposed irregularities of faith school admission policies, I would have been amazed if he had said that he was.

There are around 6,900 faith schools in the state-maintained sector, a third of all maintained schools. This figure breaks down as follows: 4,657 Church of England schools, 2,053 Roman Catholic, 36 Jewish, 8 Muslim, 2 Sikh, 1 Hindu and about 82 other Christian schools. Critics of faith-based education argue that faith schools undermine social cohesion and often discriminate against children from poorer homes. The argument for is, first, that many parents want their children to be educated in faith schools and in a democracy the state should do all it can to meet their aspirations; and, secondly, to repeat the point made by Richard Pring, that because 'the moral and educational values that shape our lives are embodied in concrete situations, in specific institutions, in particular practices which have been handed down through the generations', children educated in faith schools will develop a more secure sense of what is morally and educationally important and are likely, therefore, to contribute more positively to social cohesion in adult life than children educated in schools who have been exposed to what I have called 'the mish-mash of competing belief and non-belief of a "common culture"'.

A critical report on faith schools published by the Runnymede Trust in December 2008 made much of the social cohesion argument.[140] It quotes Sir Herman Ouseley's comment in his 2001 review of race relations in Bradford that there was 'virtual apartheid' between schools, endorsing his argument that this has 'led to polarisation, failure to prepare students for life in a multi-ethnic society, and racial tensions within and between schools'.[141] 'The notion of community cohesion based upon "shared values" has', it observes, 'become a central policy initiative. Schools in particular are identified as being crucial to breaking down barriers between young people.'

The first thing that needs to be said about this is that, while schools can and should make a major contribution to moral and religious understanding, Ouseley and the Runnymede Trust are assuming, as politicians so often assume, that schools are both responsible for and have, potentially at least, the answer to every social ill. They are not and they do not. The second thing to note is that there are only eight Muslim schools in the whole of England. The Bradford riots cannot, therefore, be blamed on faith schools. If schools are to be held responsible for the riots, then the failure is a failure of schools that promote no one religion. The third is to challenge what is always taken for granted, the assumption that faith schools must exacerbate racial tension.

When Polly Toynbee writes that we need 'look no further than evidence from Northern Ireland to see how much worse divisions grow when 95% of children meet no one from outside their sectarian schools',[142] what exactly is the evidence to which she refers? I do not, of course, deny the divisions, but I would like to know why they are assumed to stem from the existence of faith schools. My own experience visiting faith schools in Northern Ireland and the mainland is that they do all they can, often in very unpropitious circumstances, to help their children cope with social problems that are in fact caused by a complex of historical, social, economic and, yes, on occasion, religious factors. The fourth is to point to the vacuity of the statutory duty placed on schools in 2007 'to promote community cohesion'.[143] Schools are now expected to: 'encourage pupils to share a sense of belonging; help pupils develop a positive appreciation of diversity; remove barriers to equality; and build strong partnerships between people from different backgrounds'. Compared to the strength of a particular faith tradition and the ability of the faith school to educate its children within that tradition, this is feel-good twaddle.

The Runnymede report makes six recommendations.[144] The first is that faith schools should end selection on the basis of faith. 'With state funding comes an obligation to be relevant and open to all citizens.' I am not clear what 'relevant' means, and I question the general assertion. Ministers are committed to a diverse system of state schooling. They want schools to have an individual ethos and parents to be able to choose between them. The ethos of a faith school depends upon the commitment of everyone involved in the school (staff, children, parents) to its particular faith. If such a school opens its doors to any child, its ethos will change. It will become a school like any other school. A faith school in receipt of state funding which cannot fill its places should admit children of other faiths or no faiths, but why, if it can fill its places, should it be 'open to all citizens'? The citizens whose children it does admit have paid their taxes like everybody else. The recommendation is persuasive if you are opposed to the concept of parental choice, but not otherwise. Recommendations two and three – that 'children should have a greater say in how they are educated' and that 'RE should be part of the core National Curriculum' – have nothing to do with the central argument. The fourth states that 'faith schools should also serve the most disadvantaged'. They should, but it needs to be said that the extent to which they are alleged not to is strongly disputed by the Church of England. I do not understand the fifth (that 'faith schools should value all people'), but am reassured by the sixth that 'faith should play an important role in our education system'. The trust appears to recognise the value of faith education, but the proposals it makes for its future development would, if accepted by the Churches or imposed by Government, in the words of Jon Benjamin, the director-general of the Board of Deputies of British Jews, 'mould it into something that will effectively strip away that which makes it successful'.[145]

Admissions

Benjamin is right. The recommendations of the Runnymede Trust are either naïve or they are disingenuous. A school is not a fast-food outlet. Education is not a 'product' that can be 'delivered' to any customer who walks through the door. It is a conversation in which the ability of the child to listen is as important as the teacher's ability to explain. The benefit to the individual child depends both upon that child's ability to benefit and the school's ability to sustain the nature of the educational experience it offers. To a very significant extent the latter depends upon the nature of its intake. Change the nature of the intake and the school will change. This is what the Runnymede Trust and, more generally, the Government in its constant revisions to the School Admissions Code do not understand.

Ultimately, of course, the problem of admissions is a problem of supply and demand. Demand for places in good schools exceeds the number of good school places available. The problem will remain until more such places are created. At present, as the Government itself admits in its latest attempt to tighten up admissions policies, 'too many children fall short of the standards they could – and need to achieve'.[146] One in six, remember, fail to achieve one decent GCSE and under half manage five good GCSEs including English and Mathematics. Given the Government has been in power since 1997, it is unlikely that we are going to see a sudden increase in the number of good school places. What, therefore, needs to be done?

There are three possible answers to this question: the rules can be tightened in an attempt to ensure that every child has an equal chance to secure a place in a good and, therefore, oversubscribed school; all attempts to solve the problem of 'fair' access through regulation could be abandoned and lotteries used to achieve random admissions; or the negative impact of the state's attempts to equalise access to good schools could be acknowledged: we could allow individual schools to set their own admissions policies, as indeed they must if they are to retain the identity that makes them good schools.

The latter proposal runs counter, of course, to everything this Government is trying to do. Writing in his foreword to the revised School Admissions Code,[147] which was implemented on the 10th February 2009, Secretary of State, Ed Balls, asserts that 'the measures set out in this revised code will ... enable schools to have a balanced and representative intake that reflects the local community and enables them to be a community resource, raising standards in all schools, not just a few'. I wonder if he really believes that in 'enabling' schools to achieve a more 'balanced and representative intake' he is helping to raise standards? Few headteachers of successful schools will thank him for his kindness. While the nature of a school's intake is crucial to the nature of the educational success it can achieve, headteachers know that attempts to spread the misery of difficult pupils in equal numbers across all schools are more likely to damage the success of good schools than they are to raise standards in underachieving schools. The intake is important, but so, too, is the strength of leadership offered by the headteacher, the quality of teaching, and the ethos of the school, which, as I have said above, is bound to be affected by the new pupils the school is forced to admit.

Does this mean that children from disadvantaged homes should be left to drown in their sink schools? No, every effort should be made to raise standards in these schools. In saying this, I am not suggesting more of the same: more threats from the Secretary of State that schools where fewer than 30 per cent of pupils achieve five A*–C GCSEs should be shut; more central initiatives; more frenzied and futile activity from local authorities. None of this has worked. None of this will ever work. The root problem is the belief that every child has the potential to achieve academically and that the concept of the comprehensive school can be made to work. Nothing will be done for the children the system is currently failing in such huge numbers until this article of faith is abandoned. 'We can't', Lawrence wrote, 'make a highly intelligent being out of Jimmy Shepherd. Why should we, if the Lord created him only moderately intelligent? Why do we always want to go one better than the Creator?' It is time our politicians realised that this is a competition they are not going to win. They are, after all, committed, in theory at least, to notions of parental choice and to the development of a more 'diverse' system of secondary education. 'Diversity' means that there are genuine differences between different schools. By 'genuine' I do not mean (see below) the vacuous idea of 'specialist' schools. I mean a system in which schools are encouraged to think about the nature of the curriculum they want to offer and the kind of pupil they want to attract. In such a system governing bodies would be free, as in any other business, to analyse demand and to respond appropriately. Nobody would tell them what kind of school they should run and nobody would dictate the admission policies they must follow.

The stock response to any deregulatory proposal of this kind is that all schools will want to educate the brightest and nicest middle class pupils. Will they? I know of no other market in which every provider competes for one kind of customer. It certainly does not happen in the independent sector where different schools aim to recruit pupils with different abilities and aspirations, offer very different facilities and resources, and charge very different levels of fees. Some, like Winchester College, are highly selective, intensely academic institutions; others, like Summerhill, offer an extremely progressive education. Why, if state education were to be deregulated, would it be any different? To stay in business, to continue to employ their staff, schools will, obviously enough, need to attract custom. I do not actually think that every school would want to be highly selective, but even if they did they would not be able to be. There are not enough very bright children to go round. As in any other market, suppliers would need to identify their market niche and succeed within it. And, as in any other market, the result would be that prices could be driven down and quality up.

In that some children are more difficult and therefore more expensive than others to educate, the state would have to determine how much extra funding particular categories of pupil would attract. This already happens with pupils who have a statement of special educational need, so there is nothing new in principle. Schools serving disadvantaged areas receive, moreover, more funding than those situated in leafy suburbs. A government that was serious about the Jimmy Shepherds of this world would recognise that schools offering high quality vocational education are expensive to run and take the application of this aspect of existing policy further. Academically able children from disadvantaged homes should, of course, have the opportunity to go to schools that offer an academically selective education. Their less academically gifted peers should, equally, have the chance to follow a curriculum geared to their interests and abilities. Such schools would emerge in the system I envisage if the Government accepts that extra funding would be needed to run them: practical, vocational schools fit for the twenty-first century, schools that, unlike the white elephant Academies, make a real difference to the lives of children currently failed by the system.

Sadly, no political party is willing to contemplate any such solution. Instead the screw tightens on good schools in an attempt to make it impossible for any school to determine whether a child is likely to benefit from the education it offers. The Government is sympathetic to the use of lotteries to randomise admissions and the idea that every school should be forced to admit specific percentages of children of different abilities. Spread the misery. Ignore your own rhetoric about diversity and deny parents any choice over the school their child attends. Undermine the success of the schools you want disadvantaged children to attend. This is the current mindset. In ten years' time ministers will be asking themselves why one in six children leave school at 16 without a single decent GCSE to their name.

The re-invention of secondary education: Academies and Specialist Schools

Labour remains committed to comprehensive education. The Conservatives have been converted to the cause. They believe Academies and specialist schools are the way forward. Are they?

Since they are New Labour's flagship education initiative, Tony Blair's legacy to the nation, let us begin with Academies. Academies are described in the legislation, in their model funding agreements on the Department's website, and by ministers, as independent schools. They are not. An Academy is wholly dependent on money provided by the taxpayer. It operates under the terms of a Funding Agreement between its sponsors and the Secretary of State. Under the terms of that agreement, an Academy is intrusively accountable to civil servants in the Academies Division of the DCSF.

Intrusively accountable? Take the first part of clause 109:

> The Governing Body shall allow access to the premises of the Academy at any reasonable time to DfES officials. All records, files and reports relating to the running of the Academy shall be available to them at any reasonable time. The Governing Body shall provide the Department in advance with papers relating to meetings of the Governing Body of the Academy ... Two DfES officials shall be entitled to attend and speak at all such meetings.[148]

Two officials? As Deputy Chief Education Officer in Devon, which maintained a significant number of voluntary aided (VA) schools, I had no right to attend a meeting of a voluntary school governing body, and, when I did so by invitation, only spoke when invited to by the chairman. In this and a number of other ways an Academy is more constitutionally subject to outside control than a VA school and, in my experience, than any community school with a strong Chairman of Governors. The idea that Academies are 'self-governing' is a nonsense, was always a nonsense, and, if current DCSF policies continue, will become more of a nonsense in the future. Academies now, for example, have to pay much greater attention to the requirements of the National Curriculum than they once did; they have to observe local admissions protocols, which may not reflect their funding agreements; and they are now encouraged to collaborate more closely with local primary and secondary schools.

Academies are well rewarded for this lack of independence. The core funding of an Academy, which is defined as a specialist school, entitled to be funded as one even before it opens, does not differ markedly from that of other publicly funded schools. But the Funding Agreement also employs the methodology that led to huge sums of taxpayers' money being wasted in the Individual Learning Accounts fiasco: paying for students who do not exist. So if, in any one year (Clause 53),[149] the Governors' estimate of the number on roll at the start of the next financial year is too high, as long as that estimate is only 2.5% (which used to be 10% in some earlier Agreements before someone in the then DfES woke up) over the actual number then enrolled, the Secretary of State agrees to pay up and do nothing about it, although the actual numbers on roll are by then known. Being paid for 25 students, who are already known not to exist, in a school with 1,000 pupils, would not have got past any LEA finance officer or committee I have ever had to deal with. If the overestimate is more than 2.5 per cent, the Secretary of State 'reserves the right' to claw back that element of the overestimate in the following year. But does he? Now headteachers are all honourable men and women, but they are consistently over-optimistic about the number of pupils their school will attract. Any funding system under which governors, however innocently, can annually submit and be paid for a risk-free overestimate of a school's pupil numbers is unsound.

The practice of paying for students who do not exist is further extended:

> In relation to Academies which open with intakes representing only a proportion of the final planned size of the Academy (Clause 58), payments based simply on the

> number of pupils present are unlikely to be sufficient to meet the Academy's needs in the years before all age groups are present at their planned size (the 'start-up period') because of a lack of economies of scale.[150]

'All age groups'? So the Secretary of State agrees to pay an unspecified amount of grant, during a period which could last for up to seven years at an 11–18 school, for pupils who might one day be at the school but so far are not. Of course, any school which is not full has higher overhead costs per pupil than if it were (hence the drive, now faltering) to reduce the number of surplus places wherever these arise: but schools which are not Academies have had to learn to live with that for as long as I can remember.

Finally, the system of Earmarked Annual Grants works on the feeding the ducks principle. Each year, the Academies submit bids to the Secretary of State for extra capital or revenue funding for anything they want to do. It is then for the Secretary of State to decide, no doubt on the advice of civil servants, to whom it may be prudent for any Academy to remain deferential, how much extra funding he sees fit to provide.

To which the reply might be 'So what?' Academies, ministers argue, are raising educational standards in areas where standards have languished for years. Quibbles about levels of funding and degrees of independence miss the point. I do not myself think that questions concerning funding are trivial. We are talking public money, and the academy initiative remains intensely controversial. Headteachers of secondary schools close to Academies have a right to know how steeply the playing field slopes, for, obviously enough, money dedicated to Academies is money that could have gone elsewhere. I also think that the independence issue is extremely important for the Conservatives whose support for Academies is based on their supposed freedom from state control. If that freedom is illusory, Michael Gove needs to wake up.

I agree, however, that the key question concerns standards. Are Academies transforming children's lives and, if they are, is it because they are Academies?

Some are proving to be very effective schools. Mossbourne Academy in Hackney, for example, has achieved some remarkable results. Understandably enough, ministers want us to believe that all Academies are making good progress. They emphasise the fact that the 36 Academies with GCSE cohorts in 2006–07 averaged 43.7% 5+ A*–C grades at GCSE versus 22% for 2001, the last year of checked data for predecessor schools, an increase of 22 percentage points. The national average improvement is around 12%. If English and Mathematics are included, the increase is 11.2 percentage points, with an average of 25% 5+ A*–C in 2007 versus 14% in 2001. This compares to a national average improvement figure of 7.8%.[151] Any improvement is, of course, to be celebrated, but these statistics do not, for two reasons, constitute conclusive proof of the success of the academy initiative.

First, because the lower the starting point, the easier it is to deliver improvement. Nine per cent of pupils in what has become the Haberdashers' Askes Knights Academy in Lewisham achieved 5+ A*–C grades at GCSE in 2005. In 2007 the figure was 42%, a whopping 33% increase. Suppose, however, we were assessing the progress made by a grammar school where 95%+ of students routinely achieve 5 A*–C grades. With luck a comparison of the two years might demonstrate a percentage point or two increase. Does this mean the grammar school is less effective than the once poorly performing school now beginning to make strides? Only if you are a Government minister desperate to convince the electorate of the success of your policies. The second reason is that if we focus on actual achievement figures rather than progress, a very different story emerges. In 2001, the 36 Academies, or schools which preceded the Academies, achieved on average 22% 5+ A*–C grades. The national average was 50%. In 2007 the figures were 44% and 62% respectively. The statistics including English and Mathematics were 14% and 39% in 2001 and 25% and 47% in 2007 respectively. There is, once again, achievement to praise. The 36 schools are doing better than they were in 2001. It is not surprising that the Academies trail the national averages. They serve, typically, significantly disadvantaged communities and some have been set up only very recently. That said, there is no escaping the fact that 75% of the students in these schools failed to achieve 5 A*–C GCSE grades, including English and mathematics. Note, too, that the gap between the average of the academy group and the national average for 5 A*–C grades, including English and mathematics, has narrowed by just three percentage points over six years.[152] The academy programme may fulfil ministerial hopes, but as yet the jury is out.

This is the conclusion reached by the final DCSF-commissioned Price Waterhouse study on the Academy initiative: 'There is insufficient evidence to make a definitive judgement on the Academies as a model for school improvement.'[153] Indeed, and I imagine a genuinely independent study might have put the point more strongly. The most interesting thing about this study is its failure to find anything persuasive to say about how academy status per se leads to improvement. My own view, which I have repeated, boringly, for twenty years, is that what matters in a school is not plate glass, state-of-the-art buildings or sponsorship from a successful businessman, it is leadership. So I am not surprised by the fact that standards vary dramatically across Academies. The formula may be the same, but, for better or worse, each headteacher offers his own individual leadership. As a consequence, to quote Ofsted, the 'quality of teaching remains variable'. When teaching is variable, standards will be variable, too.

The Price Waterhouse report states that 'independence provides the Academies with the freedom to work outside the management and scrutiny of the Local Authority'.[154] It notes, however, a trend towards greater involvement with local schools and comments that this results from 'national education policy changes' and 'the increasing maturity of the Academies in question'. I do not know why 'maturity' should lead academies to embrace the authorities they were established to escape, and I have already remarked that in terms of their accountability to the Secretary of State, Academies are far from independent. The Price Waterhouse team choose, however, to attempt to substantiate the myth. They do not succeed. Academies, they assert, can provide a 'more flexible curriculum and a more personalised approach to learning'.[155] They do not say why greater flexibility and personalisation lead to higher standards of pupil achievement or how important these factors are to the success of those Academies that are succeeding or why Academies are in a better position to do these things than ordinary local authority schools. They further assert that 'sponsorship contributes significantly to school improvement' through the funding sponsors bring, their 'broad range of expertise', and the 'challenge' they offer to leadership.[156] The sponsors make no contribution to the revenue costs and the £2m they were originally expected to find is minimal in the context of the £30–£40m cost of a typical academy building. Any good governing body brings 'a broad range of expertise' and 'challenges' management. I would add that, while, of course, there are some honourable exceptions, most sponsors have no more understanding of education than most politicians. They are, that is, all too likely to be sucked in by the nonsense of 'personalisation' and the rest. It is an unpersuasive argument and the evidence cited to demonstrate how Academies 'have exercised their independence' is, frankly, pathetic. Many are said to have 'extended programmes of instruction and teaching hours'. So, too, have many ordinary schools. They have changed their curriculum to offer GNVQs and vocational courses. So, too, have many ordinary schools. 'Their teachers have access to a variety of technological solutions such as well based lesson plans.' So, too, have many ordinary schools, though the technological solution, I would add, is only as good as the pedagogic thought that lies behind it.

The jury, to put it kindly, is out on Academies. Those with excellent headteachers will become excellent schools. Those that do not will scrape along or fail. It is no different from any other school, but ministers have to pretend that their flagship reform is working and the drive to expand the number of Academies continues apace. What is incomprehensible is the unthinking enthusiasm of the Conservative party. My understanding has been that Mr Cameron wants to create genuinely independent state schools and to cut waste in public expenditure. The Academies are state schools run directly by central government. They waste huge amounts of public money. The hole he has dug himself into on grammar schools is too deep, I suppose, to escape, but surely a re-think on Academies would be relatively straightforward?

It was a previous Conservative government which launched the specialist schools programme in 1994. On taking power in 1997, Labour adopted the policy enthusiastically and by January 2008 95% of state secondary schools were specialist schools or Academies with a specialism. A specialist school is a school that purports to specialise in an area of the curriculum. In 2007 the number of schools choosing to specialise in different subjects was as follows: arts (498), business and enterprise (259), engineering (66), humanities (140), languages (281), mathematics and computing (302), music (43), special educational needs (45), science (367), sports (406), technology (598), combined subjects (186).[157] Those specialising in combined subjects presumably see themselves as specialist generalist schools. Despite the fact that we have specialist schools for children with learning difficulties, the possibility of specialising in the teaching of clever children is, of course, forbidden. Specialist schools can, though, admit up to 10 per cent of their pupils on grounds of 'aptitude' in their specialist subject. 'Aptitude' is deemed to be different to 'ability', though I have myself never understood the distinction, and few schools have made much use of this freedom.

The theory appears to be that specialising in a particular subject will breathe new life into the bogstandardness (to use Alastair Campbell's famous phrase) of comprehensive education. Parents will have a real choice to make between schools. Standards in the specialist subject will rise, and, though the logic is to me somewhat mysterious, standards will be driven up in other subjects, too.

In recent years, much has been made of the fact that specialist schools will co-operate with each other and with businesses in their locality. Pupils will, it is argued, be based for pastoral purposes in one school, but will attend lessons in other schools with the expertise the home school lacks. And businesses will contribute financially and ensure that the curriculum is relevant to the world of work. This, as I say, is the theory. The reality is rather different.

I remember talking to the headmaster of a successful independent school in late 1997. Labour ministers were extolling the virtues of specialist status. 'I want my school to be a good school,' he said to me, 'good across the board, in every subject, not a school which specialises in just one subject.' It is the obvious objection to the whole initiative. Why would a school want to specialise in one particular subject? The answer is equally obvious. If there are a thousand pupils on the roll, the decision to specialise means an extra half a million pounds over four years. And, if every other school is specialising, there is little option, unless you are a very popular school with a very confident head, but to do what everybody else is doing. This is what most headteachers will tell you in private. Why as a parent would you want to send your child to a specialist school? Do you want your son or daughter to specialise at 11? You may, perhaps, not worry too much if the specialism of the school matches his or her aptitude and interests, but if it does not, you might well be asking yourself whether specialist schools are a very sensible idea.

Ministers will argue that there is not a problem. Specialist schools 'have a special focus on those subjects relating to their chosen specialism, but must also meet the National Curriculum requirements and deliver a broad and balanced curriculum to all pupils'.[158] But this simply raises the question of what in practice specialisation means. If it means anything, it means that teaching in the specialist subject is somehow special: central to the identity of the school. This specialness may stem from the fact that the teachers are specially talented, or, if some pupils have been selected on grounds of their aptitude in the subject, because the pupils are specially talented. The latter condition is rarely met, and the former is not that common. There are specialist science schools without a specialist Physics teacher. It is hard not to come to the conclusion that the whole initiative is little more than smoke and mirrors, that specialist schools are pretty bogstandard comprehensive schools, albeit with a bright new label. This is reassuring if you are a parent worrying about how your musically talented daughter is going to settle in the local sports college, but it is not a ringing endorsement of the ministerial rhetoric.

Have, though, standards risen in specialist schools? The idea is that, for example, the excellence of the music department will drive improvements in science and, indeed, every other subject. My experience of schools leads me to think that it is more likely to leave the science department gnashing its teeth in frustrated, jealous fury. Why should standards in one subject inspire a general improvement across the curriculum? Let us, however, suspend judgement. If standards have improved across the curriculum in specialist schools, the wackiness of the logic might not matter.

The trouble is that, as Frances Castle and Jennifer Evans put it in a report written for RISE (Research and Information on State Education) in 2006, 'the current body of evidence about specialist schools is equivocal about their impact'.[159] This echoes the 2003 House of Commons Select Committee Report on Secondary Education: Diversity and Provision, which concluded that 'there is an absence of clear evidence as to alleged benefits of specialism'.[160]

Ofsted reports in 2001 and 2005 were positive, but at least one researcher has raised doubts about Ofsted's objectivity, pointing out that the body of the text of the 2005 report does not provide sufficient evidence to justify the very upbeat introduction.[161] I know from my own experience as Chief Inspector that the DCSF would have (how shall I put it?) taken a very close interest in a report on such a central political initiative. Setting aside any doubts we might have about Ofsted's objectivity, one thing is clear: these reports do not tell us whether it was specialist status which led to improved performance in these schools. It may have done, but the explanation could, equally, be that these schools were awarded specialist status because they were already highly effective, that any improvements are simply the result of having more money to spend, or because of 'selection practices (overt or covert)'.[162] Research funded by the then Technology Colleges Trust in 2002 is unsatisfactory for similar reasons. It purported to identify the factors underpinning the success of 20 specialist schools. These were: high quality teaching and learning; school ethos and culture; monitoring and evaluation; leadership and curriculum improvements; extra-curricular activities; and resources. Only one of these factors, as Castle and Evans point out, 'could be directly attributed to specialist status … the final one – the provision of extra resources'.[163] In every other respect the list identifies the characteristics of any effective school.

The issue of cause and effect is clearly crucial to any meaningful debate about specialist schools. The Castle/Evans review of research dating back to the late nineties shows that, as you would expect, some specialist schools have done better than others in raising standards in their specialist subjects, but generally there have been significant improvements. It has to be said that it would have been odd if there had not. In choosing its specialist subject, a specialist school presumably hopes that it is backing a winner, and, since there is a lot riding on improvements in this subject, it will presumably ensure that extra resources and support are targeted appropriately. The more interesting question is whether specialist status results in an overall improvement in examination results.

Specialist schools appear to have done better than non-specialist comprehensives when raw results (unadjusted, that is, for the prior attainment of pupils) are compared. Most researchers think, however, that it is the value-added results which matter (the difference the school makes to the achievements of its actual pupils). There is no consensus among researchers as to whether specialist schools do do better on this measure. Professor David Jesson, in a series of reports commissioned by the Specialist Schools Trust in 2001, 2002 and 2003, claims that: 'On a value added basis, specialist schools had a net value added of +4.5 compared with other schools. These excellent results strongly vindicate the Government's decision to expand the number of specialist schools by at least 2,000 by 2006.'[164] The Trust was, no doubt, delighted to learn of his ecstatic conclusions; other researchers criticised the methodology he had used, and, the point made above, questioned whether Jesson was in a position to draw a causal link between improvements in examination results and specialist status, when these improvements could have been caused by other variables not included in his analysis. It is worth adding, too, that fewer than half the pupils at specialist schools achieve five A*–C GCSE grades, including English and Mathematics. This, perhaps, is why the SSAT measures school performance in terms of the value schools add.

Given these disagreements among researchers I can only agree with Castle and Evans:

> The debate about the efficacy of specialist status as a method for improving standards of teaching and learning … has been hampered by a lack of robust research information about the impacts of the policy … Much of the evidence provided by the Government has been inconclusive or methodologically suspect.[165]

Neither is there much solid evidence about the impact of business sponsorship or the value of schools working in partnership. These key features of the initiative seem to me to be articles of faith. Do businesses know how to run schools? No. Should business interests be dictating the nature of the curriculum? No. Is it sensible to think that students can move from school to school to benefit from different subject expertise? No, it is a recipe for time wasting and truancy. Is the sharing of expertise between schools a good thing? Perhaps, if the headteachers involved want to do it, but, obviously enough, the exchange of expertise does not depend upon the schools involved having specialist status. And to state, as the DCSF states, that 'transformational change will not happen as long as schools operate as lone identities' is nonsense. Ministers need only to look at the independent sector and reflect on the virtues of competition.

Conclusion

There is solid evidence for the success of grammar and faith schools. Arguments for the 'common school' are, as we have seen, unconvincing. The best that can be said about Academies and specialist schools is that the jury is out. Labour needed initiatives to re-invent the comprehensive school and it suits Mr Cameron's egalitarian Conservative party to pick up the baton. There is no way in which politics will ever be taken out of education, but I cannot think of a clearer example of how children's education is being damaged by political ideology and electioneering.

Chapter 8

The Future of Independent Education

A confession

Starting out as a teacher at the end of the sixties, I never for one moment thought of applying for a job in an independent school. I wanted to work in the state sector. I wanted to teach children who did not have books on the sitting room walls and whose parents did not necessarily discuss current affairs over a glass of claret at dinner. I used to look down my lower middle class nose at anybody who had been educated at a public school.

Thirty years later, I can remember nodding sagely during an education 'summit' at Number 10 when the Prime Minister said that if we failed to improve standards in state schools more parents would opt for the independent sector, exacerbating the divide between the haves and the have nots. The penny, even then, had not dropped. I still saw the state as the solution and not the problem. In part this was because I still believed in Tony Blair. I thought his oft-stated determination to reform state education was serious. But it was also because I was still the grammar school boy from South London whose mum had been the lollypop lady at the local primary. We all drag our ball and chain behind us. Privilege on a plate, the chasm between the cloistered calm of the great public school and the turbulent meanness of the typical inner city comprehensive worried me.

Despite my commitment to freedom of parental choice and, therefore, to market forces rather than state monopoly provision of education, it still does. The power of old boy networks may have declined, but so too, the statistics tell us, has social mobility. Who you know still matters. I have sat in classrooms in public schools and wondered at the boorishness and stupidity and arrogance of their pupils. I can understand why members of the shadow cabinet are keen to play down their Bullingdon past. You do not have to subscribe to *The Guardian* to question the fairness of a society in which some have nothing while others cannot handle the privileges they have done nothing to earn. An argument for the reform of state education that involves, counter-intuitively, the expansion of the independent sector has to begin with these widely held and to an extent legitimate concerns.

Just how legitimate is impossible to quantify in any objective sense. My perspective on the antics of the Bullingdon Club will be different to that of an ex-Etonian. This does not matter. I simply want to register my personal sense of unease and to point to the fact that the proposals for the development of the independent sector I make in this chapter are deeply influenced by this unease.

Equally, of course, they are driven by my admiration for the outstanding education provided by the major public schools. The behaviour of pupils in a small minority of lessons might have made me cringe. My overall impression, having visited many major public schools, is of civility, humility and seriousness and excellent teaching. Too many independent schools have been tainted by the enthusiasms of the Government and its legions of advisers, but the majority remain committed to the ideal of education as a conversation between the generations, in a word, to scholarship. That is why schools like Winchester and Charterhouse have decided to abandon state examinations in favour of the IGCSE and the Pre-U. The problem of privilege and the abuse of privilege could, many argue, be solved in a flash if such schools were to be abolished. Just as, I might add, the problem of the perceived unfairness of the 11 plus test was solved by the abolition, in most areas of the country, of the grammar schools, and with similarly catastrophic results. This is not the road I shall propose we travel.

The current situation: some facts and figures

There are approximately 2,200 independent schools in the UK. Of these, 1,280 are members of the Independent Schools Council (ISC). These ISC schools educate over 500,000 pupils with non-ISC schools educating a further 120,000 pupils. ISC schools employ 46,160 teachers.

The ISC website[166] tells us that the average termly fee for member schools is £3,023 for a day school and £7,353 for a boarding school. Non-ISC school fees will be somewhat lower. Fee increases across ISC schools were 6.2 per cent in 2007–08. During 2008, ISC schools spent £689.5m on capital projects (£1,348 per pupil). Twenty four per cent of their pupils received some financial assistance from the school to help with fees.

Nearly 40,000 students in ISC schools took GCSE examinations during 2008. They were entered for an average of 9.6 subjects. 28.5% were awarded an A* grade; 59.2% an A* or A; and 93% achieved five GCSEs, including mathematics and English (compared to a national average in 2007 for state schools of 46.7%). In 231 ISC schools (41.8% of the total that had GCSE candidates) every pupil achieved five or more A*–C grades. 31,675 students were entered for the A Level examination. 50.7% achieved A grades (national average 25.9%), 76.9% achieved an A or a B grade (national average 50.8%). 92.9% of ISC students then went on to higher education.

Independence and threats to independence

Of course, the abolitionists will snort. What do you expect? Bright children from supportive and affluent homes taught in luxuriously appointed schools by highly qualified staff are bound to hoover up the A and A* grades. There is a truth here, an important, but partial, truth. A child's background, as I argued in Chapter 2, is a key determinant in their academic success and pupils in top public schools do not often lack either resources or specialist accommodation. Anybody who thinks that the latter guarantee success should, however, reflect on the very mixed record of the absurdly well-funded Academies programme and on the excellent academic achievements of many mid-market private schools, which have nothing like the facilities of their state competitors. Neither is it right to assume that bright children in effect teach themselves. Their intelligence means that they will pick up a lot on their own, but they are no different from any other child in needing a teacher to challenge their thinking and help them realise their potential. The success of the challenge in most private schools is reflected in the sector's examination successes.

Some independent schools fail to deliver the results, given their pupils, that they should deliver. The majority are privileged, but highly effective, institutions. Their most significant privilege is their independence.

They do not have to follow a state-prescribed curriculum that with each revision drifts further into politically correct propaganda and skills-based utilitarianism. They have always been able to choose the examinations they believe will motivate their pupils. Until very recently state schools have been stuck with the banalities of the GCSE. Independent schools can appoint unqualified staff that have escaped the brainwashing of a typical teacher training programme. They can decide what sort of school they want to be and can determine their own admissions procedures so that they select the pupils who will benefit from the education they offer. The state can huff and puff, but if they keep their parents happy and comply with what are admittedly ever more labyrinthine health and safety rules, they can be the school they want to be.

Why, then, are so many independent schools so very similar? Why are so many mission statements identical in their vacuous platitudes, so many glossy brochures impossible to tell apart? Why does not the independent sector as a whole, which could be a powerful force for the educational good, stand up and defend itself against the educational nonsense and, worse, the bureaucratic pressures, which threaten independence?

There are no easy answers to these questions. A few years ago my colleague at the University of Buckingham, Anthony O'Hear, and I discussed the possibility of developing a teacher training course with the Headmasters' Conference (HMC), the body which represents top public schools. The course would seek to embody the educational values HMC schools thought important. In that many HMC headteachers appeared to be critical of the content of many existing teacher training courses, the initial reaction seemed to be positive. We went ahead and established an independent qualification that promoted a particular view of the educational enterprise and ignored some aspects of state regulation. By definition, such a course could not lead to Qualified Teacher Status, the award necessary to teach in a state school. Its raison d'être as originally conceived was precisely that it would not jump through the state hoops HMC headteachers found irrelevant or wrong. We were surprised, therefore, to be told by HMC that many schools did not want to send their teachers on such a course. They were, we learnt, worried that our course would drive a wedge between the two sectors and prevent teachers who wanted to move from the independent sector to the state from so doing. On the latter point it is worth noting that in 2008 just 602 of the 46,160 teachers employed in ISC schools left to teach in state schools. On the former, I have never understood the idea that the independent sector should seek to portray itself as part of a seamless educational whole. If the state wants to impose its values on the independent sector, which it does, the independent sector can either roll over and submit or stand up for what it considers to be important. The good news is that despite the negative reaction from some individual heads and the bodies that represent them, our course now has nearly a hundred students. There are headteachers out there who do have the courage of their own convictions!

Why, though, are there not more of them? I have in front of me a review of a recently published book on the history of Stowe School. The first headmaster was the 'charismatic' J.F. Roxborough, who, the reviewer writes:

> was determined to create a school that was different from any other. He believed in the 'philosophy of the enlightenment', in the effect of Stowe's beauty on the character of the boys, rather than the forced religion and chapel advocated by the more Victorian headmasters of his time. His vision had more in common with aesthetes like Walter Pater, who felt the nobility of the Spartan character was somehow derived from its susceptibility to the 'local influences', drawing 'strength and colour' from the surrounding hills, the oleander and cypress, the plane trees and the River Eurotas, 'impetuous in winter, a series of wide shallows and deep pools in the blazing summer'. On warm evenings, Stowe boys would climb the cedar trees and recline on the branches, 'chatting idly and gazing out supposedly over five counties'. They were encouraged to ride over the hills, play music in the Grecian valley, and swim in the lakes. When these were frozen over, they skated to Strauss on the ice.[167]

I imagine that the health and safety brigade would have something to say about the tree climbing and the skating, and the ferrets the boys were allowed to keep in their bedrooms. They might even disapprove of the Strauss. Neither is it just health and safety. These days there are inspectors to satisfy and league tables to contemplate. An ever more intrusive media circles twenty-four hours a day on the look-out for scandal. Headteachers of charitable trust schools do not like to admit it, but they are the Chief Executives of multi-million pound businesses: a latter day Roxborough with a maverick vision may not always find he has the enthusiastic support of his risk-averse governors. My feeling as an outsider is that a sense of the HMC club can weigh heavily, too. What, some headteachers ask themselves, are the others going to say? What is everyone else doing? These are natural enough questions to worry about, but they strangle any impulse towards originality at birth.

In other words, the pressures on independent school headteachers to keep their heads down and conform are very significant. I nonetheless lament the fact that we do not have more independent headteachers who are prepared to stand up in public for what they believe. The sector would, I believe, be richer if there were more schools that had a genuinely individual identity. It would be safer, too, if the organisations which purport to speak on behalf of independent schools were less anxious about alienating their state school colleagues or upsetting politicians. Independent education, though the sector may not want to recognise it, is under threat. Inspectors criticise teaching methods that do not conform to the orthodoxies of the day. The General Teaching Council wants all teachers in independent schools to have Qualified Teacher Status. Universities are pressurised to accept more students from state schools. The Government's Admissions Code is used to force grammar schools to give priority to children who have been educated in state primary schools. The Independent Schools Council needs to raise itself from the torpor of its nervous complacency and fight for the cause of independence.

Charitable status

The current debate about whether charitable trust schools are true charities is an excellent example of both the pressures on independence and the inability of the independent sector to fight for what matters.

Headteachers of trust schools argue that providing education is a public benefit for two obvious and fundamental reasons. Martin Stephen, for example, High Master of St Paul's School and a former chairman of The Headmasters' and Headmistresses' Conference, wrote in March 2007 that 'we are in danger of losing an essential philosophy that determines whether a society can call itself civilised or not. This is that the teaching of knowledge is in itself an inherently charitable activity.'[168] Then, second, there is the view, put recently by Tony Little, Headmaster of Eton College, that there is a huge benefit to the public through 'the saving to the public purse'.[169] Parents who pay fees charged by private schools have already paid their taxes. Their contribution to the 'public purse' can be used to enrich the education of children who cannot pay such fees. The first of these two arguments is confused; the second, which, given current policy on the funding of state education, is compelling, would have less force if parents were to be given a voucher that they could use to fund or part fund the education of their children in state or private schools. I discuss each argument below.

First, though, it is important to note that the Charities Act 2006 explicitly challenges the idea that the provision of education is a public benefit in itself.

Private trust schools now have to demonstrate how exactly they provide a direct benefit to the public. A key principle here for fee charging charities is that people on low incomes must be able to benefit. Guidance provided by the Charity Commission states that: '"Not excluding" people on low incomes does not mean providing some "token" benefit to a person or person on low incomes; it must be more than a minimal benefit or a benefit which occurs merely by chance.'[170] Acceptable benefits include: providing access for those on low incomes through scholarships, bursaries, or assisted places, sharing facilities with local state schools, partnerships between fee-paying and state schools, and loans of teaching staff.[171]

How much access has not been quantified; neither has the extent of the partnerships with state schools. The courts will, presumably, in time decide. Meanwhile, the latest Guidance published by the Commission offers a fictional example of a school which, in attempting to meet the new requirement, dedicates 5% of its fee income to the allocation of 16% of its places to pupils who cannot afford the normal fees, and, in addition, spends a further 6% of its income on the provision of support to state schools.

This example will prompt the parents who pay the fees at this fictional school to ask the obvious question: can this expenditure be found without damaging the education of their children or inflicting further damage on their pockets? To which the answer is equally obvious: it cannot. There are only two means by which the 11 per cent can be found. Services can be cut or fees increased. Neither is good news for parents who have paid their taxes before finding the money to meet the by no means insignificant fees charged by most private schools. One headteacher was quoted recently as saying that his school could increase its fees 'ten times over' and his parents would not even notice. There may, I suppose, still be such parents, but I suspect he was wise to make his comments anonymously.

I know as Chairman of the schools group Cognita that many of our parents work overtime and forgo expensive summer holidays in order to pay for their children to attend our schools. Nothing is more important to them than the education of their children and they are prepared to make real sacrifices to ensure that they have the best possible start in life. We are a for-profit company, so the new charity legislation does not affect us. If it did, I would not like to be embarking on a tour of our schools to explain that we were putting the fees up by 11 per cent in order to fund bursaries and support failing state schools.

Those responsible for the running of private schools have, in my view, a moral responsibility to their parents to deliver the best possible value for money. It is disingenuous of the Charity Commission to assume or private trust schools to pretend that the new public benefit requirements can be met without disadvantaging the parents who pay the fees. They cannot. How can a headmaster and his governors dedicate themselves to the development of a new City Academy without affecting the school they are meant to be running? Every minute that headmaster spends liaising with DCSF officials is a minute he should have spent in his school. So, too, with teaching staff. If the head of science is spending an afternoon a week down at the local comprehensive, he is not in the school that is employing him. These points are so obvious that they should not need to be made. Nobody else seems, however, to be making them. Parents are being duped; students will suffer; and so, too, as the penny drops, will the reputation of individual schools. Ultimately, it is the reputation of the sector which will be tarnished. This, I might feel if I were more of a cynic, is the political game plan. Mr Brown's socialist Government does not approve of private schools. It cannot rival their achievements, but it does not have the courage to legislate for their abolition. It can, and apparently is, happy for the Charity Commission to undermine their performance.

The loss of charitable status would mean that trust schools would have to pay corporation tax. Bursars of trust schools estimate that this might necessitate a 5 per cent increase in fees. Martin Stephen is more worried by the fact that donors to a charity 'can make their gift worth 20% more than their actual outlay', and that such donations are crucial to his campaign at St Paul's to raise funds for bursaries for children who cannot afford the fees. The question then becomes whether parents might prefer this 5% increase to an 11% increase which guarantees that more parents will have their children educated at discounted rates and that facilities and resources and above all staff time are going to be dedicated to the education of other people's children. If I were a parent, I know what my answer would be.

But this is not a rational debate. The idea that education is a charitable activity is widely held and deeply felt within the world of private education. Later in the article I have already quoted, Martin Stephen wrote that:

> Loss of charitable status would mean completing a further lap in the lamentable trek to see education simply as a business. Fine: many of us are a business in at least some senses of the word – we charge a fee in exchange for a product. But

> as a charity we plough back all profit in to the business, are prepared to run some activities at a loss simply because they have huge educational value and can put the human value of what we do before its monetary value. A school-charity is more likely to find its employee staying on voluntarily to comfort a distressed child than it will ever find a profit-maker-lawyer staying on for anything unless the clock is ticking up the earning hours.

In that this latter comparison should be between the teacher in the trust school and the teacher in the for-profit school it is silly; in that it demeans the latter, it is insulting. To return to the statement I quoted from Stephen's article earlier: the teaching of knowledge is no more 'an inherently charitable activity' than any other activity that costs a great deal of money to provide. That money has to come from somewhere. In the case of St Paul's it comes, in the main, from parents wealthy enough to pay the fees the school charges; in the case of state schools, it is the taxpayer who foots the bill.

Sir Eric Anderson, the recently retired Provost of Eton College, believes, like Stephen, that: 'Charitable status is a guarantee that schools are out to do the best for their pupils, not make the most money.'[172] Do these highly intelligent and extremely experienced educationalists really believe that a commercial company does not set out to do the best for its customers? Do they not understand that the profit such a company generates depends upon the satisfaction of its customers? As Chairman of Cognita, a for-profit schools company, I have a vested interest, but the basic economic truth was clear to me forty years ago when I took O Level Economics: a company which sets out to make money at the expense of its customers is a company that will fail. In Cognita's case, every commercial decision is driven by a fundamental educational imperative: will what we are about to do or not do result in an improvement to the education our pupils receive? Sometimes we cannot do what we would like to do because the sums do not stack up, but this is true for every trust school in the country. Or, to be more accurate, it should be true. Most weeks at Cognita we are contacted by a school that has taken on more debt than it can manage. Some governors, sadly, show the same lofty disdain for economics that Stephen and Anderson demonstrate. Schools are businesses. Trust schools make an operational surplus rather than a profit, but they have to balance the books like any other business. The real question concerns how they use the surpluses that are generated if they manage their business well.

If Martin Stephen, along with many others, argues that charities must offer better value for money than for-profit companies because the latter have to generate a profit for their shareholders, he ignores the fact that the costs of running a school are the same irrespective of whether the school is a trust or for-profit, and that the need to generate a profit concentrates the mind in a way that, in Cognita's experience, the minds of some trust schools' governors are not concentrated. My colleagues have, frankly, been shocked by the lack, not just of financial control, but of basic financial information in some of the schools which have joined our group. A for-profit company like Cognita has, of course, significant advantages over a stand-alone independent school. It has, for instance, immediate access to expert financial and legal advice which many schools may not. Real economies in purchasing flow from the size of the group. We have the funds to invest if investment is needed. But the main advantage is not tangible. We are a new company and we know that to succeed we have to convince our parents that a Cognita school should be the school of choice. This means offering the best possible education at the lowest possible price.

For 17 years many independent schools have had it easy. Demand for places has outstripped supply. They have not had to worry too much about fee increases. Their headteachers have been able to sit back and pontificate about the wickedness of schools run to make a profit. They have been able to bow to the demands of the Charity Commissioners and the Government and dedicate time and money to partnerships with state schools. The recession will probably not make much difference to elite public schools such as Eton and St Paul's, but many independent schools are going to have to re-think the economics of their provision and their commitment to charitable status. They are going to have to fight for their independence.

Widening access

Most people assume that charities exist to help people who cannot help themselves. The only public school in the country which is a genuine charity on this definition is Christ's Hospital. This is the one school which has the resources to fund the education of any child who can benefit from the education it offers irrespective of the ability of that child's parents to pay the normal fee. Others, like St Paul's and Eton, aspire to be able to do this. Eton offers some kind of financial support to 150 of its 1,300 pupils. This is a long way from open or 'needs blind' access, but it is a lot more than most schools are able to do.

That last comment is not meant critically. Most private schools cannot educate large numbers of children for free. They have not the funds. They are businesses which depend upon the income they receive from parents who can afford their fees. It is the pretence that they are charities, coupled with the fact that so little has been done to widen access over the last decade and a half of boom years, which I find offensive.

'Widening access' is the moral crusade through which the private sector wants to purge itself of its divisive and elitist sins. I would be more impressed if I thought that the sector had done anything to deliver on this noble aim. The demand for private education may be slackening because of the recession. Until very recently it was extremely strong. Good, but not outstanding, schools had waiting lists; survey after survey demonstrated that fifty per cent or more of parents would send their children to independent schools if they could afford the fees. Has the sector responded to the strength of this demand? Has it increased capacity and lowered fees? No, of course, it has not. Fee inflation has materially outstripped almost every other category of consumer price inflation over the last twenty years and capacity growth has been minimal.

It is extremely difficult to start a new independent school. In areas where demand for independent schooling is greatest, land values tend to be highest. The only affordable possibilities are sites already restricted by planning for educational use. Even if a site can be found, the economics are difficult. The new school has to be built year by year. Parents are understandably reluctant to commit their children to a school that has yet to build a reputation. Very substantial overheads have to be carried for, typically, six years when the school will have, hopefully, a full roll. These factors combine to make genuine green field school creation in the UK very rare. If the independent sector is to meet extra demand, then capacity in existing independent schools has to be increased.

It has not happened because most independent schools are trust schools, and, despite the professed commitment to widening access, where there is no profit motive there is no incentive to expand capacity. Instead, trust schools have tended to use their untaxed surpluses to build ever more elaborate facilities, which entrench the elite nature of the institution and avoid the risks and challenges of expansion. It is hard to think of an ownership system less well designed to expand capacity and access, or, for that matter, a pattern of behaviour that is less appropriate for a charity.[173]

If trust schools could point to a significant expansion in free or subsidised places, they would have some defence. But most cannot. Instead they talk about building bursary funds to be used for such subsidies. I would myself be very surprised if many, or, indeed, any, succeeded. The problem is that the sums involved are huge. Suppose a school admits 100 pupils each year, that it charges fees of £10,000 a year, and that it wants to offer free or subsidised places to 50 pupils each year. Suppose, further, that the subsidy averages out at £5,000. This would mean that the interest on the fund would have to deliver £250,000 for one year's pupils, a sum that needs to be multiplied by seven if each cohort of pupils is subsidised. At the time of writing, interest rates are zero. In normal circumstances with, say, a 5 per cent return, this means a fund of some £35m. If we are talking about a major public school, like Eton, then the number of pupils will double or more and the fees will be £25,000 plus a year. And in the years that it takes to build the fund, fees, of course, will continue to rise at, if we base future predictions on recent history, around 6 per cent a year.

A solution

My analysis appears to lead to a depressing conclusion. Independent schools in the UK are for the most part excellent schools. They charge, however, fees beyond the reach of most parents. As I said in the introduction to this chapter, I would like more children from less affluent homes to benefit from the education they offer. I do not believe that trust schools (with the exception of Christ's Hospital) are charities in any meaningful sense of the term. I think, therefore, that the Charity Commission is in principle right to ask hard questions about the public benefit these schools offer. In practice, I fear that its campaign to force trust schools to do more to justify their status will do very significant harm. The more such schools do to meet the Commission's demands, the more likely it is that the quality of the education they currently provide will be jeopardised. Parents should not have to pay a third time for an education they have already paid for twice. This, however, is what is going to happen. If trust schools want to retain their charitable status, and most at present do, they will have to meet the Commission's public benefit test. It would be nice if they were able to create bursary funds large enough to widen access without raising fees for existing parents, but I do not think that this is possible. The likely future, therefore, is that the quality of the education they offer is going to be prejudiced or the fees they charge will be higher. Without large bursary funds, the impact on access will be small. And, for the next two or three years at least, the recession is going to exacerbate the problems they face.

There is, however, a further possibility. This is that the law allows an educational charity to sell its assets and the business of its school or schools to a commercial company in order to use the proceeds of the sale to further its aims by providing bursaries for children whose parents cannot afford the normal fee. If such transactions were to become common, the potential capital released would be huge. The schools would benefit from professional management by a business dedicated to the provision of high quality, cost-effective education. Such businesses would have a strong motive to increase capacity, partly to meet existing demand and partly because demand would increase given the increased availability of financial support.

In that Cognita has bought four trust schools which were facing an uncertain future and is in discussion with other trust schools that are financially secure, I must, of course declare an interest. It is quite clear, however, that the governors of the schools with whom we are talking are attracted by the logic of the proposition. They want to widen access and they cannot see how else to do it. They appreciate the fact that the availability of bursaries will strengthen the future security of their school. What worries them is the thought that Cognita might change the nature of the school. To which the answer is: why would we? Parents want continuity. If the school is succeeding, then it makes no sense for a new owner to come in and change the winning formula. Questions are also asked, understandably, about what might happen if Englefield Capital, the private equity firm which owns Cognita, were to decide to sell the company. Here again, I do not think there is a problem. When Cognita is sold it will be sold as a successful schools' group and the new owners will want to build on that success. There is no more point in a new owner changing what works than there is Cognita changing a successful school. These are understandable questions to ask, but they do not challenge the logic and the attractiveness of the essential proposition.

Conclusion

So will it happen? Will the independent sector become less, as it is at its worst, complacent and self-deceiving? Will more children from less privileged homes have the opportunity to benefit from the excellence of the education that, at its best, it provides? I think that, to an extent, they will. There is a genuine desire to widen access, and, among some headteachers at least, a growing realisation that what is important in the sector will not survive if it is not defended. There are the pressures of the public benefit test. There is the fact that changes to company law and personal liability have revealed the exposure to personal risk of individual governors, particularly in the context of health and safety and care of children. The recession may help to concentrate minds. But the forces of conservatism (with a small 'c') are strong, and we are unlikely to see any rapid change.

The question I discuss in the following chapter is whether a future Conservative government would facilitate the developments I believe are needed. It could, for example, introduce a voucher scheme in which parents were given a sum of money which equates to the cost of educating their child in a state school. This would stimulate demand and therefore encourage new providers to enter the market. There would be more competition between and among schools. It could, moreover, though Mr Cameron has already, of course, vetoed the idea, encourage the creation of more grammar schools. It was, remember, the headmaster of Eton, Michael McCrum, who thought that competition from the grammar schools was threatening the very existence of public schools. There is nothing like competition to encourage a business to sharpen its act. If, that is, trust schools could be persuaded to see themselves as businesses and the Conservative party could bring itself to reaffirm the virtues of markets and competition.

Chapter 9

Gove, or yet more Balls?

TONY BLAIR PROMISED us 'a world class education service'. He did not deliver. The Pisa studies which compare education standards in advanced economies show that in most tests of educational achievement England has slid down the international league tables during the last eight years. Nothing has happened since Gordon Brown became Prime Minister to suggest that new, more effective policies are to be adopted to halt this decline. The key question, therefore, is whether David Cameron, if he were to win the next election, would offer a different approach to the reform of state education.

He might. Last Autumn, Michael Gove, the Conservative spokesman on education, gave a speech in which he made it very clear that the transmission of knowledge should be at the heart of the educational enterprise. He attacked the education establishment for its commitment to progressive educational ideals and lambasted ministers for their 'centralised, bureaucratic, one size fits all, don't change till we tell you, don't get ahead of yourself sonny'[174] approach to the management of state education. The way forward, he said, is 'to give control over education to the people who really matter – to parents and children'. He is right. It is. How, though, is Gove going to achieve this transfer of power? We need answers to a number of critical questions.

Is his commitment to parents as consumers real? As the next Conservative education minister would he really be prepared to relinquish the levers of power? Will parents have genuine freedom to choose the school they want for their child or will their choice be restricted by constraints the Conservatives impose for political or educational reasons? How exactly does Gove intend to deal with the academics and officials who have exercised such influence for so long? Does he remain committed to the National Curriculum and the various mechanisms of state regulation, and, if so, how does he square this commitment with the belief that diversity and choice are the way forward? Are we convinced that the Conservatives have learnt the lessons of these last twelve Labour years? Gove may talk about wresting power from the educational establishment and restoring rigour to the curriculum and public examinations, but his meritocratic credentials remain, in my view, shaky. In the speech I have just quoted, for example, he states that 'there are those who say that university education, by definition, can only ever be enjoyed or appreciated by a minority'. There are, and I am one of them. Does Gove want more and more young people to waste three years studying for a meaningless degree which leads nowhere? Does he really think that the huge increase in the number of students attending university over the last years has had no impact on academic standards? Or is it that, like Labour ministers, he is less interested in academic standards and a genuinely meritocratic society than he is in the quick and fallacious fix of social engineering?

The Education Reform Act twenty years on

You either believe in the effectiveness of the market as a mechanism for the distribution of public services, or you don't. You either think that parents care about their children's education, and that, given the opportunity, they can be trusted to exercise an intelligent choice over the school their children might attend, or you don't. Labour does not believe in markets and does not trust parents. Mr Cameron's Conservatives don't know whether they do or they don't.

In 1988 when the then Secretary of State, Kenneth Baker, masterminded the Education Reform Act (ERA), the most significant piece of education legislation since the 1944 Act, through the Commons, the Conservative party was similarly ambivalent about whether market forces would raise standards in state schools.

On the one hand, the ERA introduced two measures to free schools from Local Authority control: 'Local Management of Schools', which sought to ensure that a school's budget was determined by the number of pupils it attracted, and 'Grant Maintained Schools', which was a more radical measure offering secondary schools the opportunity to opt out of Local Education Authority control completely. The idea underpinning these initiatives was that state schools should have the same freedom to determine their own ethos and to compete with one another in the market place as independent schools. Baker also believed, however, that schools should be forced to follow a National Curriculum. Driven by a frustration with the education establishment at least as intense as that now felt by Michael Gove, he wanted to raise expectations of what children should achieve as they moved through primary and secondary school, to challenge progressive teaching methodologies and to ensure an entitlement to key areas of learning irrespective of the school a particular child might attend. These were noble aspirations, but they betray a doubt about the market's ability to deliver improvements which sat uneasily with the drive to liberate schools from the shackles of state control.

Michael Gove is wrestling with the same dilemma. His desire to liberate schools from the constraints of state bureaucracy is clearly genuine. He believes it is better to trust parents than bureaucrats. But he wants, it seems, to retain the National Curriculum, inspection, admissions codes, and other levers of political power. The lesson of the ERA, which he has yet to learn, is that you can't have your cake and eat it.

This is not to deny that the Conservative reforms of the early 1990s had a plausible managerialist logic. The National Curriculum spelt out the expectations schools had to meet. LMS devolved the responsibility and the resources needed to meet these expectations to the unit of delivery. National Curriculum tests, public examinations and Ofsted inspections held schools accountable to the communities they served and to Government. If you are happy to have the man or woman who happens to be sitting in the Secretary of State's office in the DCSF impose his or her version of the educational good on the nation's schools, this, in theory at least, is a sensible approach to raising standards. It is, after all, what every good business tries to do. Define what needs to be done; delegate; monitor progress. Why not?

The theory might be fine; the history of what actually happened to the Conservative reforms of the early 1990s suggests that there are any number of reasons why not. I will take the National Curriculum and school inspection as examples of the lessons Gove should learn from the failures of his predecessors.

When Margaret Thatcher first thought about a National Curriculum it must have all seemed very simple. She wanted this curriculum to spell out what should be taught in English and mathematics. Things became more complicated when Baker decided eight other subjects should be included. But the fun really started when committees of subject specialists were brought together to draw up detailed specifications. Many of those involved did not want a subject-based National Curriculum at all. There were interminable debates about the place of skills and what were known (see Chapter 4) as 'cross-curricular themes'. Primary teachers disagreed with secondary teachers. The progressives fought bitterly with the traditionalists. Needless to say the end result was a fudge, better, in my view, than what had been the norm in many schools, but a long way from what ministers had envisaged. Political dissatisfaction grew and a review of the National Curriculum was ordered in order to stiffen rigour and eliminate all trace of wishy-washy progressivism. Teachers, particularly primary teachers, were, however, equally unhappy. Protests escalated and in the end John Patten, who had the misfortune to be holding the parcel when the music stopped, had to call in Sir (as he then was) Ron Dearing to lead a review into the mess. That review resulted in a further fudge, but one which was more palatable to those within the profession who hated either the principle of a national curriculum or the detail of the individual subject specifications or both.

That was more or less that until Labour came to power in 1997. Since then constant revisions have been made to the programmes of study, teachers, who have to change their schemes of work on an annual basis, have been driven to despair, and we have ended up with the curriculum described in Chapters 4 and 5. The National Curriculum has become a vehicle for the enthusiasts of the education establishment and for social engineers generally. Kenneth Baker's solution to the ills of state schools has, ironically, morphed into one of the most difficult and urgent problems facing Michael Gove if he becomes the next Conservative Secretary of State for Education.

Gove would no doubt like to be able to rely on Ofsted, which now inspects most aspects of education and child care, as a natural ally in his drive to challenge the damaging orthodoxies of the education establishment. He will find that Ofsted has become part of that establishment. Its reports are no longer worth reading. Those on schools, as we saw in Chapter 7, are written to a formula and are riddled with highly contestable assumptions about education and teaching. The recent Baby P tragedy in Haringey demonstrates that the child care reports are no better. A year before Baby P died, Ofsted inspected Haringey's children's services and concluded that they were 'good'. Sent in by a Secretary of State desperate to be seen to be doing something in the aftermath of this child's death, Ofsted found such appalling standards that its report could not be published. How, we might reasonably ask, was the wool pulled so comprehensively over the inspector's eyes on their first visit?

The answer to this question tells us a lot about what has happened to Ofsted since 1997. Blair retained my services as Chief Inspector in order to ensure that Ofsted continued to deliver objective reports that told parents what was going on in the classrooms of the schools their children attended or might attend. To an extent, I suppose, I was politically useful, a lightning conductor to deflect the cries of anguish from the teacher unions. As far as I was concerned, that was fine. We were never going to see standards rise if problems in schools were to be allowed to continue to fester. Regular and rigorous inspection was needed to expose these problems, and I was grateful for Mr Blair's Prime Ministerial support. That support did not, however, translate into effective policy development in the Department for Education and Skills (DfES) as it was then called. I became increasingly disillusioned and resigned in November 2001. Sir Mike Tomlinson stepped in to hold the fort. He immediately announced that 'inspections would now be done with schools rather than to schools'. Inspired, no doubt, by the DfES, his logic may have been faulty, but his message was clear. The days of punitive rigour were over. From now on inspection was going to be a partnership between the inspection team and the school. The unions and the gathered ranks of ex-teachers on the Labour back benches were pacified; a new era of collaboration between the Government and the teaching profession could begin. In 2002 David Bell, who is now the Permanent Secretary in the DCSF, took over from Tomlinson. He decided that the notion of partnership should be at the heart of the inspection methodology: inspectors would in future concentrate on a school's evaluation of its own performance. This, of course, killed off any notion of objectivity. The time inspectors spent in school was, moreover, reduced radically. Lesson observation, which used to be at the heart of inspection, was scaled right down. Inspectors were now to spend their time discussing data with the school's management team in an attempt to authenticate the school's assessment of its own performance. This is what Ofsted did in its first Haringey report. It is why that report was so fatally flawed, and it is why Michael Gove needs to think very hard about whether Ofsted is worth its multi-million pound budget.

Nobody will ever be able to determine who drove these changes to inspection. What drove them is clear. Ministers decided that the battle to open up the performance of schools was politically too difficult. Estelle Morris, who succeeded Blunkett as Secretary of State in 2001, had been an NUT official when she was a teacher. Temperamentally, she was on the side of the teachers and she clearly disapproved of what she took to be my punitive excess. But, equally, strong voices in the inspectorate were advocating a slimmed down model of inspection that focused on what became known as 'the school's central nervous system' – its ability to improve. Tomlinson, who had once inspired a *Guardian* headline when he told reporters at a press conference that 'Ofsted was on the side of children and did not give a monkey's toss for teachers who found inspection stressful',[175] clearly decided to move with the times. Bell would not have been appointed Permanent Secretary if, as Chief Inspector, he had obstructed ministerial wishes.

There was, let us say, a meeting of minds. Who drove which decisions in the end is irrelevant. What does matter is that lessons are learnt. Given the necessary majority, politicians can pass the legislation. That is the easy part. Their problems start when they try to flesh out the operational detail. Take the curriculum, which, if Gove is serious about challenging the anti-educational ideas that currently distort classroom practice, he is going to have to reform. Who will he persuade to drive through his ideas? Is the development of a revised curriculum going to be a consultative process, involving representatives of the different subject associations, the teacher unions, and everyone else? If it is not, it is unlikely ever to win any professional assent; if it is, the squabbles and compromises of the past are almost certain to be repeated. Suppose a new curriculum is, somehow or other, drawn up. What then? Despite all the sound and the fury, it is a moot point whether the original National Curriculum ever had that much effect in schools. My own sense, having been closely involved in the latter stages of its implementation and in the subsequent Dearing review, is that take up was, to the say the least, patchy. Secondary English teachers, for example, who have always been a bolshy lot, tended to go their own sweet way. Primary school teachers, who, through no fault of their own, lacked the subject knowledge needed to teach the nine subjects they were meant to cover, did all they could to hang on to a topic-based approach. Secretaries of State for Education, like all politicians, assume that once Parliament has pronounced that is it. It is not. It is only the beginning, and, in the world of education, the political will all too often evaporates in the face of the operational challenge.

Gove, moreover, will find himself in a more difficult position than Baker. Twenty years on, opposition to central direction of schools has hardened to the point where outright rebellion is quite likely, particularly if Gove's reforms threaten, as they must if he is to restore traditional educational values, the progressive status quo. The Chief Executive of a commercial company who sets out to change the company's product has levers he can pull, middle managers upon whom he can rely to make things happen. The Secretary of State for Education is in a far weaker position. If the Conservatives win the next election and Michael Gove finds himself in charge of the nation's 24,000 schools, he will very quickly discover that he is very much on his own. The Permanent Secretary and his senior colleagues will, I am sure, uphold the apolitical traditions of the civil service. The fact remains that these are the men and women who presided over the blitz of centralised initiatives and the corruption of the curriculum Gove, rightly, deplores. Are the various organisations described in Chapter 7 suddenly going to dance to a completely different tune? Labour relied on these organisations to brainwash the profession into an acceptance of its 'agenda'. Officers and advisers in local authorities are unlikely to prove to be any more reliable. If Gove has any sense, he will view the sincerity of post-election conversions with a great deal of scepticism. If he is wise, he will abandon any ambition to impose a Conservative agenda from the centre.

For the lesson of the ERA is that the teachers will win. A Labour government which wishes to implement reforms that the education establishment has itself proposed can, as we have seen, ensure that the teaching profession does what is expected of it. A Conservative minister who wants to challenge that establishment is in a very different position. His ideas will be undermined every step of the way. He needs the bureaucracies to impose his agenda on 24,000 schools, but these bureaucracies are responsible for the problems he is trying to solve. He may, for a while, achieve some success, but it will not last. He will depart and new ministers, perhaps a new government, will arrive. The establishment will remain, and, in the end, it will have its way.

That is the bad news. The good is that Gove does not have to try. He does not need the National Curriculum or Ofsted. He does not need the bureaucracies Labour has created to impose its will. He could learn from Kenneth Baker's mistakes and trust to markets and parental choice. Why not? His dilemma boils down to a very simple choice. Given the fact that the bloated bureaucracies and frenzied initiatives of the last 12 years have resulted in a decline in educational standards, who should we trust: politicians and their officials or teachers and parents? Gove has observed that decline. He is a Conservative. He knows that there is only one answer.

A Conservative education policy

Let us, for a moment, forget the operational challenges which will have to be faced if the Conservatives were to win the next election. Let us ignore, too, the tactical positioning inevitable in the run up to that election. Are there fundamental Conservative attitudes which should determine the nature of the education policies pursued by a future Conservative government? There are, but they have had insufficient impact thus far on the development of Conservative thinking. Mr Cameron appears too often to be more interested in the findings of the latest focus group than he does the wisdom of Burke.

Burke, as Roger Scruton writes in his introduction to *Conservative Texts*, argued that 'political order is always threatened by enthusiasm, and by the attempt to realise, through the institutions of political power, the aims and ideals of an all-encompassing programme'.[176] What programme could be more all-encompassing than that set out in the Children's Plan? 'So long as people seek, through social and political change, for a solution to problems which cannot be solved, just so long, the conservative argues, is the body politic threatened by the malady of agitation.'[177] It does not, Scruton reminds us, matter whether the means chosen are violent or constitutional. The result, in either case, is a threat to the body politic. State education is a part of that body politic, and I cannot find a better phrase to describe what has happened to our schools since 1997 than 'the malady of agitation'. Most union representatives in schools do not, in my experience, tend to vote for the Conservative party. I cannot think of one who would not endorse Scruton's words.

Cameron wants to 'give people more responsibility'. He believes that 'if you trust people, they will tend to do the right thing' and that 'they will make better decisions than those the state would make on their behalf'.[178] He is, however, quick to add that 'while we must be aware of the limitations of government, we should never be limited in our aspirations for government: to protect our security; to guarantee the provision of high quality, efficient public services; and to work tirelessly for social justice and a responsible society'.[179] He wants, in other words, to have it both ways. No government, however centralist, can 'guarantee' high quality, efficient public services. That is the lesson of the last 12 years. The more power a government devolves to the citizen as consumer, the less likely it is that it can guarantee anything. What, moreover, does the commitment 'to work tirelessly for social justice and a more responsible society' mean? What exactly is a Conservative government headed by Cameron going to do to achieve 'social justice'? How will what it is going to do differ from what Brown and Blair before him have tried to do? Will Cameron's ministers meddle tirelessly in the running of schools in a continuing and futile attempt to find remedies, as Roger Scruton puts it, for 'the unhappiness of man'? Is the 'malady of agitation' to continue? If Cameron means what he says, it will.

'A spirit of innovation', Burke stated emphatically, 'is generally the result of a selfish temper and confined views.'[180] As a member of the gloriously misnamed 'Standards Task Force', a group of the great and good David Blunkett convened to solve our educational problems, I used to reflect on this. Innovation was the thing; new ideas were conjured out of the air with huge conviction. Everything that moved and much that did not was to be modernised. I reflected, too, on Michael Oakeshott's quietly ironic comment in *On Being Conservative* that 'a man of conservative temperament' will not be 'an ardent innovator'.[181] Such a man, Oakeshott suggested, knows that 'innovating is always an equivocal enterprise, in which gain and loss ... are so closely interwoven that it is exceedingly difficult to forecast the final upshot: there is no such thing as an unqualified improvement'.[182] He believes that the more closely an innovation resembles growth (that is, the more clearly it is intimated in and not merely imposed upon the situation), the less likely it is to result in a 'preponderance of loss'. He thinks that 'an innovation which is a response to some specific defect ... is more desirable than one which springs from a notion of a generally improved condition of human circumstance, and is far more desirable than one generated by a vision of perfection'.[183] He 'favours a slow rather than a rapid pace, and pauses to observe current consequences and make appropriate adjustments'.[184] And he 'considers the most favourable occasion for innovation to be when the projected change is most likely to be limited to what is intended and least likely to be corrupted by undesired and unmanageable consequences'.[185] A man of conservative temperament will not, that is, see himself as 'the heir to Blair', driven by a compulsion to modernise every aspect of state education. He is the heir to Hume and Burke, and the defence of custom and tradition will be dear to his heart.

The vision since 1997 has been a vision of perfection. Blair promised a 'world class education system'. The current Secretary of State, Ed Balls, has pledged to make England 'the best place in the world to grow up'.[186] Our children will be successful learners, confident individuals and responsible citizens. They will be creative and resourceful problem-solvers with enquiring minds. They will have a sense of self-worth and personal identity and will relate well to everyone they meet. They will appreciate the benefits of diversity and will challenge injustice of all kinds. They will sustain and improve the environment. They will be literate and numerate and, because they make healthy lifestyle choices, will be thin. Yes, all of them. The National Curriculum says so. Every school in the land will be a successful school and the rights of the many will have triumphed, of course, over the privileges of the few.

Does anybody, other than ministers and their officials, believe any of this? We know that nothing will change because nothing ever does change. This, the man of conservative disposition will argue, is because the state is not very good at running anything. The privilege-sodden bureaucracies spawned by these idle dreams grow larger, but their impact on the real world is negligible. If anything, as Oakeshott warns might well happen, the innovations deemed necessary to achieve the utopian fantasies have made things worse. The National Curriculum, which was once a reasonably serviceable statement of academic knowledge, has, for example, become a vehicle for the inculcation of politically correct attitudes. The pursuit of equality of opportunity through an admissions system based on a lottery threatens the existence of excellent schools. The belief that all must have prizes has ruined an examination system that once identified those who really did deserve the top grades. The state should, of course, do what it can to deal with what Oakeshott calls 'specific defects', but, in seeking to improve the conditions of our 'human circumstance', it often makes things worse. A Conservative education policy should be rooted in this fundamental tenet of Conservative faith.

Labour has imposed its political agenda upon state and independent education. Our man of conservative temperament probably has a nostalgic affection for the old-fashioned idea that schools exist to teach children things they would not otherwise know. He recognises that new technology has the potential to make teaching more effective, but he knows that the usefulness of the technology depends entirely on the professionalism of the teacher using it – by which I mean that teacher's knowledge of and passion for his subject, the expectations he has of his children, and, of course, his mastery of the craft of the classroom. Teaching in the twenty-first century, the man of conservative temperament will feel, is not fundamentally different from teaching in the twentieth or nineteenth centuries. He is unlikely to sympathise with the idea that learning should be 'personalised' or that children need to be taught 'the metacognitive skills of learning how to learn'. Michael Gove and his education team need to scrutinise each and every orthodoxy that has been imposed upon teachers and their pupils from a position of similar scepticism. Thus far, we have some promising signs (Nick Gibb's support for synthetic phonics, for example, and Michael Gove's clear commitment to the teaching of worthwhile knowledge), but we await any comprehensive demolition of the theorising that has done so much damage in recent years.

That said, our man accepts that education is a contested concept. Different parents will have different ambitions for their children. If people are to be given 'more power and control over their lives', then ways will need to be found to encourage a real diversity of provision within the system. Here again, the current Conservative position is open to the charge of wanting to have it both ways. On the one hand, Gove has spoken a great deal about how he will allow parents and other interested parties to start schools that reflect their personal views on what education should involve; on the other, he thinks all schools should teach children to read using synthetic phonics and wants to persuade all secondary schools to adopt aspects of what he considers successful practice. I happen to agree that synthetic phonics is the most effective way to teach reading and that successful schools have 'strict uniform policies' and a 'system of prefects', but , as a man of conservative temperament, I know that no government has a monopoly of educational wisdom and that different parents will have different beliefs and expectations. It is not possible to square the circle. I believe, to push my argument to the limits, that if there are parents who want to send their children to a school like Summerhill (the progressive school A.S. Neill set up in Suffolk where children are expected to decide which lessons they wish to attend), but who cannot afford the Summerhill fees, then there should be a state-funded alternative. Why not? 'Conservatives have always believed', Cameron tells us, 'that if you trust people, they will do the right thing.' I agree. But who is to determine whether the thing is right or not? The individual parent or Cameron's Secretary of State for Education?

There is only one Conservative answer to these questions. To quote John Stuart Mill's famous diatribe:

> A general State education is a mere contrivance for moulding people to be exactly like one another: and as the mould in which it casts them is that which pleases the predominant power in the government, whether this be a monarch, a priesthood, an aristocracy, or the majority of the existing generation, in proportion as it is efficient and successful, it establishes a despotism over the mind, leading by natural tendency to one over the body.[187]

Children are not the property of the state, and, as part of their freedom and responsibility, the duty to educate children lies primarily with parents, with the state acting only as a default mechanism.

Finally, there is the market. Mr Cameron may not feel that this is quite the time to launch policies which celebrate the power of the market over the futility of state bureaucracy, but, in endorsing the Swedish model of 'free schools' (see pp. 191–9), this is what, in a limited way, he is doing. My argument, the conservative argument, is that he should have the courage of his Conservative convictions and go further. Scruton puts it succinctly:

> Some defend the market as the most efficient form of distribution and exchange – the form which in the long run, maximises the social benefit, and minimises the social cost. Others have defended it as a paradigm of human freedom, whereby people, acting freely in their own interest, secure a beneficial result which, in Adam Smith's famous words, was 'no part of their intention'.[188]

The point here, which I accept is politically problematic for Cameron, is that, as Hayek has insisted, 'the price or value of a commodity is fully determined within the context of free exchange: and only in such circumstances is price an effective measure of what people are prepared to sacrifice in order to obtain anything'. This is because, Hayek argues, 'the price of a commodity embodies an extremely complex piece of information, concerning the social behaviour of all those to whom the purchaser is economically related'.[189] In other words for the market to function effectively so as to enable real choices, prices cannot be centrally controlled or directed.

If he adopts the Swedish approach, Cameron will cut through the complexity inherent in a genuine market, by imposing a fixed price to be charged by all who wish to run free schools. In that Labour will seize upon any decision to allow some schools to charge more than the funding state schools receive as evidence of a wicked Tory plot to destroy state education, politically he may feel that he has no alternative. Economically and educationally, the consequences of his decision are, however, dire. I explore them later in this chapter. Suffice to say here that the options he is offering to those who wish to supply education, and the choices he is offering parents as consumers of education, are seriously limited. The market upon which he wants to rely is not a market in any real sense of the word.

Raising the bar, closing the gap

'Raising the Bar, closing the Gap' is Policy Green Paper No 1: 'An action plan for schools to raise standards, create more good school places and make opportunity more equal' published by the Conservative party. The starting point for this plan is the argument that has run through this book, namely that 'Gordon Brown places his faith in the state, believing that it should take upon itself ever greater responsibility and moral authority.'[190] The Conservative alternative is that 'the role of government is to be an engine of independence'.[191] What is needed is 'real empowerment through the transfer of power and control from the state to the citizen'.[192] I could not agree more. But what do the words mean and how exactly is this transfer of power to be achieved?

Read on a page or two in this policy paper and you come to these paragraphs:

> Conservative education policy is driven by a moral imperative – the need to make the most of every individual talent. We believe in raising the bar for achievement in Britain, helping every child to acquire a more comprehensive array of skills and providing them with the knowledge to become authors of their own life stories.
>
> We believe that ensuring every child has an excellent education is the principal role the state can play in making opportunity more equal. We plan to raise the standards of the worst-performing schools so they can catch up with the best. We will reverse the trend in Britain's schools which has those from disadvantaged backgrounds falling further and further behind with each year that passes. We will ensure those whom the state has failed most badly are given fresh hope by making our state education system excellent for all. And we will ensure that coasting schools face searching new scrutiny to guarantee improved standards for everyone.
>
> Our education reform plan, outlined in these pages, is driven by our commitment to social justice – a society made more equal by dispersing opportunity both more widely, and more fairly. We believe that education is the most powerful means by which individuals can be given the opportunity to shape their own futures. And we think there is a moral duty to secure change as quickly as possible before the gap between the fortunate and the forgotten grows wider.[193]

Take out the word 'Conservative' and this could be New Labour at its most sanctimoniously utopian. Does it matter? Papers like this are, after all, written to make a political point, and, it might be argued, should not be taken too seriously. I think that it matters a great deal. Ends may not justify means, but they have, as we have seen, a nasty habit of leading to initiatives which, to quote Oakeshott, are 'corrupted by undesired and unmanageable consequences'. This is 'a vision of education driven by a passion for social justice'.[194] It has as 'its central mission the defeat of ignorance'. The rampant utopianism of these sentences worries me as it would have worried Oakeshott. I am reassured by the fact that the authors 'believe that each new generation has a right to be introduced to the best our civilisation has produced, to encounter the best that has been thought and written, to be given equal access to the knowledge which liberates'.[195] This is what I have been arguing for the best part of two decades. The very next sentence states, however, that 'we reject the principle that academic excellence should be rationed to a few and embrace the challenge of spreading knowledge more widely than ever before'. Who has done the rationing? Previous Conservative governments which supported grammar schools? I agree, of course, that every child should have the opportunity to make as much intellectual progress as they can, but, like D.H. Lawrence, I think we have to accept that many children are going to make little progress. The challenge is to stomach this unpalatable truth and to develop curricula that will allow such children to fulfil the potential that they do have. To pretend otherwise will result, whatever Michael Gove may think and hope, in a further dumbing down of knowledge.

I would feel more optimistic if I felt that Gove knew how to achieve his cosmic aims. His policy paper divides into two sections: 'Immediate action driving urgent improvements' and 'The Supply Side Revolution'. Neither is convincing.

He makes six proposals for immediate action:

1 Improve discipline and behaviour in schools, shifting the balance of power in the classroom back in favour of the teacher.

2 Get every child who is capable of doing so reading by the age of six, so that every minute in the classroom thereafter is productive.

3 Reform the testing regime in primary schools to reduce bureaucracy and focus on every pupil's real needs.

4 Deliver more teaching by ability, which stretches the strongest and nurtures the weakest.

5 Reform the inspection procedure to ensure there is tougher, more effective and more searching scrutiny of under-performance.

6 Champion excellence in the comprehensive sector by evangelising for the best professional practice in the state system, and more generously rewarding those who deliver for the poorest.

Proposals two and four are beyond his control, and, as I have noted above, if the next Conservative government wants schools to be free from state direction, should be beyond his control. The paper notes that the Rose review on the teaching of reading has had precious little impact in the classroom, but seems to believe that changes to teacher training will deliver the desired improvements. Having tried to change the way in which teacher training institutions taught the teaching of reading when I was Chief Inspector, I can tell him that it will not be that easy. Neither is he likely to make much progress with proposal four. In 1997 the Labour manifesto announced that setting was to be a priority. Nine years on in 2006 the percentage of academic lessons set by ability had risen by three measly percentage points, from 37% to 40%. The Conservative solution is apparently to use Ofsted to enforce setting, a suggestion which, even if it were to work, would further corrupt the inspectorate and undermine the idea that schools should be autonomous, self-governing institutions. Proposal six is doable in that anyone can evangelise. There is no reason to expect that schools will listen. Proposal one is essentially a matter for the individual school, though the paper is right to want to give greater power over exclusion to the headteacher and to improve the quality of education in Pupil Referral Units provided for children who have been excluded. Proposals three and five are within the Secretary of State's power. Nobody, however, should underestimate the difficulties that will be encountered in trying to deliver these ends.

The authors of this paper understand the problems. They want for the most part to do the right thing. They have very little idea about the practical difficulties they will face and they have not thought through the basic contradiction in wanting to tell schools what to do while simultaneously wanting the state to be less intrusively managerial. The lesson of the mistakes made in 1988 has not been learnt.

New Academies: the Swedish model

The starting point for what the Conservatives are calling 'the supply side revolution' is 'the simple fact that there are not enough good school places, especially in the most deprived areas of the country'.[196] This is, of course, true, and no amount of tinkering with admissions procedures is going to solve the problem. I applaud, therefore, the drive 'to generate an environment in which many more good schools can be created'. These schools will be known as New Academies.

'New Academies', the paper tells us, 'will be free, non-selective, and within the maintained system. They will be smaller than comparable, existing schools; they will be set up and run by existing educational providers, charities, trusts, voluntary groups, philanthropists and co-operatives on behalf of parents and pupils; they will be not-for-profit organisations and they will compete with surrounding local authority schools, helping to exert pressure for higher standards in the surrounding schools.'[197] The state will provide capital funding for organisations that need it and steps will be taken to ease planning and other regulations that make it difficult to start new schools. Revenue or recurrent funding will come from the DCSF in the form of the Dedicated Schools Grant. Each pupil, that is, who moves from a Local Authority school to a New Academy will increase the New Academy budget by the sum of money that would have been spent on their education in the Local Authority school – £5,966 in 2007–08. The paper proposes what is called a 'pupil premium for pupils in disadvantaged areas'. It is not clear how this premium will differ from the existing additional funding which children from deprived areas attract, but the intention is that Academies will be incentivised to recruit pupils they might not otherwise have wanted to recruit. Somewhat mysteriously, the authors of the paper appear to believe that 'the freedom to innovate has been a crucial part of the success of the existing academy programme'.[198] They reach, however, in principle at least, the right conclusion: 'the only constraints on New Academies, and indeed on existing Academies, should be the curriculum requirements which apply to independent schools'. If 'New Academies abide by the Admissions Code, ensure that the needs of pupils with special educational needs are taken into account, and levy no charge or fee in respect of admissions, they will be free from burdensome regulation'.[199]

What is new here? In essence two things: the encouragement to parents and others to set up schools and the determination to ease regulations to make this possible. These changes mark an important shift in policy from the current statist model. They go, however, nowhere near far enough. Mr Cameron is giving parents a little more 'power and control' over their and their children's lives, but not in reality very much. He may well have calculated that this is as far as he could go politically at this stage, and he may well be right. The limitations of his proposals need nonetheless to be spelt out.

First, though, let us take a brief look at the Swedish reforms upon which the Conservative proposals are based.[200] In 1992 the Swedish government changed the law to allow any individual or organisation to apply to set up a school. The process of approval of an application, which can, incidentally, take up to eighteen months, involves assessing whether it is viable, educationally and financially, and, significantly, the impact it will have on existing state schools. If the impact is deemed to be excessively disruptive to existing schools, then the proposal can be turned down. New schools have to follow the Swedish national curriculum and conform to strict admissions criteria which for most mean first-come, first-served. Initially, they were allowed to charge top-up fees, but this freedom was abolished in 1997. Now a voucher system, identical to that proposed by our Conservative party, means that the funding allocated to each pupil attending a new independent school equates to the cost of educating that pupil in an ordinary state school. In 2005 the number of independent schools catering for children in the 7–16 age range had risen from 90 in 1992 to 585, and the number of independent upper schools educating 16–18-year-olds from 57 to 266. These figures represent 12% and 33% respectively of the total number of schools in each age range. Academically and in terms of parental satisfaction, the initiative has proved to be successful:

> In 2006, the average merit rating for pupils leaving compulsory education (age 16) was 20 points higher in independent schools than municipal schools (225.3 compared to 205.3). Among pupils leaving independent schools, 93.5 per cent were eligible to attend an upper secondary school, compared with 89.2 per cent from municipal schools. Results at the upper secondary school level were also encouraging. Average grade points at independent schools were 14.5 (out of 20) compared to the 14.1 national average.
>
> In addition, a study conducted by the National Agency for Education suggests that school choice now commands a high level of support among families. Parents tend to be more satisfied when they make a choice of school, especially if they choose an independent school: 'favourable assessments apply in particular to those who chose independent schools'. In contrast: 'There is … a small proportion of parents who state that they are not happy with

> the schools. These are mainly those who did not choose a school.'[201]

These are promising results, which suggest that the Conservatives are right to seek to implement reforms based on the Swedish experience. The question is whether a great deal more could be achieved if Mr Cameron were to show a little less tactical sophistication and a little more political conviction.

The aim of these reforms is, remember, to create more good school places. 'Good' means, in this context, independent of the state and attractive to the customer, although, as noted above, current Conservative policy shows considerable ambivalence on both of these points. An increase in good school places can be achieved through the creation of good new schools, the option the Conservatives favour, or through making access to existing good schools, state or independent, possible for children for whom at present it is impossible. Other than meddling with admissions arrangements for good state schools and threatening, therefore, their identity, there is little that can be done to widen access to state schools that are already oversubscribed. The independent sector is a different matter. Why make it an either/or? If parents are to be given a voucher that equates to the cost of educating their child in a state school, why should they not be able to cash this voucher in as payment or part payment of fees in an existing independent school?

Most people who accept the idea of independent, state-funded schools will have no trouble with the idea of the voucher being used to purchase a place in a school where the fees are not higher than the value of the voucher. Many are worried by the idea that parents who can afford to do so should be allowed to make a top-up payment. They dislike the idea of subsidies being given to the rich, and they feel that the proposal in some way offends against notions of fairness and social justice. If a future Conservative government were to give £6,000 to every parent who sends their child to an independent school it would cost the state, very roughly, £3 billion a year. This is money, many will argue, which should be spent on disadvantaged children whose parents have little or nothing, not wasted on subsidies for the rich. They find the idea morally indefensible and the tacticians of the Conservative Party deem it, therefore, to be too great a political risk.

It may be politically risky; it is not morally indefensible. Parents who choose to educate their children privately have, after all, already paid their taxes. Why should anyone, however wealthy they might be, pay for a service they do not use and then have to pay additional fees charged by their provider of choice? If the reply to this question is that this is their choice and that social justice demands the redistribution of income, then we should note statistics from the Office for National Statistics which show just how redistributive our taxation system is already. 'In 2006–7, before taxes and benefits, the ratio of the total income of the richest 20% of people to that of the poorest 20% was 15:1. After taxes and benefits it had narrowed to 4:1'[202] Given this degree of effective redistribution , the moral argument for making the rich pay twice if they choose to educate their children privately is perhaps not that compelling. Nobody, moreover, should assume that every parent who sends their child to a private school is that well off. Many scrimp and save. They forgo a foreign holiday and stick with the old car because nothing is more important to them than the education of their children.

A Conservative government that purports to trust individuals to make the right choices should be doing all it can to help them do what they choose to do. There are those who argue that education is too important to our economic prosperity and social cohesion to allow any parent to buy an advantage for their child. The counter argument, rooted in a sense of how hopelessly the state has failed to deliver the education the individual and the country needs, is that education is too important for the state not to help any parent who wishes to send their child to a private school. Current Conservative policy sits uneasily between the two positions. If Mr Cameron cannot stomach the idea that parents should be allowed to use this voucher to help pay independent school fees, he should stop talking about empowering parents and, logically, announce that he intends to abolish all private schools. If he wants to develop an alternative to Labour's commitment to state control, then he needs to understand that public policy should not be framed negatively. It is wrong to deny a benefit to one group within society because another group may not be able or willing to use that benefit. Social justice may require a significant redistribution of wealth, but a society in which the needs of the disadvantaged dictate every policy decision on the provision of public services is neither just, nor sane.

It is insane for two reasons. First, because the politics of envy spawns a punitive taxation regime which ultimately demotivates the individual and impoverishes the exchequer and undermines, therefore, the ability of the state to support those who need its support; and, second, because an approach to public services that, in order not to allow anybody to purchase an advantage over anybody else, fixes funding at the level the state can 'afford' and prohibits the individual top-up, militates against the competition among service providers that is essential if the quality of services is to be improved.

A genuinely radical supply-side revolution would use the concept of the education voucher to open up existing independent schools to more children. It would also recognise that there is only one way to create the number of good new places that is needed. The Conservatives' current proposals, again no doubt for political reasons, rule out for-profit education companies setting up New Academies. They assume that individual parents, livery companies, charities, and the like will react enthusiastically to this initiative and establish sufficient numbers of good schools. This assumption begs two questions: will there be such interest and, if there is, will the interested parties have the competence to do the job?

In Sweden about half the independent schools are owned by for-profit companies. Michael Sandstrom, the Swedish Prime Minister's senior adviser, believes that the decision to allow for profit companies to run independent schools explains the rapid rise in numbers:

> Since larger (for-profit) companies running several schools are allowed, the expansion of independent schools has been more rapid than it otherwise would have been ... while successful non-profit schools have no incentive to expand, for-profit schools do. In Sweden ... for-profit schools have expanded rapidly and established subsidiary schools, the non-profit schools instead tend to create waiting lists.[203]

F. Bergstrom, noting the fact that the highest levels of growth in the independent sector were experienced in the first two years of the reform, at 58.6% in 1992 and 26.2% in 1994, reducing to 6.8% in 2004, writes: 'A possible explanation for this may be that independent schools are not allowed to charge any school fees and hence the incentives for starting up schools may decrease.'[204]

The Conservatives would do well to reflect on these observations. In England, opinion surveys repeatedly tell us that many parents would like to send their children to independent schools if they could afford the fees. The sector has done very little, however, to respond to this potential demand, and the number of pupils attending independent schools has remained static for many years. The key question, given this potential demand and an economy that until recently was benefiting from strong growth, is why?

There are approximately 2,500 independent schools in the UK, of which some 1,500, including most of the largest, have charitable status. Charitable status schools typically lack the kind of professional management that drives efficiency, as well as the skills to implement and risk-manage complex capacity expansion projects. More fundamentally, as Michael Sandstrom suggests, where there is no profit motive there is no incentive to expand capacity. It is more congenial to avoid the risks and challenges of expansion and instead to channel ever-increasing surpluses into ever more elaborate facilities, which entrench the elite nature of the institution. Surpluses, which could achieve high returns on investment if re-invested in capacity creation, are used to build state of the art, five star facilities for the tiny minority of pupils whose parents can afford the highest fees. It is hard to think of an ownership system less likely to expand capacity and widen access.

Cameron and Gove might reply that their model is not the traditional charitable status independent school, but the City Academy. Where, though, is the evidence that the Academy movement is succeeding? Individual schools, like Mossbourne Academy, have made excellent progress, but examination results across the existing Academies (see Chapter 7) are far from compelling. Reading the latest DCSF-commissioned Price Waterhouse report,[205] it is hard to see what aspect, if any, of the Academy model explains the success we do see. The success of individual schools is down to the exceptional leadership of the headteachers responsible for them. As noted in Chapter 7, in what is, given the fact the DCSF was paying the piper, a remarkable admission, the Price Waterhouse report concludes that there is insufficient evidence to back the Academy initiative as a template for the future of secondary education. Will other, new organisations come forward to run New Academies? Universities, perhaps, or existing private schools? I can't myself see it, or not, anyway, in the numbers that are needed to generate the 220,000 plus new school places the Conservatives calculate are needed. And, if they do, what evidence is there that they will have the expertise necessary to deliver? Parents? Yes, some, no doubt, and they will most probably be middle class parents interested in starting schools in middle class communities. The Conservatives, of course, want these New Academies to be concentrated in areas of deprivation. I do not think they will find many working class parents with the time, entrepreneurial energy and professional expertise needed to set up a new school.

The success of this initiative depends, in my view, upon a willingness to involve for-profit companies, such as Cognita, the schools group I chair. I would, of course say that, wouldn't I? Indeed I would. As Chief Inspector I observed the huge problems faced by many inner city schools and I witnessed the failure of local and national government to solve these problems. As Chairman of Cognita, I know that the success of an education company depends upon a very particular combination of educational and business expertise which is very difficult to get right. To assume that any parent or charity, however enthusiastic they might be, is likely to succeed in setting up a school or, what is really needed, chains of schools, is naïve in the extreme. I want this Conservative initiative to succeed because I care about the education of disadvantaged children and I know that there is no alternative. That is why I argue that the policy must be re-thought.

If it is to attract companies like Cognita, it needs, moreover, to be re-thought in another way. As it stands, the policy proposes that 'the only constraints' on New Academies 'should be the curriculum requirements which apply to independent schools'.[206] It further states that New Academies must 'abide by the admissions code'.[207] Michael Gove may not realise it, but these are very significant constraints.

In assessing the nature of the constraints, what matters is not so much the 'curriculum requirement' as the inspection demand. The DCSF divides the Independent Schools Standards into seven sections or 96 regulations.[208] A school that is judged by inspectors to be lacking in respect to any of these standards is said to be 'non-compliant', and can, if immediate 'improvements' are not made, be shut down. The first section of these Standards requires inspectors to make judgements upon the quality of the education provided by the school, which means they must comment upon the quality of the curriculum and the quality of the teaching and assessment. This might be fine if the inspectors were suspending their own educational prejudices and working to a broad notion of minimal standards, but, all too often, as we saw in Chapter 6, neither of these conditions holds. Take, for example, regulation 1:3:c: 'The teaching at the school shall involve well-planned lessons, effective teaching methods, suitable activities and wise management of class time.' Each of these adjectives ('well-planned', 'effective', 'suitable' and 'wise) is open to interpretation. To put it charitably, inspectors tend to be highly inflexible in the criteria they employ. If Gove is serious in wanting to establish a network of 'free' schools, he needs, therefore, to revisit this crucial question of independence and constraints upon independence. Only two of the DCSF's seven standards (the welfare, health and safety of the pupils and the suitability of the proprietor and the staff) have anything to do with the state, and, even here, it is arguable that parents should be left to exercise their own judgements. Gove should leave everything else to the school and the market.

So, too, as I argued in Chapter 7, with admissions. The identity of a school depends upon the curriculum it offers, the teachers it employs, and, crucially, the pupils it admits. The Conservatives' current proposals, for obvious political and painfully illogical reasons, require New Academies to conform to state admissions arrangements. Cameron and Gove believe that the state should trust us to make intelligent decisions on issues that matter to us. Few issues matter more to more people than the education of their children. A decision is only possible when there is a choice to be made. Real choice in education is not possible when all schools have to conform to state regulation, particularly, because the nature of the intake is such a major factor in defining the identity of a school, when the regulations dictate the kind of pupil they can admit. Eton College wants to build up a bursary fund to open up entrance to any child bright enough to pass its entrance examination, irrespective of the ability of that child's parents to pay the fees. It is a noble aspiration, but it will fundamentally change, for better or worse, the nature of the school. Eton will become an extremely luxurious grammar school. If it were a New Academy it would not, of course, be allowed to select more than 10 per cent of its intake so it would become a comprehensive school. Cameron and Gove want a diverse education system that allows parents to choose between and among schools. They have, therefore, to allow schools to develop their own individual identities. This means allowing them to decide their own admissions policies.

Conclusion

Schools, funded by, but otherwise independent of the state, free to decide their own admissions policy and to define their own individual ethos, competing one with another in the market place: then we would have some clear blue educational water.

Conclusion

The Road to Freedom

Fifty years ago the novelist and philosopher Iris Murdoch asked whether 'we (can) maintain educational standards while making education more "democratic"?'[209] The experience of the last twelve years has taught us that we cannot. We can abandon our responsibility to initiate the young into the best that has been thought and written. We can impose a skills-based, socially relevant, politicised curriculum on teachers and their pupils. We can reduce the intellectual demand of public examinations so that more students appear to succeed. We can force successful schools and universities to abandon their supposed elitism and accept more students from disadvantaged homes. We can and we have done all these things. We have neither maintained educational standards, nor, if by 'democratic' we mean that every child has an opportunity to fulfil their potential, have we made education any more 'democratic'.

A little earlier in the same essay Murdoch wrote: 'Education is no longer seen as the road to freedom; it is seen as the road to a higher salary.'[210] She thought that education in art and ideas and knowledge was that road to freedom. She knew it from her own life, just as I know it is from mine. By freedom I mean: an appreciation of what the greatest human beings have achieved; a sense of what other people in other ages knew to be important and possible; a liberation from the tyranny of the majority view; a release from the monotony of the quotidian. I want every child, every 'disadvantaged' child in particular, to walk as far as they can down that road to freedom.

This, you may be thinking, is what Labour ministers have been saying since 1997. It is the drum the Conservative party is now banging. I would love to be able to join them and mosey hand in hand towards the horizon. I cannot. First, because I am talking about the road to freedom and they appear to have no conception of education beyond the utilitarian; second, because I do not think that every child is capable of travelling very far along this road; and, third, to return to the democratisation of education, because I know that attempts to pretend otherwise have damaged, perhaps irrevocably, our sense of what education must involve.

On the first point, I accept, of course, that it is not an either/or. Employers are right to complain that too many school leavers are unemployable. Our failure to develop proper vocational courses for students at the upper end of secondary school is indefensible. We have failed hundreds of thousands of young people and we have failed business and industry. My argument is that, in their obsession with what logically and honestly should be called 'training', successive governments, but, particularly our current Government, have lost sight of what 'education' ought to involve. You only have to glance at the National Curriculum, or flick through the 'competences' the Training and Development Agency expects trainee teachers to demonstrate, or skim the blurb poured out by the National College for School Leadership to see that nobody in power has any understanding that education is an activity which needs no external justification. To pick one statement from hundreds of others which say exactly the same thing, education today is deemed important because it is 'a route to equality of opportunity for all, a healthy and just democracy, a productive economy and sustainable development'. We may or may not think that these goals are more complex and morally difficult than governments like to pretend. We may or may not share in ministerial confidence that teachers can deliver what are undeniably elusive aspirations. What we should not do and what we have done is forget that children go to school to learn things they would not otherwise learn so that they come to see things in a different way and are freed from the poverty of their own immediate circumstance.

This freedom depends, paradoxically, on the child's willingness to submit. To submit to the authority of a teacher who knows what the child does not know and to the body of knowledge, wisdom and values it is that teacher's duty to transmit. Education cannot be democratic in the sense that the child is an equal partner in the activities of the classroom. The child does not and cannot judge the importance of what he is taught, and should have no say, therefore, in the content of his lessons. So much for 'personalisation' and what is now known in the jargon as 'student voice'. So much, too, for the Government's drive to render the curriculum 'relevant' to the immediate 'needs' and experiences of the child and to dumb the demand of examinations down to an egalitarian minimum.

Every child in primary school should have the opportunity to learn about the mystery and magic of the world beyond their own experience. The Rose review denies them this opportunity and should, therefore, be rejected. What, though, of post-primary education? Do we agree with Lord Adonis, who, when he was an education minister, said that every child was capable of five good GCSEs? Those who want to pursue an academic education should, of course, have the chance to do so. Those who do not should have the opportunity to follow more practical vocational courses. The opportunities will be different because the abilities and the aspirations of the students are different, but, if they each lead to a goal that is valued by the student and his family they will be of equal value. The attempt to pretend that one curriculum and qualification can cater for every student has led to the introduction of a qualification – the Diploma – which will neither inspire the academically able nor motivate those who are sick to death of academic study.

In that when Iris Murdoch wrote the essay from which the above questions were taken, grammar schools were an essential part of state education, education was in one important sense more democratic than it now is. Labour has done everything in its power to make all schools the same, changing the admission rules in a never-ending attempt to equalise intakes; lobotomising the teaching profession so that every teacher thinks and acts in the same way; and imposing diplomas which have been introduced to eliminate the divisions between education and training. The premise has been that if every school is the same school then every school will be a good school. I, needless to say, disagree. I think standards will rise when schools are allowed to develop their own particular identity and purpose and to compete one with another in the market place. Some will offer an education that is very different from that which I would choose for my children and grandchildren. That is fine. It is not the wrongness of the Government's vision which, ultimately, concerns me: it is the arrogance with which it has imposed this vision on every school, every teacher and every parent. Ministers have talked constantly about the importance of parental choice while undermining that choice through ceaseless legislative change and manic bureaucratic activity. I want choice. State education must become less centralist and, in this particular sense, more democratic.

I would like to end this book on a positive note and say that if the Conservatives were to win the next election we would see the radical changes that are necessary if our children are to receive the education they deserve. Mr Cameron makes much of his wish to empower the individual citizen and Michael Gove has stated that he wants to introduce reforms based on the Swedish model of 'free schools'. The devil, as always, is in the detail, and, thusfar, that detail shows a continuing confidence in the instruments of state control and a reluctance to trust either parents or markets. We shall see.

Notes

1 *The Independent*, 7th February 2008.
2 *Philosophical Remains of Richard Lewis Nettleship*, quoted by Geoffrey Hill in *Collected Critical Writings*, ed. Kenneth Haynes (Oxford: Oxford University Press, 2008), p. 138.
3 *The Guardian*, 30th January 2009.
4 DCSF press notice, 16th May 2008.
5 *The Times*, 28th August 2008.
6 Ibid.
7 DCSF press notice, 21st May 2008.
8 *The Times*, 28th August 2008.
9 *The Times*, 15th September 2008.
10 Children, Schools and Families Committee, Uncorrected Transcript of Oral Evidence, 24th November 2008.
11 *Daily Telegraph*, 26th November 2008.
12 Christopher Ray, 'The Retreat from Scholarship', *The Head Speaks*, ed. Julian Lovelock (University of Buckingham Press: 2008).
13 BBC News, 1st July 2008.
14 Ray, 'The Retreat from Scholarship', pp. 58–9.
15 International Baccalaureate Organisation 'Mission and Strategy' page: http://www.ibo.org/mission/.
16 Cambridge Pre-U Diploma publicity brochure, University of Cambridge International Examinations. Available for download from the Cambridge Pre-U page under 'Qualifications': www.cie.org.uk/qualifications.
17 D.H. Lawrence, *The Education of the People*, originally published 1918, reprinted in *Lawrence on Education*, ed. Joy and Raymond Williams (Harmondsworth: Penguin Education, 1973), p. 133.
18 Ibid., p. 129.
19 *The Times*, 21st August 2008.
20 *The Sunday Times*, 28th September 2008.
21 DCSF press notice, 21st May 2008.
22 Level One Engineering Diploma, Qualifications and Curriculum Authority, 16th November 2007.
23 See 'About Diplomas' webpage, Office of the Qualifications and Examinations Regulator (Ofqual), under Types of qualifications/Diploma/About the Diploma (http://www.ofqual.gov.uk).
24 *The Spectator*, 27th September 2008.
25 Frank Musgrove, *School and the Social Order* (Chichester: John Wiley & Sons, 1979).
26 DCSF press notice, 23rd June 2008.
27 'Safer children in a Digital World', the Report of the Byron Review, published 27th March 2008. Available for download from: http://www.dcsf.gov.uk/byronreview/.
28 DCSF press notice, 7th May 2008.
29 T.S. Eliot, *East Coker* (Faber, 1940).

30 Charles Leadbeater, *Living on Thin Air: The New Economy* (London: Penguin, 1999) p. vii.
31 Alison Wolf, *Does Education Matter?: Myths about Education and Economic Growth* (London: Penguin, 2002), p. 48.
32 Ibid., p. 27.
33 Ibid., p. 49.
34 Ibid., p. 29.
35 Ibid., p. 30.
36 Ibid., p. 42.
37 Ibid., p. 97.
38 Ibid., p. 96.
39 *Nonesuch*, Summer 2008.
40 'The Universities', in *The Voice of Liberal Learning: Michael Oakeshott on Education,* ed. Timothy Fuller (New Haven: Yale University Press, 1989), pp. 127–8.
41 Allan Bloom, *The Closing of the American Mind: How higher education has failed democracy and impoverished the souls of today's students* (Penguin Books, 1988), p. 246.
42 Ibid., p. 247.
43 Ibid.
44 Ibid., p. 249.
45 From the National Curriculum homepage: http://curriculum.qca.org.uk.
46 'The Aims of the Curriculum' (QCA, 2008). Available for download at: http://curriculum.qca.org.uk/key-stages-3-and-4/aims/.
47 Ibid.
48 *'Towards an aims-led curriculum'*, Conference at the Institute of Education, 4th June 2008. See www.qca.org.uk/futures for further background on the Futures initiative.
49 'The Aims of the Curriculum' (QCA, 2008).
50 Key Stage 3 and 4 Programmes of Study by subject. See http://curriculum.qca.org.uk/key-stages-3-and-4/subjects/.
51 'The role of functional English in supporting progression and success'. Available for download from the DCSF website under Secondary/Secondary Frameworks/English Framework/Planning or at: http://nationalstrategies.standards.dcsf.gov.uk/node/47081.
52 Ibid.
53 Ibid.
54 Key Stage 3 and 4 Cross-curriculum dimensions. See http://curriculum.qca.org.uk/key-stages-3-and-4/cross-curriculum-dimensions/.
55 *'The Global Dimension in Action: A Curriculum Planning Guide for Schools'*. Available for download at: http://www.qca.org.uk/qca_15333.aspx.
56 See Key Stage 3 and 4 Programmes of Study under 'Subjects' and 'Physical Education' or go to: http://curriculum.qca.org.uk/key-stages-3-and-4/subjects/physical-education/keystage3/ to download a pdf.
57 See Key Stage 3 and 4 Programmes of Study under 'Subjects' and 'History' or go to: http://curriculum.qca.org.uk/key-stages-3-and-4/subjects/history/ to download a pdf.
58 Ibid.
59 See Key Stage 3 and 4 Programmes of Study under 'Subjects' and 'Geography' or go to: http://curriculum.qca.org.uk/key-stages-3-and-4/subjects/geography/ to download a pdf.
60 See Key Stage 3 and 4 Programmes of Study under 'Subjects' and 'Modern foreign languages' or go to: http://curriculum.qca.org.uk/key-stages-3-and-4/subjects/modern-foreign-languages/ to download a pdf.

61 See Key Stage 3 and 4 Programmes of Study under 'Subjects' and 'Personal, social, health and economic education' or go to: http://curriculum.qca.org.uk/key-stages-3-and-4/subjects/pshe/ to download a pdf.
62 See Key Stage 3 and 4 Programmes of Study under 'Subjects' and 'Citizenship' or go to: http://curriculum.qca.org.uk/key-stages-3-and-4/subjects/citizenship/ to download a pdf.
63 Ibid. Key Stage 3 Programme of Study.
64 Ibid. Citizenship 'Attainment target'.
65 Key Stage 3 and 4 Programmes of Study under 'Subjects' and 'Personal, social, health and economic education' and 'Personal wellbeing' or go to: http://curriculum.qca.org.uk/key-stages-3-and-4/subjects/pshe/ to download a pdf.
66 Ibid. Key Stage 3 Programme of Study.
67 Ibid.
68 Key Stage 3 and 4 Programmes of Study under 'Subjects' and 'Personal, social, health and economic education' and 'Economic wellbeing and financial capability' or go to: http://curriculum.qca.org.uk/key-stages-3-and-4/subjects/pshe/ to download a pdf.
69 Ibid.
70 'Education: the engagement and its frustration', in *Education and the Development of Reason*, ed. R.F. Dearden, P.H. Hirst, and R.S. Peters (London: Routledge, 1972), pp. 21–2.
71 *'Children and their Primary Schools'*, aka. 'The Plowden Report' (London: HMSO, 1967). Available to download at: http://www.dg.dial.pipex.com/documents/plowden.shtml.
72 'Ed Balls' remit letter to Sir Jim Rose'. Available for download at: http://www.dcsf.gov.uk/primarycurriculumreview/.
73 Ibid.
74 Rose, 'Interim Report'.
75 Ibid.
76 'The Children's Plan: Building Brighter Futures', pp. 62–3. Available for download at: www.dcsf.gov.uk/childrensplan/.
77 Balls, 'Remit letter'.
78 Rose, 'Interim Report', p. 6.
79 Douglas Barnes, *From Communication to Curriculum* (Harmondsworth: Penguin Education, 1976).
80 Rose, 'Interim Report', p. 6.
81 Balls, 'Remit letter'.
82 Rose, 'Interim Report', p. 35.
83 Ibid., p. 27.
84 Balls, 'Remit letter'.
85 'The Cambridge Primary Review'. Available at: www.primaryreview.org.uk.
86 Rose, 'Interim Report', p. 33.
87 BBC Radio 2, 8th December 2008.
88 Rose, 'Interim Report', p. 38.
89 Ibid., p. 18.
90 Ibid., p. 38.
91 'Emerging Perspectives on Childhood', Keynote lecture presented at the conference on Childhood, Wellbeing and Primary Education, Westminster, 17th March 2008. Available for download from the Cambridge Primary Review website at: http://www.primaryreview.org.uk/Downloads/ThePrimaryReview_Emerging-perspectives-on-childhood_RJA2_170308.pdf.
92 Follow the link to the Professional standards from the 'Teachers' box on the homepage: www.tda.gov.uk or go direct to http://www.tda.gov.uk/teachers/professionalstandards/standards.

93 The '2007–10 Corporate Plan' is available for download from the TDA website: www.tda.gov.uk. Go to About us/Plans, policies, and reports/Plans; the Corporate plan archive is accessible from the panel to the right of the screen.
94 Ibid., p. 3
95 See 'Integrating 14–19 Diplomas into Initial Teacher Training'. Available for download at: www.tda.gov.uk.
96 Follow the link to the Professional standards from the 'Teachers' box on the homepage: www.tda.gov.uk or go direct to http://www.tda.gov.uk/teachers/professionalstandards/standards.
97 Email from Paul Moses, Head of Standards in ITT, to Professor Anthony O'Hear, October 2008.
98 The NCSL Corporate Plan 2008–09 is available for download from the NCSL website: www.ncsl.org.uk. Go to Publications/Publications A–Z/Corporate plan NCSL or go direct to: http://www.ncsl.org.uk/corporate-plan-08-09.pdf.
99 NCSL Corporate Plan 2008–09, p. 4.
100 Ibid., p. 7.
101 The NPQH Final Stage Residential Think Piece February 2006, National College for School Leadership, 2006. See Find a programme/Aspiring headteachers for further background.
102 See About the SSAT at: www.specialistschools.org.uk (Corporate website).
103 Available for download at: www.specialistschools.org.uk. Go to Publications (external)/Electronic publications.
104 Hargreaves, 'A New Shape for Schooling', p. 3.
105 Ibid., p. 16.
106 Milbourne Lodge Senior School Inspection Report, p. 2. Ofsted School Inspection Reports are available at: www.ofsted.gov.uk.
107 Ibid., p. 3.
108 Ibid., p. 5.
109 Ibid., p. 2.
110 Ibid., p. 6.
111 Musgrove; School and the Social Order, p. 92.
112 Ibid., ch. 5.
113 Ibid., p. 94.
114 And, one should add, two other very influential studies, Colin Lacey's *Hightown Grammar* (Manchester: Manchester University Press, 1970) and H. Himmelweit's 'Social Status and Secondary Education since the 1944 Act', in D.V. Glass (ed.), *Social Mobility in Britain* (London: Routledge & Kegan Paul, 1954).
115 Musgrove, *School and the Social Order*, p. 99.
116 Anthony Sampson, *The New Anatomy of Britain* (London: Hodder & Stoughton, 1971).
117 Richard Pring, 'The Common School', in the *Journal of Philosophy of Education*, Vol. 41, Issue 4 (November 2007).
118 Ibid., p. 504.
119 Ibid.
120 Adam Swift, *How not to be a Hypocrite: School Choice for the Morally Perplexed Parent* (London: Routledge, 2003).
121 Ibid., p. 35.
122 Ibid., p. 36.
123 Pring, 'The Common School', p. 510.
124 Ibid., p. 518.

125 Ibid., p. 511.
126 Ibid., p. 517.
127 Ibid., p. 520.
128 DCSF Statistical First Release, 16th October 2008. Available for download at: www.dcfs.gov.uk.
129 Hansard Written Answers, 6th June 2005. Available for download at: www.publications.parliament.uk.
130 'University Admissions by Individual Schools', Sutton Trust, February 2008. Available for download at: http://www.suttontrust.com/annualreports.asp (at the time of going to press, misfiled under '2007 Reports').
131 'Social Selectivity of State Schools and the Impact of Grammars', Sutton Trust, October 2008. Available for download at: http://www.suttontrust.com/annualreports.asp.
132 Statistics from Mark Tweedle, 'Value Added and Grammar Schools' (National Grammar Schools Association). Available for download at: http://www.ngsa.org.uk/research/.
133 A and AS Level headline statistics 2008 webpage, Department for Education Northern Ireland (DENI). Go to: www.deni.gov.uk, then follow the links to Curriculum and assessment/Qualifications/AS and A Level Headline Statistics 2008.
134 GCSE headline statistics 2008 webpage, Department for Education Northern Ireland (DENI). Go to: www.deni.gov.uk, then follow the links to Curriculum and assessment/Qualifications/GCSE Headline Statistics 2008.
135 'Schools and pupils in Northern Ireland 1991/92 to 2008/09.' Available for download at: www.deni/index/32-statisticsandresearch.gov.uk.
136 DENI Statistical Press Release, 6th August 2008. Available for download at www.deni.gov.uk/schoolleavers_0609.pdf and DCSF Statistical First Release, on results in England in 2006–07. Available at: www.dcsf.gov.uk.
137 John Marks, 'The Betrayed Generations', Centre for Policy Studies, January 2000. Available for download at: www.cps.org.uk.
138 Fred Naylor and Roger Peach, *The Truth about Grammar Schools* (National Grammar Schools Association, September 2005). Details at: http://www.ngsa.org.uk/publications/.
139 *The Independent*, 10th January 2008.
140 Rob Berkeley, *Right to Divide? Faith Schools and Community Cohesion* (London: Runnymede Trust, 2008) Available for download at: http://www.runnymedetrust.org/publications/115/74.html.
141 Ibid., p. 4.
142 *The Guardian*, 9th February 2008.
143 'Guidance on the Duty to Promote Community Cohesion' (DCSF, 2007). Available for download at: http://publications.teachernet.gov.uk.
144 Berkeley, *Right to Divide?*, pp. 5–6.
145 'Board responds to the Runnymede Trust report on faith schools'. See the Press Office webpage at: www.boardofdeputies.org.uk.
146 *School Admissions Code* (London: TSO, 2009), p. 12. For details go to: http://www.dcsf.gov.uk/sacode/.
147 Ibid., p. 7.
148 'Academy Model Funding Agreement', p. 39. Available for download at: www.standards.dfos.gov.uk/academies/publications.
149 Ibid., p. 24.
150 Ibid.
151 Statistics from DCSF 'Academies Evaluation Fifth Annual Report', p. 19. Available for download at: http://www.standards.dfes.gov.uk/academies/publications/?version=1 (Pick

area: Academies, then follow link from menu to Publications and Documents and scroll down to locate from list.)
152 Ibid.
153 Ibid.
154 Ibid., p. 9.
155 Ibid.
156 Ibid., p. 11.
157 Statistics from the Specialist Schools Programme. Available at: www.specialistschools.org.uk/schools/specialistschoolsprogramme/.
158 'What are Specialist Schools?' www.standards.dcsf.gov.uk. (Pick area: Specialist Schools, then follow link from menu to What are Specialist Schools? page.)
159 Frances Castle and Jennifer Evans, *Specialist Schools – What do we know?* (London: RISE, 2006), p. 2. Available for download at: http://www.risetrust.org.uk/specialist.html.
160 Select Committee on Education and Skills Fourth Report, paragraph 125. Available at: www.parliament.the-stationery-office.co.uk.
161 R. Glatter, 'Just how independent is Ofsted?', *Education Journal*, Issue 87 (2005), p. 7.
162 Castle and Evans, *Specialist Schools*, p. 2.
163 Ibid.
164 'Educational outcomes and value added by specialist schools – 2003 analysis', p. iv. Available for download at: www.specialistschools.org.uk. Go to corporate site and search on title.
165 Castle and Evans, *Specialist Schools*, p. 3.
166 See www.isc.co.uk. Statistics are from the Facts & Figures page of the website.
167 *The Spectator*, February 2009.
168 *Daily Telegraph*, 10th March 2007.
169 'Proving the Benefit', *Attain*, Vol. 3, Issue 8 (Spring 2009).
170 'Charities and Public Benefit', p. 23. Available at: www.charity-commission.gov.uk. Click on 'About Charities' and scroll down to Charities and Public Benefit.
171 Ibid., p. 25.
172 *Daily Telegraph*, 7th March 2007.
173 This analysis draws upon a private paper submitted by Edmund Lazarus, a Founding Partner of Englefield Capital, to Michael Gove, Conservative Spokesman on Education.
174 Michael Gove, Speech to the Conservative Party Conference, 30th September 2008.
175 *The Guardian*, 4th February 1997.
176 *Conservative Texts: An Anthology* (Basingstoke: Macmillan, 1991), p. 11.
177 Ibid., p.1
178 'Raising the Bar, Closing the Gap', Policy Green Paper No. 1, Conservative Party (November 2007), p. 3.
179 Ibid.
180 Michael Oakeshott, *On Being Conservative: Rationalism in Politics and Other Essays* (London: Methuen, 1981), p. 31.
181 Ibid, pp.245–6.
182 Ibid.
183 Ibid.
184 Ibid.
185 Ibid.
186 Edballs.com, 8th June 2008.
187 John Stuart Mill, *Utilitarianism, Liberty, and Representative Government*, intro. by A.D. Lindsay (New York: Dutton, 1950), p. 88.

188 Scruton, *Conservative Texts*, p. 4.
189 Ibid.
190 'Raising the Bar', p. 4.
191 Ibid., p. 5.
192 Ibid., p. 6.
193 Ibid., p. 10.
194 Ibid.
195 Ibid.
196 Ibid., p. 36.
197 Ibid., pp. 36–7.
198 Ibid., p. 43.
199 Ibid., p. 44.
200 I have based this account on Nick Cowen's very useful pamphlet, *Swedish Lessons*, published by Civitas in 2008.
201 Ibid., p. 26.
202 David Green, article in *The Sunday Times*, January 2009.
203 Cohen, *Swedish Lessons*, pp. 14–15.
204 Ibid, p. 15.
205 'Academies Fifth Annual Report'. Available for download at: http://www.standards.dcsf.gov.uk/academies/publications/?version=1.
206 'Raising the Bar', p. 43.
207 Ibid., p. 44.
208 'The Education (Independent School Standards) (England) Regulations 2003', Office of Public Sector Information: opsi.gov.uk
209 'A House of Theory', Iris Murdoch, in *Essays in Conviction*, ed. J.S. Mackenzie (1958), reprinted in *Existentialists and Mystics* (London: Chatto & Windus, 1997), p. 184.
210 Ibid., p. 182.

Index